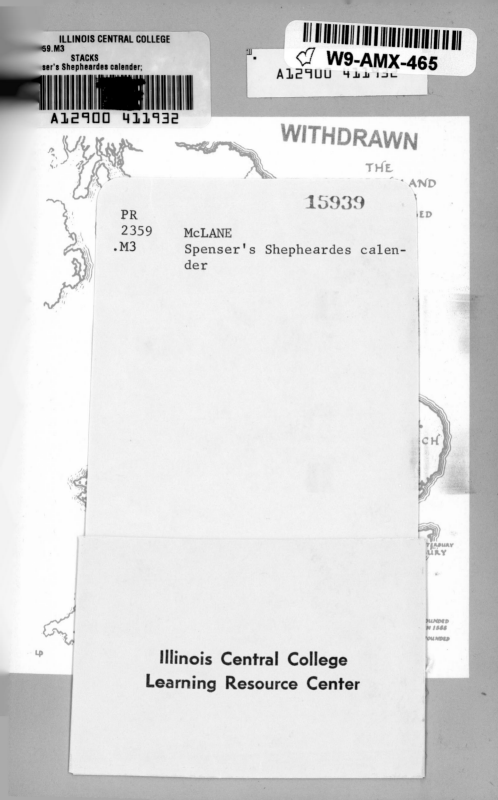

Spenser's Shepheardes Calender:

A STUDY IN ELIZABETHAN ALLEGORY

₭ " . . . the Poet devised the Eglogue . . . ,
not of purpose to counterfait or represent the
rusticall manner of loves and communication,
but under the vaile of homely persons and in rude
speeches to insinuate and glaunce at greater matters."

--- George Puttenham, 1589

spenser's shepheardes calender:

A Study in Elizabethan Allegory

BY

PAUL E. McLANE

University of Notre Dame Press

Notre Dame, Indiana

1961

to

All those who worked on the
Variorum Spenser

Contents

vii

Illustrations

I gratefully acknowledge permission to reproduce photographs: to the Huntington Library for the portrait of Queen Elizabeth from Saxton's *Atlas* and for the woodcuts from the 1579 edition of the *Shepheardes Calender*; to the Ashmolean Museum for the Wyngaerde drawing of Greenwich Palace. I also wish to thank Hollis and Carter, Publishers, for permission to reproduce the map of the Sees of England and Wales (taken from Philip Hughes, *Reformation in England*, London, 1954, III, 125).

—P.E.M.

ix

Publication of this volume
was assisted by a grant from
The American Council of Learned Societies
as a result of a contribution from the United States Steel Foundation.

✤

Grateful acknowledgement is also made to the Ford Foundation.

Preface

In spite of its great importance in the history of literature, the *Shepheardes Calender* has never been closely or accurately studied in relation to the age that produced it. In particular, it has never been so studied in relation to Spenser's closest friends and associates and the political and religious events of the year in which it was published. Furthermore, allegory is a genre much misunderstood today, for we no longer instinctively comprehend the allegorical mode as did the Elizabethans. Then, too, scholars have been constantly extending our knowledge of the Elizabethan period, and we are now able to better understand early works of literature. For these reasons a reinterpretation of the *Calender* as historical allegory has long been needed, and this book has been designed to fill that need.

The arrangement of my material is that which seemed most practical to me. After justifying my interpretation of the *Calender* as allegory, I give the necessary background just before the chapters on the political and religious allegory. Because of the complex and confusing state of religion in the decade that produced the *Calender*—and the consequent misinterpretation—I found it necessary to picture in fuller detail than usual the religious situation in England of the late 1570's. Even in my chapters on the specific religious allegory I tried to clarify the poem further by setting forth the slightly varied religious attitudes of the allegorized leaders of the Established Church and to relate these attitudes to Spenser's. And though the political, religious, and personal allegory is closely entwined, it was easier to divide my material in this threefold fashion and then, in the fourth section, to show in general how the allegory affected the *Calender* as a work of art.

Although my background material has been subordinated to my main intention—explaining the historical allegory of an important allegorical poem—the background as well as the allegory deals with notable people, events, and institutions, and will have, I think, an independent appeal to those interested in Elizabethan biography, politics, and church history. At all times, however, the relevance of this background material to my subject has been carefully considered. This relevance is the sole criterion for including the historical material that appears in this book.

All quotations from Spenser are taken from the Oxford *Spenser*, edited by J. C. Smith and E. de Selincourt (Oxford, 1912). In all crucial or disputed readings of the *Calender*, however, this text was checked against that of the *Variorum Spenser, The Minor Poems*, I (Baltimore, 1943). In transcribing quotations from the Elizabethan period I have expanded contractions, observed the modern usage in regard to u and v, and capitalized important words of titles. In dating, I have followed the "new style," changing to the new year at January 1 instead of March 25 (and hence do not use the double year date during this period).

Some parts of this book have appeared in an earlier form in the *Huntington Library Quarterly, Publications of the Modern*

Language Association of America, *Journal of English and Germanic Philology, Studies in Philology,* and *Modern Language Quarterly.* I wish to thank the editors of these journals for permission to reprint. I also wish to thank the staffs of the Huntington and University of Notre Dame libraries, where I did all of my research.

Work on this study was aided tremendously by a half-year Huntington Library fellowship. Hence I wish to thank the trustees of the Library and its research staff—notably French Fogle, who patiently guided my work through its early stages. I am grateful to the administrative officers of the University of Notre Dame for their relieving me of teaching duties for a semester so that I could complete this book. I also owe more than can be well expressed to my wife for her constant encouragement and help.

Spenserians have been exceedingly generous in giving me the benefit of their judgment and in sending me items of information on various aspects of my work. I particularly wish to thank Professors Rudolf Gottfried, William Ringler, Leicester Bradner, Charles E. Mounts, De Witt T. Starnes, James E. Phillips, Josephine Bennett, T. W. Baldwin, John Hankins, and Virgil Whitaker. I am also grateful to my colleagues Frank Moran, Mortimer Donovan, John Murphy, and Elias Schwartz for many helpful suggestions.

My indebtedness to the editors of the *Variorum Spenser* should be apparent in every chapter: I am grateful to the late Frederick M. Padelford, who long ago taught me Spenser and encouraged me to write this book; to Charles G. Osgood, whose gathering of scholarship on the *Calender* has been of incalculable aid to me; and to Alexander C. Judson, whose encouragement and friendly criticism have helped me greatly, and whose excellent biography of Spenser I have heavily relied on.

Spenser's Shepheardes Calender:

A STUDY IN ELIZABETHAN ALLEGORY

I

Introduction

SPENSER's *Shepheardes Calender* ushers in the great age of Elizabethan poetry. As Frank Kermode recently wrote, "It is generally regarded that the publication of the *Shepheardes Calender*, in 1579, was one of the most important events in the history of English poetry, and not only in the history of the Pastoral."[1] But however important this event, and however important this pastoral poem, there is perhaps no other work of the period which has presented more difficult problems. And despite the valuable contributions of such scholars as Edwin Greenlaw, Percy W. Long, and A. C. Judson[2]—to name but three—the fundamental allegory of the *Calender*, as well as a good many of its minor mysteries, is still obscure.

[1] *English Pastoral Poetry* (New York, 1953), p. 41.
[2] Scholars of the *Calender* are grateful to these men. Further, they are particularly grateful to C. G. Osgood and H. G. Lotspeich (assisted by Dorothy E. Mason) for an evaluative summary of scholarship on the *Shepheardes Calender* in the *Variorum Spenser, The Minor Poems*, I (Baltimore, 1943). All subsequent references to the *Variorum* (hereafter *Var.*), unless otherwise noted, will be to this volume.

3

The purpose of this study is to set forth as clearly as possible the complete allegory of the *Calender*—a project often before attempted but one that has hitherto led to highly uncertain or unacceptable results. For instance, in 1912 James J. Higginson published his *Spenser's Shepheardes Calender in Relation to Contemporary Affairs*, a book attempting to do essentially what I am doing in this study. But Higginson somehow missed the published fact that Spenser in 1578 had been secretary to Dr. John Young, bishop of Rochester—a fact that would have put the poem in the proper perspective of its religious allegory. Higginson's ignorance, then, of an essential part of Spenser's background, as well as his acceptance of certain assumptions about Spenser's Puritanism not in keeping with this background, seriously discredited his work.[3]

In 1930 W. L. Renwick brought out his scholarly edition of the *Shepheardes Calender*. He analyzed the poem in a brilliant fashion but refused to come to grips with its allegory. And although admitting that the pastoral normally dealt with contemporary affairs, Renwick offered three reasons for avoiding the discussion of personalities: first, evidence is too scanty to provide certain identifications; second, Spenser's choice of pastoral pseudonyms is too unsystematic to afford help; third, in inspiration and origin Spenser's eclogues were not personal but literary. Moreover, the significance of identifications is slight: "personalities are secondary and attached to real men only partially and vaguely."[4] All of these points will be considered in this study. It is my contention that enough evidence exists to uncover the allegory of the *Calender*; that Spenser is reason-

[3] Percy W. Long, *JEGP*, XIII (1914), 344–50, justly points out the limitations of Higginson's book.

[4] (London, 1930), pp. 241–42. An earlier edition of the *Calender* by C. H. Herford (London, 1895) is equally valuable for its introduction and notes, but Herford also finds the allegory too difficult.

ably careful in his use of pastoral names in relation to contemporary characters and events; and that Spenser's primary intention is to reflect his attitude on these characters and events.

It should not be difficult to demonstrate that the *Calender* is an allegory, for the history of the pastoral since the time of Virgil indicates that allegory is always to be suspected in this genre. In his study of pastoral poetry, W. W. Greg maintains that the pastoral is usually allegorical. He writes: "The pastoral, whatever its form, always needed and assumed some external circumstance to give point to its actual content. The interest seldom arises from the narrative itself."[5] And even those like Renwick, who think the allegory of a pastoral is often not worth the effort to dig it out, admit that it is there. Two later scholars (who have been mainly interested in defining the conventions of the pastoral) also acknowledge the usual presence of allegory in this literary form. Hallett Smith declares that "in the English Renaissance the pastoral was inherently a criticism of life" and that we should not be surprised "that sometimes the criticism became explicit."[6] Frank Kermode asserts that the pastoral "was a genre critically regarded as allegorical by nature and tradition, and as particularly apt for veiled personal and ecclesiastical references."[7]

Renaissance critics of poetry who wrote within a decade after the appearance of the *Shepheardes Calender* likewise emphasize the allegorical nature of the pastoral. In 1589 Puttenham wrote:

> The Poet devised the Eglogue . . . not of purpose to counterfait or represent the rusticall manner of loves and communications: but under the vaile of homely persons, and in rude speeches to insinuate and glaunce at greater matters,

[5] *Pastoral Poetry and Pastoral Drama* (London, 1906), p. 67.
[6] *Elizabethan Poetry* (Cambridge, Mass., 1952), p. 57.
[7] P. 29. Both Kermode and Smith give an illuminating account of the meaning of the pastoral in terms of its conventions.

and such as perchance had not bene safe to have disclosed in any other sort, which may be perceived in the Eglogues of *Virgill*, in which are treated by figure matters of greater importance then the loves of *Titirus* and *Corydon.*[8]

Writing three years earlier, William Webbe was equally emphatic. The earlier writers of the pastoral, he wrote, in their rustic characters "would eyther sette foorth the prayses of theyr freendes, without the note of flattery, or enveigh grievously against abuses, without any token of bytternesse." He then adverts to the *Calender* and its author.

There is also much matter uttered somewhat covertly, especially the abuses of some whom he would not be too playne withall; in which, though it be not too apparent to every one, what hys speciall meaning was, yet so skillfully is it handled, as any man may take much delight at hys learned conveyance, and pick out much good sence in the most obscurest of it.[9]

No writer of a pastoral, of course, wishes to be intentionally obscure in his allegory—unless it is dangerous for him to be otherwise. Usually he deals with important contemporary matters and wants to be understood. Often he feels that it is artistically unnecessary to explain his purposes, for he can rely on his readers—or at least on the initiated—to catch his meaning. Nevertheless, writers of Renaissance pastorals were sometimes misunderstood. As Petrarch once wrote on the nature of the pastoral, "if the author does not provide a commentary, its meaning may perhaps be guessed, but can never be fully understood."[10] This statement sheds light on Spenser's intentions. Spenser provided a commentary! The introductory epistle and

[8] *Arte of English Poesie*, ed. G. D. Willcock and A. Walker (Cambridge, 1936), pp. 38–39.
[9] *A Discourse of English Poetrie. Elizabethan Critical Essays*, 2 vols. (London, 1904), G. G. Smith, ed., I, 262–64. (Also in *Var.*, pp. 571–72.)
[10] Quoted by Herford, p. xxx.

gloss by the mysterious E. K., Spenser's wary but well-informed commentator, was in large part added so that the allegory would not be overlooked. In his Epistle to Harvey E. K. tells us (with a quick glance at Skelton) that "the basenesse of the name" *Colin Clout* indicates that Spenser "chose rather to unfold great matter of argument covertly." E. K. further writes that he composed his glosses because otherwise he "knew many excellent and proper devises both in wordes and matter would passe in the speedy course of reading, either as unknowen, or as not marked." E. K. also declares that the allegory of the *Calender* as a whole is specifically personal: a gloss to the September eclogue tells us that Hobbinol is Gabriel Harvey and that the other characters represent Spenser's "familiar freendes and best acquayntaunce."

Further considerations which guided me in this study should perhaps be here declared—particularly the problems of Spenser's use of sources and of literary conventions. Spenser, as we all know, was thoroughly familiar with the pastoral tradition—and with all other literary traditions as well that lent themselves to allegory—and easily followed the footsteps of his great predecessors. As E. K. informs us, Spenser employed all the established conventions of such pastoral poets as Theocritus, Virgil, Petrarch, Mantuan, and Marot. But in imitating these poets Spenser was merely using the externals of their art. Decorum decreed that the poet should thus proceed—even though his world was quite different from that of earlier poets who used these same literary conventions. The evils that Spenser attacks, the great matters of argument he deals with, are those of his own age and not those of Mantuan or Virgil. And while it is interesting and often revealing to note how closely Spenser followed this or that earlier pastoral poet, in order to understand his purposes it is certainly just as important to fit the content of his eclogues to the condi-

tions of his own time. Spenser was expressing himself, his hopes
and fears, in terms of England of 1579. He was free to use or
modify whatever conventions helped him to express his views
on the pressing realities of Church and State in the England
of his own day. In the *Calender* he was not writing an artificial
schoolboy exercise or using frigid literary conventions that had
no relation to contemporary problems. Rather, he was primarily
interested in these problems, wished to reflect on them, and as
a poet chose the recognized way of dealing with them—that
lowly kind, the pastoral.

It is probably idle to speculate whether Spenser's interests
were mainly artistic or ethical; they were both. However rare
the combination, the *Shepheardes Calendar* is both good poetry
and—as I will demonstrate—good propaganda. Hence I would
strongly disagree with, or at least radically qualify, the following
statement by W. J. Courthope—a judgment fairly common in
Spenserian scholarship: ". . . the true significance of Spenser's
allegorical matter can only be discovered by tracking the sources
of his allegorical forms. His motives are artistic rather than
ethical, and he is concerned less with matter of thought than
manner of expression."[11] In this book I do not minimize Spenser's artistry; my purpose, however, is to emphasize Spenser's
matter of thought and to ask the reader to judge its supreme
importance.

It is most reasonable, I believe, to discover the allegory of
the *Calender*, especially the identity of the "familiar freendes
and best acquayntaunce," among those that Spenser lived and
worked with in the two years before the *Calender* appeared.
Hence we are fortunate in knowing that Spenser was secretary
to Dr. John Young, bishop of Rochester, in 1578; and that
Spenser was in the employ of the Earl of Leicester, serving probably as a secretary or as a confidential agent, in 1579. The

[11] *CHEL*, III, 250.

political and religious issues that preoccupied Leicester and Bishop Young in the late 1570's, and Spenser's friendships with important members of the Young and Leicester circles, will furnish most of the evidence and arguments of this book on the meaning of the *Calender*.

The composition of the *Shepheardes Calender* is a problem that has on occasion harried scholars. As it affects my argument I will briefly deal with it here. It has been generally believed that Spenser wrote most of the *Calender* during 1578 while he was secretary to Bishop Young. My research, however, and the implications of the allegory, suggest that Spenser wrote a good part of his poem in the five months prior to its licensing on December 5, 1579. There is, of course, the April 10, 1579, date attached to E. K.'s Epistle to Harvey. This date was probably a fiction designed to protect Spenser from the wrath of the Queen for his allegorical portrayal of more recent events. But even if we grant that it is a true date, substantial changes and revisions could easily have been made in the various eclogues in the seven-month interim before licensing. Events, then, which occurred between April and November, 1579, could very well have influenced either the writing of certain eclogues or—if the poem existed in an earlier form—the substitutions which Spenser incorporated in the *Calender* before handing it to the printer, Hugh Singleton, in early December, 1579. (And Singleton, if he followed his usual practice of dating, rushed the printing through before the end of the month.[12]) I wish to make it clear, however, that there exists no independent evidence on the dating of the eclogues. My suggestions on the composition of the *Calender* rest entirely on the allegory.

[12] The most complete information on Singleton can be found in H. J. Byrom, "Edmund Spenser's First Printer, Hugh Singleton," *The Library*, Fourth Series, XIV (1933), 121–56. On Singleton's practice of dating, see p. 154. Most Elizabethan printers used the calendar year system of dating. Cf. W. L. Edgerton, "The Calender Year in Sixteenth-Century Printing," *JEGP*, LIX (1960), 441.

A complete study of the *Calender* as poetry is not the kind of book I am writing. I am interested here only in the allegory and the way the allegory helps the understanding of the poetry. Hence, in the final section of the book, I discuss only those artistic considerations which relate to the allegory and to the extent that they are influenced by the allegory.

In writing this book I have not tried to evade any problems— or not to meet them honestly. In certain cases I know that I have failed to explain contemporary allusions; in other cases, I realize that my identifications are not capable of absolute proof and that we still remain in the realm of probability. The problem of historical allegory has long been a stumbling block in the poetry of Edmund Spenser and perhaps will always remain so. There are, I know, many scholars who question either the possibility or significance of definite identifications: to them the volumes of the *Variorum Spenser* bring home the sad fact that many identifications are idle and worthless conjectures. And although at times I am inclined to agree, it is my firm belief that we cannot make any final judgments on Spenser as a humorist or as a satirist, or fully understand him, until we determine the personal allegory in his poems. And even when an identification is not too certain, if sensibly based on Spenser's immediate background, it often leads to a closer study and surer knowledge of Spenser's environment and of his relations to his contemporaries. In addition, the exploration of real-life counterparts for characters in literature often reveals aspects of an author's mind and art that have been hitherto overlooked.

With this apologia, I will set forth fully in the next chapter the political crisis of 1579, a crisis that not only disturbed England but particularly agitated the group of poets and statesmen at Leicester House, where Spenser was employed in some capacity by the Earl of Leicester.

Political Allegory

II

Alençon Courtship

THE YEAR 1579 was indeed a time of crisis for the Earl of Leicester and his closest political associates. And in his service for Leicester Spenser was at the very center of the whirling events of this year.

In 1579 the projected marriage of Queen Elizabeth with Francis, Duke of Alençon, younger brother of the French king and heir to the French throne,[1] produced bitter divisions in Elizabeth's Council and hysteria in her Protestant subjects. And al-

---

[1] Francis of Valois, Duke of Alençon, became Monsieur of France (nearest collateral heir to the throne) in 1573; in 1576 he was created Duke of Anjou. A good many historians, however, continued to call him Alençon— as I do here, following Conyers Read, *Mr. Secretary Walsingham*, 3 vols. (Cambridge, Mass., 1925), II, 1–30, where a full account of the second Alençon courtship (that of 1579) can be found.

My summary account of this courtship is largely taken from Read, with a few added details from J. H. Pollen, *English Catholics in the Reign of Queen Elizabeth* (London, 1920), pp. 313–28; and from M. W. Wallace, *The Life of Sir Philip Sidney* (Cambridge, 1915), pp. 211–18. Anything not in these books will be documented.

though in the perspective of history this excitement proved to be a tempest in a teapot, at the time it seemed as crucial as any that had as yet disturbed Elizabeth's reign. Since the frenzy over the contemplated marriage and the events of this year produced a good part of the allegory of the *Shepheardes Calender*, the marriage negotiations and the ensuing national turmoil will be treated in sufficient detail here so that we may see in subsequent chapters how the world of high politics was transmuted into pastoral poetry.

The question of an Elizabeth-Alençon marriage was first broached in 1572, after Prince Henry, Duke of Anjou, abandoned his courtship of the English Queen when he realized that her ministers would not tolerate his Catholicism. So the Queen Mother of France, Catherine de Medici, suggested as a suitor his younger brother, the seventeen-year-old Alençon, who was reputed to be indifferent in religious matters. Both Catherine and Dale, the English ambassador to France, thought Alençon would quickly become a Protestant to marry Elizabeth. But this first Alençon courtship was not taken too seriously, for his youth and his looks (he was twenty-three years younger than the Queen and his face was deeply pock-marked) were against him. Shortly afterward occurred the massacre of St. Bartholomew, which put a stop to all negotiations. They were taken up briefly later when Alençon went over to the Huguenot side.

No real progress was made in bringing about the marriage until the last few months of 1578, when the Privy Council began anew to explore the arguments for and against the marriage. The Earl of Sussex from the very beginning strongly supported the match, and Lord Burghley, with his usual caution, also approved it. Foreign political advantages aside, a strong argument for those who supported the marriage was that it would weaken Leicester's well-nigh royal power.

In early January, 1579, Jean de Simier, Alençon's agent in the negotiations, arrived in England with full power to conclude the arrangements. An accomplished courtier, Simier soon won his way to the Queen's heart with his vicarious courtship. Tongues started to wag and scandalous rumors of the Queen's conduct were bruited about. Simier became Elizabeth's favorite, her "ape"—le petit singe, she affectionately nicknamed him. And even though it was understood that Elizabeth would marry no man unless she had seen him, the members of the Privy Council who opposed the marriage (Leicester, Walsingham, and their political allies) grew fearful and started their campaign against it.

In March, 1579, Castelnau and Mendoza, French and Spanish ambassadors to London, were confident that the marriage would take place. In March also, the preacher at the Royal Chapel declared in the presence of the Queen that England did not need another foreign marriage: Queen Mary's experience was sufficient. Incensed, Elizabeth gave orders that no one was to preach upon a text that lent itself to inveighing against the French marriage.

In April, Richard Cox, bishop of Ely, wrote a letter attempting to dissuade Elizabeth from the marriage. Elizabeth, however, unreceptive to all advice, was willing to settle the details of the marriage contract at once—on the condition that she could cancel these arrangements if Alençon were not to her liking. By the end of April Elizabeth put the question of marriage up to her Council and demanded that individual answers be given in writing. Since she had expressed herself so strongly in favor of the marriage, those councillors who opposed it dared not speak their mind but contented themselves with listing the advantages and disadvantages of the match.

Walsingham's memoranda on the marriage, written in the

spring of 1579, give a good insight into the psychology of those opposing the marriage. Walsingham thoroughly distrusted the French nation and the French duke, thought England would be torn asunder by religious diversity (God's providence and England's prosperity obviously depending on the strict following of the Reformed faith), stressed the traditional national hatred of the French, emphasized the dangers of childbirth to the forty-six-year-old Queen, and noted the augmented problems of the succession and of Mary Stuart if the marriage took place. And if Alençon became king of France, England would be subjected to all the discomforts of an absentee consort. The obvious advantages of the union—a possible heir and the elimination of dangers from Spain and Scotland (which Burghley and Sussex dwelt upon)—Walsingham was inclined to minimize.

If we can believe the optimistic reports of the French ambassador at London (letter of May 29, 1579), the Catholics in England were beginning to take heart. The Queen was said to be looking with new favor upon them, and the Puritans were fearful that when the Queen married Alençon she might prefer to rely on Catholics rather than on the Protestant group in power. The latter and their supporters were so outspoken in their opposition that the Queen imposed silence on them and went less, it was said, to the Protestant services.

And then a new blow fell. In early July Simier informed the Queen that her favorite, Leicester, had secretly married her cousin, Lettice Knollys, Countess of Essex, a woman Elizabeth thoroughly detested. The Queen was furious. While denying Elizabeth her marriage, Leicester was apparently enjoying his own. According to Camden, Leicester was ordered not to stir from Greenwich Castle, and Elizabeth was dissuaded from sending him to the Tower only through the intercession of his long-time political enemy, the Earl of Sussex. Sussex could afford to be generous, for he undoubtedly thought that Leicester's power would now forever be curbed both because of his marriage and of the probable union of the Queen and Alençon. But Leicester, after a bitter and humiliating interview with the Queen, was allowed to return to court in six weeks.

The tension increased in August. Alençon made a short visit to England, arriving on August 17, and the marriage appeared to be a foregone conclusion. Elizabeth seemed to be enthralled by her young suitor, and the wooing was termed a great success. Leicester and his group grew despondent, talked of thwarting the marriage by Parliamentary action, and, encouraged by the Spanish ambassador, fomented Puritan agitation against the marriage. The Puritans, however, appalled at the prospect of the Queen's marriage to a Papist, a Frenchman, and the son of Catherine de Medici (who was popularly blamed for the massacre of St. Bartholomew), needed little encouragement. They composed books, posters, and letters, inciting the people of England to oppose the marriage. They even foretold a new massacre of St. Bartholomew with the Queen as the first victim. The ruin of England and of the English Church was at hand.

One of the Puritan books, John Stubbs' *The Discoverie of a Gaping Gulf Whereinto England Is Like To Be Swallowed by Another French Marriage, if the Lord Forbid Not the Banes, by Letting her Majestie See the Sin and Punishment Thereof*, a bold, vitriolic attack on the marriage and on the character of Alençon, was brought out in late August or early September without the author's or printer's names. Violently angry, Elizabeth ordered the responsible parties to be apprehended, and imposed still stricter silence on the Court and the preachers of London. During August the Countess of Derby, Elizabeth's chief matron of honor, and a daughter of the Earl of Bedford were placed under arrest for talking about Alençon.[2] And during this month, in front of the French commissioners, there occurred the sensational tennis court quarrel between Philip Sidney and the Earl of Oxford. The latter, Burghley's son-in-law and Sussex's protégé, was a strong advocate of the marriage.

Other books appeared, attacking the French marriage by implication. For instance, in 1579 that arch-Puritan, John Field, a protégé of Leicester's and co-author of the famous Puritan manifesto, *The Admonition to Parliament* of 1572, brought out his translation of Philippe de Mornay's *A Treatise of the Church* (a work so popular that four editions appeared in three years, two of them in 1579). In his dedication to Leicester, Field exemplified admirable caution—the safe way of proceeding—by attacking Catholicism in general rather than Alençon in particular. In his lengthy dedication, Field called for strong action against Catholics. Leicester was adjured (but no doubt Burghley and Sussex were silently addressed) "to stoppe youre eares against the enchaunting and fawning whisperings of hollowe harted Papists and dissolute Professors."[3]

On September 27 a royal proclamation prohibited the circulation of Stubbs' *Gaping Gulf*. Those directly responsible for this inflammatory pamphlet were captured in early October. The author, John Stubbs, the publisher, William Page, and the printer, Hugh Singleton, were tried on October 13 and condemned to lose their right hands and to be imprisoned. Many lawyers questioned the legality of the proceedings. One of the judges of

---

[2] For this detail, see *Calendar of State Papers, Spanish*, 1568–79, p. 692. The unnamed daughter of the Earl of Bedford was either the Countess of Warwick or the Countess of Cumberland. (Hereafter *Calendar of State Papers* will be cited as *C.S.P.*)

[3] Eleanor Rosenberg, *Leicester: Patron of Letters* (New York, 1955), pp. 244–50, gives a full analysis of this dedication. In adjacent pages she writes an interesting account of other books brought out at this time, many of them obviously written with the Alençon marriage in mind.

Common Pleas, Robert Monson, openly called them illegal; he was sent to Fleet prison, and, after refusing to retract, was removed from the bench. Meanwhile, Hugh Singleton, through the intercession of someone with power at Court, received his pardon. On November 3 Stubbs and Page were brought from the Tower to the marketplace at Westminster. Before a large and sullen crowd Stubbs declared his loyalty to the Queen. After his right hand was chopped off, he took off his hat with his left, cried out "God save the Queen," and then lapsed into insensibility. And Page, while his bleeding stump was being seared with a hot iron, exclaimed, "There lies the hand of a true Englishman."[4]

A significant fact to remember here is that the printer of the *Gaping Gulf*, Hugh Singleton, little more than a month after the unpopular punishment of Stubbs and Page, brought out the *Shepheardes Calender*. Why Spenser chose him has never been explained on artistic grounds, for normally Singleton would have been the last printer in London that one would employ to bring out what was to be an example of the new poetry.[5] But if we examine Singleton's career, we discover that his connections with the group at Leicester House were both political and religious. As a henchman of the Dudleys, Singleton had been involved in the Jane Grey affair (for which political offense he was denied citizenship at Strasbourg in 1557). At Strasbourg and at Basle (Singleton's main residences on the continent while he was a Marian exile), Singleton would probably have had the opportunity to become acquainted with such roving Marian exiles (now prominent members of Leicester's circle) as Walsingham, the Earl of Bedford, Thomas Randolph, Sir Francis Knollys (father of Leicester's wife and Privy Councillor), and Daniel

[4] *DNB*, "John Stubbs."
[5] Byrom, p. 152.

Rogers.[6] Rogers, a close friend of Singleton's, was also a close friend of Spenser in late 1579, one to whom Spenser was allowed to show Harvey's verses.[7]

When the Privy Council, on the Queen's orders, met on October 2 to discuss the marriage, the sessions lasted for five days. Leicester and his allies had so well organized the opposition that Burghley was startled at the great change in the sentiments of the councillors since the marriage had last been discussed by them, but he and Sussex still favored the match. The majority were bitterly opposed but were unwilling to commit themselves until the Queen had made her views clear. The evasion angered the Queen, but they refused to shoulder the responsibility of a decision. Elizabeth stormed at them, particularly at those who opposed the marriage. She even considered adding four influential Catholics to her Council to counterbalance the opposition. Mendoza, the Spanish ambassador, predicted civil war if the marriage took place.

Things carried on in a tense manner for the next two months, with Simier pressing for a decision. On November 10 Elizabeth summoned her Council, announced her determination to marry, and forbade any further objections. Two days later, agitated and unsure of herself, she sought another expression of opinion from her Councillors and tried to coerce them into writing a joint letter to Alençon to hasten his coming. At their refusal, she stormed again. The matter appeared to reach a climax on November 20, when Elizabeth appointed a select group of her Councillors, from which Leicester and Walsingham were excluded, to arrange the terms of the marriage contract with Simier. On

[6] C. H. Garrett, *Marian Exiles* (Cambridge, 1938), "Census" of these men.

[7] A. C. Judson, *The Life of Edmund Spenser* (Baltimore, 1945), p. 59. All general information on Spenser, particularly of the period under discussion in my book, can be found in this excellent biography.

November 24 they came to a hasty agreement with him. But Elizabeth, disturbed at the opposition of her Council and of their Puritan supporters, provided herself with an avenue of escape. She declared that she could not marry without the consent of her subjects and must be allowed two months to win them over. Otherwise the agreement was off.

When her emissary, Sir Edward Stafford, returned from France in early January, 1580, with expressions of French enthusiasm for the marriage, Elizabeth changed her mind and grew strangely cold. She had found that she was not strong enough to defy public opinion and the majority of her Council. As a result, those Councillors who opposed the marriage slowly began to find favor in her eyes. Leicester appeared again at Court, and Walsingham (who had been angrily called a protector of heretics shortly after Singleton received his pardon) returned after a two-month exile.

In early January, 1580, Elizabeth wrote Alençon, clearly intimating the marriage was off, principally because of the religious difficulty. Her Council and her people would never allow him the public exercise of his Catholic faith. After this period, up to Alençon's death in June, 1584, the marriage talk was sometimes revived for political reasons. But Elizabeth's ministers realized that she no longer desired the marriage, was not emotionally involved, and that there was no reason to become concerned. Alençon even took a second trip to England in early November, 1581, and was publicly entertained by the Queen. But during his visit Campion was executed, an event that doubtless assured the Puritans that no concessions to Popery were being contemplated.

Among the Catholic records there is no evidence that the Catholics had much hope, even if the marriage took place, of improving their situation. In general, they were not enthusiastic about a foreign marriage for their Queen (they remembered the tragedy of Mary Tudor), even though the marriage of the Queen to a Catholic prince offered the only real hope of freedom for the Old Faith or a possible return of England to the fold. Castelnau, the French ambassador, optimistic by nature, thought that the French marriage would relax the persecution of Catholics and that they would gain some measure of toleration. In the long run, however, the Alençon episode augmented the frenzied attack of the Puritans on the English Catholics and led to the stricter Parliamentary act of 1581. The Puritans, too, had a chance to win a temporary tolerance for themselves by helping Leicester and his party achieve their mutual goals by stirring up anti-Catholic propaganda.

Spenser, then, a protégé of Leicester's and a friend of Philip Sidney, was so placed that he not only knew most of the developments of 1579 enumerated above, but also, as we shall see, entered the paper war against Alençon by reflecting the opinions and the feelings of his group in the Shepheardes Calender. While Stubbs was writing the Gaping Gulf in August of 1579, Spenser probably began to revise the Calender to accommodate the same events that had moved Stubbs to fury and consternation. His eclogues, then, are, as we shall see, the abstract and brief chronicle of the period, revealing to the age and body of the time its form and pressure. Sidney's letter to the Queen (outlining the reasons against the Alençon marriage), Stubbs' book, and Spenser's poem all deal with the same great matter of argument that so agitated the English people in the last six months of 1579. And since the contributions of Stubbs and Sidney to the Alençon controversy were written about the same time, and since both writers were somehow connected with Spenser (Stubbs slightly through Singleton, and Sidney mainly through Spenser's employment by Leicester), it is tempting to quote fully the main points made by both, for the Gaping Gulf and the Letter are vigorous pieces of Elizabethan prose and faithfully reflect the extreme and moderate position of the English Protestant mind regarding the French marriage. I will restrict myself, however, to those statements that have a bearing on material in the *Calender.*

The *Gaping Gulf* forcefully reveals the attitude of English Puritans on the Alençon marriage. The burden of the book is that the marriage is extremely dangerous to the "Church of Christ," the English State, and the person of the Queen. Stubbs calls the marriage unreasonable, unlawful, and monstrous, and cites Biblical precedent against it. The marriage will kindle the wrath of God, be the death wound of the English Church, set on fire the Church and the Commonweal—and this fire will spread to other Protestant countries. Moreover, it is sinful to match a Christian lady, a daughter of God, a member of the Church of Christ, to a son of man, of Rome, of France—that "den of idolatry, a kingdom of darkness, confessing Belial and serving Baal." Stubbs then asks:

> And can [it] be saufe that a straunger and Frenchman should as owner possesse our Queene, the chiefe officer in England, our most precious rych treasure, our Elizabeth JONAH and ship of good speede, the royall ship of our ayde, the hyghest tower, the strongest hold, and castle in the land?[8]

The French, declares Stubbs, are utterly untrustworthy. In terms of the St. Bartholomew massacre of seven years before he prophesies that if the marriage takes place, the French, instead of going up to the knuckles in French blood, will go up "to the elboes in English blood" and that Elizabeth would be " a doleful bryde in theyr bloody brydchambers." Furthermore, for the Queen to have a child at her age would be extremely dangerous: her death might be expected, and then the land would be left a

[8] *Gaping Gulf*, sig. C2. The paraphrased material and short quotations have been taken from sigs. A2ᵛ, B2, B3, C3ᵛ, C4, D1, F4, and F4ᵛ. Huntington Library copy was used.

spoil to foreign invasion. Stubbs concludes the *Gaping Gulf* thus:

> . . . thys French mariage is the streightest line that can be drawne from Rome to the utter ruine of our Church: and the very rightest perpendicular downfal that can be imagined from the point France to our English State: fetching in within one circle of lamentable fall the royal estate of our noble Queen, of her person, nobility, and commons. Whose Christian, honorable, healthful, joyful, peaceful and long sovereigne raigne without all superior overruling commander, especially French, namely Monsieur, the King of Kings hold on, to his glory and his assurance of true glory in that other kingdom of heaven. Amen. Amen. Amen.

We do not know exactly when Sidney wrote his letter to the Queen on the Alençon marriage. Wallace suggests that he began it (probably at the request of Leicester, Walsingham, the Earl of Pembroke, and Sir Henry Sidney) in late August of 1579. As Philip Sidney later told Languet, his continental friend, he followed the orders of those he was bound to obey in the matter. And when the letter was given to the Queen we again are not sure: most biographers of Sidney suggest the last two months of 1579 or early January, 1580.

Sidney's letter, then, represents not only his own thoughts on the marriage, but probably the reasoned view of the majority of the Privy Council. The letter makes clear that Sidney had earlier discussed the marriage with the Queen, who feared that her popularity was waning because of her long reign and the uncertainty of the succession. Sidney brings out in a restrained fashion many of the points made by Stubbs. The marriage is not only a hazard to the Queen's safety but is also totally unnecessary. Her strength and the stability of the state depend on her loyal Protestant subjects.

> These how their hartes will be galed, if not aliened, when

they shall see you take to husband a Frenchman and a Papist, in whome howsoever fine wittes may finde either further daunger or painted excuses, yet very common people will know this that he is the sonne of that Jezabel of our age: that his brothers made oblacion of their owne sisters mariadge, the easier to make massacres of all sexes: That he himself contrary to his promise and against all gratefullnes, having had his liberty and principall estate cheefly by the Hugnotes meanes did sack la Charité and utterly spoiled Issoire with fire and sworde. This I say at the first sight geveth occasion to all the truely religious to abhorre such a master, and so consequently to diminishe much of their hopefull love they have long held in you.[9]

The Catholic faction, on the other hand, has been responsible for the Northern rebellion and other plots and cannot be trusted. The Catholics are characterized thus:

men whose spirites are full of angushe, some being forced to othes they accompte damnable, some having their ambition stopped because they are not in the way of advancement: some in prison and disgrace, some whose best friendes are banished, practisers, many thinking you an usurper, many thinking the right you had disannulled by the Popes excomunicacion, all greved at the burdenous weight of their consciences, men of great number, of great riches, because the affaires of the Estate have not lyen upon them: of minds united as all men that deame themselves oppressed naturally are, . . .

Sidney stresses Alençon's unstable mind and French disposition, manifested in the past in both political and romantic projects, mentions the French race's "unhealthfulness," but refrains from repeating other disgraceful truths about Alençon. And since Alençon was not content to be second in power in France, would he be satisfied to be a royal consort without power in England? And his brother, the French king, to satisfy old grudges and

[9] Philip Sidney, *Complete Works*, Albert Feuillerat, ed. (Cambridge, 1923), III, 52. Other quoted and paraphrased material can be found between pp. 51–60.

to divert Alençon from troubling France, would no doubt encourage him to cause mischief in England. Unless the Queen delivers Alençon the keys of the kingdom and lives at his discretion, he would never be content.

Sidney does admit that marriage could bring the "bliss of children," but any marriage, without the attendant disadvantages of this one, could do that. Indeed, the Queen and Alençon represent contrary principles:

> He of the Romishe religion, and if he be a man, must nedes have that man-like propertye to desire that all men be of his mind: you the erector and deffendour of the contrary and the onely Sunne that dazeleth their eyes. He Frenche and desirous to make Fraunce great: your Majesty English and desiring nothing lesse then that France should be great.

Sidney then declares that Elizabeth is the support of God's Church. He even recommends his pet project, the Protestant League: if Elizabeth supports Protestant allies abroad she will be safe.

> If you make that religion upon which you stand to carrye the onely strength and have abroade those who still mainteine the same cause, who (as being as they may be kept from utter falling) your Majesty is sure enough from your mightiest enemies." [sic]

Sidney concludes with an appeal for Elizabeth to support her Council—men whose minds and characters, as he had earlier declared in the letter, were dedicated solely to her safety and welfare: "Lett those in whome you finde trust and to whome you have committed trust in your weighty affairs, be held up in the eyes of your subjectes."

The first section of my book, on the political allegory of the *Calender*, will indicate how many of the characters whose fortunes were involved in the Alençon marriage controversy underwent a literary incarnation in the shadowy world of pastoral poetry.

III

Elizabeth as Rosalind

ONE OF the unsolved mysteries of Elizabethan literature, a mystery that has been a fascinating challenge to scholars, is the identity of Rosalind, Spenser's fickle lady-love of the *Shepheardes Calender*. In the *Variorum Spenser* Professors Osgood and Lotspeich carefully list the various bits of evidence in the *Calender* and its glosses, the Spenser-Harvey letters, and *Colin Clouts Come Home Againe* which serve as the basis of speculations concerning Rosalind; they then summarize and briefly evaluate the many theories on her identity. Since none of these theories has proven generally acceptable, and since they are all conveniently summarized in the *Variorum*, it should not be necessary to review them in advancing a new speculation concerning the identity of Rosalind.[1] The purpose of this chapter is to argue

[1] Var., pp. 651–55. Through their organization and evaluative summary of this mass of material, Professors Osgood and Lotspeich have made my task much easier. All my references to Rosalind scholarship, unless otherwise noted, can be found in the above listed five pages of the *Variorum*. Many of the Rosalinds are imaginary country maidens or purely ideal beings with no flesh and blood existence.

27

that Rosalind represents Queen Elizabeth—a suggestion, as far as I know, never before made.

That Spenser, in various characters of the *Calender*, should represent different aspects of the public and private character of the queen should not be surprising, for such was his usual allegorical practice. In the *Faerie Queene*, for instance, Elizabeth is represented by Gloriana, Una, Mercilla, Belphoebe, and Britomart—all of whom embody in one way or another the virtues of Elizabeth as queen and woman.[2] So too with the *Shepheardes Calender*. In the April eclogue the beauty and virginity of "fayre Elisa, Queene of shepheardes all," is presented in lilting verses replete with classical, medieval, and Renaissance poetic conceits. Colin's "Lady," "flowre of Virgins," is worthy enough to become a fourth Grace "and reigne with the rest in heaven." Classical lore and pastoral convention are strangely intermixed as Henry VIII and Anne Boleyn are thus commended:

> *Pan* may be proud, that ever he begot
> such a Bellibone,
> And *Syrinx* rejoyce, that ever was her lot
> to beare such an one.
> Soone as my younglings cryen for the dam,
> To her will I offer a milkwhite Lamb:
> Shee is my goddesse plaine,
> And I her shepheards swayne,
> Albee forswonck and forswatt I am. (91–99)

In the November eclogue, as I will show in the next chapter, Spenser laments the death of the Queen as Dido: this death is both figurative (in the sense of the loss of the Queen's favor by the Leicester-Sidney group) and real (in the sense of political

[2] For instance, see Elkin Calhoun Wilson, *England's Eliza* (Cambridge, Mass., 1939), pp. 355, 362. This book proved most useful to me in writing this chapter.

Clemens et Regni moderatrix usta Britini
Hac forma insigni conspicienda nitet.

Tristia dum gentes circum omnes bella fatigant,
Circ̄q; errores toto graſsantur in orbe.
An˚ D̄ni   pace beas longa. Vera et pietate Britannos   1572
Iustitia moderans miti sapienter habenas.
Chara domi, celebriſ; foris, longævaꝗ; regni
Hic teneas, regno tandem fruitura perenni.

Plate 1: THE ENGLISH QUEEN

Frontispiece to Christopher Saxton's *Atlas of England and Wales*, 1579: Queen Elizabeth, enthroned, as Patroness of Geography and Astronomy. Probably by Remigius Hogenberg. (Cf. A.M. Hind, *Engraving in England*, I, 74)

The Latin verses stress the mercy and justice of the English Queen; the unbroken peace and the true religion she has blessed her Britons with; the grateful love of her people at home, and her fame abroad.

In the oval above the Queen's head is represented, in the person of the Queen, the reconciliation of the virtues of Justice and Peace—Peace holding her olive-branch; Justice, her sword.

The engraving also illustrates something of the atmosphere of religious prophecy surrounding the Queen. In the bottom right-hand corner, a man gazes through a telescope at a sign in the starry heavens—"a representation of Virgo-Elizabeth as a celestial portent whose advent has been mysteriously foretold." (Frances A. Yates, "Elizabeth as Astraea," p. 60)

This engraving, which appeared in Saxton's *Atlas* the year of the printing of the *Shepheardes Calender*, portrays some of the same attributes of the Queen that are emphasized in Spenser's poem—particularly in the April eclogue and the woodcut before *August*.

prophecy a real death is being forecast for England and Elizabeth if the Alençon marriage takes place, a prospect that seemed
inevitable in the last four months of 1579). The same details
that Spenser uses for Dido—the sun of all the world now dim
and dark—he also uses for Elisa in *April*. Elizabeth is also the
eagle who drops the shellfish on the head of the unfortunate
Algrind (or Archbishop Grindal) in *July's* fable, and the husbandman who, because of the lying complaints of the Briar, cuts
down the oak in *February's* fable.[3]

In order for us to understand how Rosalind represents Elizabeth, it is of primary importance to keep in mind the course of
the Alençon marriage negotiations as outlined in the last chapter.
But also significant, as Professor Elkin Calhoun Wilson has
amply demonstrated in his *England's Eliza*, is to remember the
extent to which Elizabeth was idealized in popular ballad, courtly
and pastoral verse, and epic. As Wilson points out, much of
this glorification of the Queen and woman during the latter half
of Elizabeth's reign was rooted in Spenser's beautiful song to
Elisa in the *Shepheardes Calender*. The Platonizing spirit of
the Renaissance, the Petrarchan concept of love, the stirring
spirit of English nationalism—these found their adequate center
and symbol in the virgin Queen who represented so thoroughly
all that was good and beautiful in sovereignty and womanhood.
Elizabeth was not only the "incarnation of the perfect idea of
feminine majesty, beauty, and virtue," but also the symbol of
amor patriae, the love of England itself, the dear, dear land now
so happily personified by a brilliant and beautiful virgin Queen.[4]

The question, of course, arises why Spenser should find it
necessary to disguise some of the representations of Elizabeth in
the *Calender*. The answer is obvious. Whenever Spenser in his

---

[3] See later chapters on Grindal and Oak and Briar.
[4] Wilson, pp. 238, 336, 394, 270, 164.

allegory becomes critical of the Queen and her policy, whenever he—against the Queen's express command—is alluding to the Alençon affair he of necessity must be as vague and ambiguous as possible. Hence the air of mystery that surrounds Dido. And hence also, as I intend to show, the similar air of mystery enveloping Rosalind. If Spenser had wished to compliment a real lady-love, or to honor some patron who had befriended and helped him, no secrecy would have been necessary. E. K., the *Calender's* wary and well-informed annotator, could have been as open in identifying Rosalind as he was with Hobbinol as Harvey. But open protest against the Alençon marriage, such as was indulged in by Stubbs' *Gaping Gulf* (printed by Hugh Singleton about four months before he printed the *Calender*), was much too dangerous. Realizing that Stubbs' frankness had cost him his right hand, Spenser proceeded by indirection, with E. K. and the engraver of the woodcuts before each eclogue sometimes giving a few hints and sometimes keeping a discreet silence. The details of the eclogues, the political and personal events at Court which were veiled in pastoral or fable would most certainly be understood by those who were in the center of these events and vitally concerned over their outcome.

Let us now run through the *Calender* and determine how closely the details referring to Rosalind would fit the Queen, the symbol of England and love of country, who in late 1579 was stirring up a whirlwind of controversy by her determination to marry the Duke of Alençon.

As a member of the Leicester group and a friend to Philip Sidney and Edward Dyer, two of Leicester's most vigorous younger supporters, Spenser expressed his feelings, as well as those of this group, in a pastoral allegory that, while obvious enough to the initiate, was sufficiently vague and clever to save him from the Queen's wrath.

In the Argument to the January eclogue we are told that the shepherd boy Colin Clout complains "of his unfortunate love, being but newly (as semeth) enamoured of a countrie lasse called Rosalinde." Then in the eclogue itself Colin mentions the "neighbour towne" wherein he saw "so fayre a sight" as Rosalind. But Colin's passion is not particularly sharp, and it suggests the conventional and the allegorical rather than a real emotion. At times the verses have the highly self-conscious rhetorical quality indicative of the courtly poetic exercise.

> I love thilke lasse, (alas why doe I love?)
> And am forlorne, (alas why am I lorne?)
> Shee deignes not my good will, but doth reprove,
> And of my rurall musick holdeth scorne.
> Shepheards devise she hateth as the snake,
> And laughes the songes, that Colin Clout doth make.
>   (61–66)

Then in the gloss we are told that the neighbor town is the "next towne" and that "Rosalinde is also a feigned name, which being wel ordered, wil bewray the very name of hys love and mistresse."

The "countrie lasse" is of course a pastoral term and perhaps not of too much significance; but, as will later appear, this phrase might also suggest someone who is living outside London in the country. The "neighbour or next towne" would probably be a significant hint if we recall that at this time in late 1579 Spenser's chief abode was Westminster and London—the hub of the English universe and the point of common geographic reference—and the Queen's was the royal palace of the neighboring town of Greenwich. This circumstance might have some bearing on the emphasis on Kent in relation to Rosalind in the *Calender*. The only place that the Queen resided in the last half of 1579—

except for the period of her short progress through Essex and
Suffolk in August and early September—was the royal palace at
Greenwich, Kent.[5] All of the bitter meetings of the Privy Council over the Alençon marriage in October and November, 1579,
took place in Greenwich, and it would not be an unpardonable
exaggeration to say that at this time the eyes of all England were
focused on this corner of Kent.

The problem of working out the anagram of Rosalind's real
name is not too difficult if we take *Elisa*, R (abbreviation for
Regina), and the first syllable of *England*. If we take R first,
spell *Elisa* backwards, and change the g of *Eng* to d for the purpose of euphony and of achieving a recognizable girl's name, we
get *Rasilende*, a name close in sound and spelling to *Rosalind*.
Ironically, four scholars—Malone, Grosart, Hales, and Long—
have suggested identifications for Rosalind (based on the correct
ordering of the letters) which have Elisa as the first name, but
have overlooked the most important Elisa of the time. Perhaps
also significant is the final e of E. K.'s spelling of *Rosalind* both
in the Argument before *January* and its gloss (Rosalinde, a spelling, by the way, also used by Gabriel Harvey in the Spenser-
Harvey letters), a spelling which accommodates the e of the first
syllable of England. Besides being an anagram for Elisa Regina,
Rosa linda, Keightley tells us, is pure Italian or Spanish for beautiful rose. As Wilson has indicated, Elizabeth was the rose of
England, the Tudor rose, the flower which in earlier times symbolized a far holier virgin but now was appropriated by poets for
a Queen who incarnated all beauty and virtue.[6]

If we recall from Spenser's letter to Harvey of October 15,
1579, that Spenser was presented to the Queen shortly before

[5] See the *C.S.P.* for these months.
[6] Wilson, pp. 134–35.

this date,[7] such lines as the following might be significant:

A thousand sithes I curse that carefull hower,
Wherein I longd the neighbour towne to see:
And eke tenne thousand sithes I blesse the stoure
[meeting]
Wherein I sawe so fayre a sight, as shee. (49–52)

These lines suggest that Colin saw Rosalind only once—as at this time, as far as we know, Spenser had seen the Queen only once —and, if we properly interpret pastoral conceits, there is nothing in the *Calender* that contradicts this impression. These lines suggest reality. Later lines in which Colin reports that the gifts received from Hobbinol are turned over to Rosalind suggest convention, mere pastoral ballast. We can be fairly sure that Harvey, the Cambridge scholar, would not express his regard for Spenser through gifts of "kiddes, cracknelles, and early fruit"; hence Spenser neither could, nor would, give such gifts to Rosalind, no matter who she was.[8]

A final important bit of evidence must not be neglected. In the woodcut before *January* Colin is looking wistfully towards what appears to be a royal palace.[9] Whoever made the woodcuts was surely aware of the allegory. For instance, this artist knew

[7] Perhaps *presented* is too strong a word. Spenser's words are his "late beeing with her Majestie." This may mean no more than that Spenser was taken to court by Sidney, Dyer, or Daniel Rogers and had an opportunity to see the Queen, who may have nodded in his general direction. Spenser probably refers to this visit in *November*: "Als Colin Cloute she [Dido] would not once disdayne (101)."

[8] Harvey and Spenser were exchanging verses, but it does not seem probable that these are being referred to. The lines on the conventional pastoral gifts are derived from Virgil, Second Eclogue, 40–57. See *Var.*, p. 250.

[9] The woodcut, as we might expect, is a generalized picture of a royal palace rather than a specific sketch of Greenwich. I checked it against the Palace of Placentia, Greenwich, as pictured in the drawing of Anton van den Wyngaerde. Sutherland Collection, Bodleian Library. Published by Whitlock and Hyde (London, 1849).

that the husbandman who cut down the Oak in *February's* eclogue was the Queen, and in the woodcut sketched a figure—a country lass if you will—who in dress, hips, and manner of holding the axe is decidely feminine.[10]

The next important bit of information on Rosalind is E. K.'s statement in a gloss to *April.* "He [Hobbinol] calleth Rosalind the Widowes daughter of the glenne, that is, of a country Hamlet or borough, which I thinke is rather sayde to coloure and concele the person, then simply spoken. For it is well knowen, even in spighte of Colin and Hobbinoll, that shee is a Gentle woman of no meane house, nor endewed with anye vulgare and common gifts both of nature and manners: but suche indeede, as neede nether Colin be ashamed to have her made knowne by his verses, nor Hobbinol be greved, that so she should be commended to immortalitie for her rare and singular Virtues."

The mystery here tantalizes—and is intended to tantalize. Like Dido of *November*, the daughter of "some man of high degree," Rosalind, "a Gentle woman of no meane house," is undoubtedly a Personage deserving the highest idealization and poetic encomiums. The "widow's daughter of the glen," as E. K. writes, is not to be taken literally, for this term is intended to "coloure and concele the person, then simply spoken." I explain it thus: in early Tudor political plays (such as *Respublica* and Bale's *King Johan*) the widow represents England. Rosalind would then be the daughter of England or the Queen. (Incidentally, it might be here mentioned that the *Calender* has interesting points in common with both *Respublica* and *King Johan*. In *Respublica*, People protests his love for the widow Respublica, just as in the *Calender* Colin Clout—who, as we will see, also

---

[10] The Oak, of course, was Leicester. The husbandman is addressed in terms that would apply only to the Queen: "My soveraigne, Lord of creatures all," and "my liege Lord." See Chapter V.

represents the people of England—protests his undying affection for Rosalind, who as Queen would both symbolize and be identified with England. In Bale's *King Johan*, in the earliest version written about 1536, the poor widow who represents England would, in terms of the Elizabethan patterning of history,[11] be identified with the then King Henry VIII and, in this way, the "widow's daughter" would be Henry's daughter, or Elizabeth.) Further, and perhaps more important, in medieval thinking the widow represents the Church.[12] In the agitation against the French marriage, a common objection (as in Stubbs' *Gaping Gulf*) was that the contemplated match was one of a Christian lady, a daughter of God and the true Church of Christ, to a son of man, of Rome, of Antichrist, of France—that "den of idolatry, a kingdom of darkness, confessing Belial and serving Baal."[13] From this point of view, Rosalind, as "widow's daughter," in the political context of late 1579 would be the daughter of the true Church of Christ or the Queen. *Glen* (which as Fletcher remarks here makes its first appearance in English literature)[14] is, I suggest, an anagram of the first four letters of *England*. Inasmuch as Spenser used the word *glen* (meaning a "wild valley") correctly in the *Faerie Queene* and the *View of the Present State of Ireland*, it would be rather naive to consider, as some have considered, that E. K. or Spenser here made a mistake. A better principle to follow is that when E. K. feigns ignorance, or makes

---

[11] For the Elizabethan patterning of history, reflecting the present through the past, see Lily B. Campbell, *Shakespeare's "Histories": Mirrors of Elizabethan Policy* (San Marino, Cal., 1947), particularly chapter on *King John*.

[12] See St. Augustine, *P.L.*, XXXVII, 1726; St. Ambrose, *P.L.*, XVI, 3; Alcuin, *P.L.*, C, 626. These references were furnished by my colleague, Professor Mortimer Donovan.

[13] *Sig.*, A2V.

[14] *Var.*, p. 278.

what seems to be an obvious error, he is not being obtuse but is offering a hint on the allegory of the poem.

The "country Hamlet or borough" is perhaps another reference to Greenwich, which in the late sixteenth century—in comparison to nearby London at least—could be considered a hamlet, that is (according to a common meaning of the term) a village without a church, one that would be included in the parish belonging to another village or town.[15] This was true of Greenwich, for the Church of the Observant Friars, whose land adjoined the royal palace, was no longer used after the Friars were expelled by Elizabeth shortly after her accession.[16] *Borough* would be an even more significant term in reference to Greenwich. As before mentioned, Elizabeth was at this time holding court at the royal palace of Greenwich: in Lambard's *Perambulation of Kent* (published just three years before the *Calender*) *borough* was used in the sense of a Court, or place of assembly. Greenwich was also a fortified town (it contained the Tower of Greenwich where Leicester was sequestered in late 1579), had special privileges granted by royal charter, was not large enough to be considered a city, and could even be regarded as a suburb of London, a part lying outside the wall—all possible meanings of *borough* in the sixteenth century.[17]

The June eclogue brings us to the heart of the matter. In the Argument E. K. writes that Colin, "having (as semeth) founde place" in Rosalind's heart, "is nowe forsaken unfaithfully, and

[15] *NED.*
[16] This was the church in which Henry and Catherine were married, the princesses Mary and Elizabeth christened, and Cardinal Pole consecrated Archbishop of Canterbury. *Victoria History of County of Kent*, II, 194–98.
[17] *NED.* Another definition of a borough is a town which sends representatives to Parliament. Greenwich would not here qualify. See *Victoria History of Kent*, III, 302–303.

in his steede Menalcas, another shepheard, received disloyally."
In the eclogue proper Colin complains:

> And thou Menalcas, that by trecheree
> Didst underfong my lasse, to wexe so light,
> Shouldest well be knowne for such thy villanee.
>
> (102–104)

Then in a gloss to this passage E. K. writes that Menalcas is the name of a shepherd in Virgil "but here is meant a person unknowne and secrete" against whom Colin "often bitterly invayeth."

Here it may be noted that chiefly because of the *Calender's* protest against the Alençon marriage Spenser was forced to seek anonymity. So he adopted Skelton's Colin Clout, the symbol of the people of England. Behind the protective mask of Colin, by name representative of the people, Spenser can voice a common criticism of the sovereign and Burghley, the Wolsey of his time. Colin Clout is in love with Rosalind, the Queen of England, because Colin represents *vox populi*.[18] The people of England love their Queen, who at her accession, by placing a wedding ring on her finger, plighted her troth to England and her people. Hitherto, "as semeth" (to use E. K.'s phrase), the Queen has been faithful to this pledge. But now the Queen is contemplating marriage to a foreign prince whose country is the enemy of England and England's religion. If the marriage took place, the people of England, and England herself as symbolized by the Queen, would be betrayed to their traditional enemy. In the light of these facts, the people (i.e., Colin Clout) can protest; in the light of these facts, the Queen can now be regarded as faithless

---

[18] See Robert S. Kinsman, "Skelton's *Colyn Cloute*: The Mask of Vox Populi," *Essays Critical and Historical Dedicated to Lily B. Campbell* (Berkeley and Los Angeles, 1950), pp. 17–23.

and fickle. Now her "flowre is woxe a weede" and her earlier "faultlesse fayth is turned to faithlesse fere [mate]."

Menalcas—Virgil be thanked!—is of course a daringly close anagram for Alençon. And Alençon, though unnamed and "secrete," was most certainly a person against whom the people of England (again Colin Clout) were bitterly inveighing. E. K. glosses *underfonge* thus: to "undermine and deceive by false suggestion." This definition embodies the opinion that Walsingham, Leicester, and the Sidneys had long entertained about French policy. In a gloss to the May eclogue the whole purpose of the fable of the Fox and the Kid is declared to be to warn Protestants against the "unfaythfull Catholique" and a pointed reference is made to the massacre of St. Bartholomew's. As I will point out later, this fable, though ostensibly dealing with Scottish affairs, is in reality an attack on Alençon.[19] In the gloss on the emblem of *June* E. K. writes that Colin is now "cleane forlorne and rejected" of Rosalind; his hope "cleane extinguished and turned into despeyre," Colin "renounceth all comfort and hope of goodnesse to come." If, as argued, Colin represents the people of England, this remark would be a perfect description of the general reaction to the contemplated marriage.

Colin Clout, then, represents both the people of England in the political allegory of the *Calender*, and Spenser himself, who as an individual Englishman and poet would swell the chorus of voices opposing the Alençon marriage. In the Epistle to Harvey and in the very first gloss to the poem E. K. tells us that Colin "shadoweth" the poet. But in the next paragraph of the Epistle E. K. writes that the "basenesse" of the chosen name Colin Clout indicates that Spenser chose "to unfold great matter of argument covertly"; and in the same first gloss to the poem—

[19] See Chapter VI.

lest we forget—E. K. pointedly reminds us that Skelton wrote a poem under the title of Colin Clout.

The mystic marriage of Queen and Country was, as we all know, a common theme in Elizabethan literature, so I will cite only a few examples here. (This theme, of course, is found earlier than the accession of Elizabeth: in *Respublica* [1553] the allegorical People protests his love for the widow Respublica.) One of the early ballads of Elizabeth's reign, William Birch's *A Song Betwenc the Quene's Majestie and England*, celebrates, in a charming dialogue between England and "Bessy," the betrothal of Queen and Country, as the following two stanzas reveal:

> E. I am thy lover faire,
> Hath chose thé to mine heir,
> And my name is mery Englande;
> Therefore, come away,
> And make no more delaye,
> Swete Bessie! give me thy hande.
> B. Here is my hand
> My dere lover Englande,
> I am thine with mind and hart,
> For ever to endure,
> Thou maiest be sure,
> Untill death us two do part.[20]

When Elizabeth visited Audley End in the summer of 1578, Gabriel Harvey presented his *Gratulationes Valdinenses* which contained (by the vice-chancellor of Cambridge) these verses in her honor:

> Et Populam quod ames, Populo quod amata vicissim
> Semper es, hic constans SEMPER et UNA manes.[21]

[20] Wilson, p. 4.
[21] Wilson, p. 78.

The Alençon courtship caused a rift in the hitherto untroubled love between Queen and Country and produced a good deal of metaphorical jealousy, soul-searching, psychological frustration— and bad poetry, as in an anonymous lyric written to "Elisa: Regina upon Mounzeur's Departure." (The title would probably date it sometime after Alençon left England, following his short visit with the Queen, in late August, 1579.) The first of the three stanzas reads:

> I greefe and dare not shewe my discontent
> I love and yet am forced to seeme to hate
> I doe, yet dare not say, I ever meant
> I seeme starke mute but inwardly doe prate
>   I am and am not, I freese and yet am burnd
>   Since from myself, my other self I turnd.[22]

A few more references to Rosalind remain to be noted in the *Calender*. In *August* Cuddie rehearses the love-lament of Colin, in the form of a sestina, written apparently upon Rosalind's temporary absence from home:

> Thus all the night in plaints, the daye in woe
> I vowed have to wayst, till safe and sound
> She home returne, whose voyces silver sound
> To cheerefull songs can chaunge my chereless cryes.
>   (179–82)

This artificial lament, I suggest, refers to the Queen's leaving Greenwich for a short progress during the month of August— perhaps a good reason for putting it in the August eclogue—and expresses the sorrow of the Court in the temporary loss of its Queen and mistress. But the lament, in terms of its extreme and elaborate emphasis on Colin's woe and the near approach of "dreery death," could also express the national sorrow over the Alençon courtship and the feeling that the marriage would in-

[22] Wilson, p. 262.

evitably involve the death of England, Queen, and people. "Leaving home" could metaphorically depict the straying of the Queen's affections from the English people to the French prince. Another reference occurs in a November gloss when E. K. doubts whether Dido's father is, "as some vainely suppose," the God Pan. But in an *April* gloss Pan is clearly identified as Henry VIII.[23] All of this, of course, is high irony and slick procedure. The gloss suggests what some are concluding (and correctly) but teasingly throws up a handful of dust to protect the allegorist.

The December eclogue, largely imitative and conventional, reviews Colin's life, in pastoral fashion, in terms of the four seasons of the years, but sheds no light on the identity of Rosalind. The eclogue ends with Colin in his wintry desolation, now awaiting "timely death," asking Hobbinol to relay his adieus to Rosalind. But again, if we understand pastoral convention and keep in mind the historical background of the *Calender*, the "deathes wound" that Colin has received, and the fragrant flowers of his poetry—now withered—that should properly adorn Rosalind's garland, could be a figurative expression of the blight that the Alençon negotiations had cast over England.[24]

If Rosalind is Elizabeth, the Spenser-Harvey letters make much more sense, and the *Calender* better harmonizes with the known facts of Spenser's life. The important facts to consider are these: first, Spenser probably married Machabyas Chylde on October 27, 1579;[25] second, Spenser was still working on the *Calender*

[23] Pan at other times in the *Calender* represents Christ, the Pope, or the Shepherd god, but a gloss or the context always makes Spenser's meaning clear.

[24] In *October* Cuddie is encouraged to write of Elisa and Leicester in the epic vein, and in *October's* glosses Elizabeth and Burghley are at least implicitly criticized for their failure to support and encourage poets and poetry.

[25] Judson, *Spenser*, p. 63.

(licensed on December 5, 1579) during the months of October and November, 1579, and a good bit of the allegory, as I will make clear later, deals with the events of these months. Since Spenser was probably married before he had completed the *Calender*, it would not be likely that in Rosalind, Spenser, as some have argued, was representing his bride as a fickle and hardhearted mistress. Finally, it should be remembered that the storm over the Alençon match had almost completely subsided by late January, 1580, when it became generally known that Elizabeth had heeded the will of her people and no longer seriously desired the marriage.[26]

The Spenser-Harvey letters carefully distinguish between Rosalind and Spenser's wife. In the letter to Spenser of April 23, 1580, Harvey speaks of Spenser as one "whom gentle Mistresse Rosalinde once reported to have all the Intelligences at commaundement, and another time Christened her Segnior Pegaso." This could very well be a remark of the Queen's that was reported to Harvey, for the Queen would certainly respond to the poetry of the *Calender* and Spenser's panegyric to her in the April eclogue —an effective counterbalance to the Rosalind and Dido eclogues—especially since the bitterness over the Alençon affair had now died down.

In Spenser's letter to Harvey of April 10, 1580, a reference is made to Spenser's wife: Spenser's sweetheart sends her commendations and wonders why Harvey has not answered her letter. In his reply Harvey promises to make immediate amends and writes the much noted passage, "Per tuam Venerem altera Rosalindula est," etc., which Hamer translates: "Through your love

---

[26] Until Alençon's death in June, 1584, political expediency often revived the discussion of the marriage, but apparently no one—at least not in the Privy Council—thought the Queen was serious in her later negotiations.

she is a second little Rosalind: and not another, but the very same old Hobbinol loves her (as before with your kind leave) with all his heart. O my lady Immerito, my most beautiful Collina Clouta, good-better-best bye and farewell."

Like Hamer, Banks holds that these sentiments refer to Spenser's bride; but as translated by Hamer he believes that they would be extremely tactless and inept, and that even the blundering Harvey would know better than to suggest to a bride that she was almost the equal of the predecessor in her husband's affections. So he translated *altera* not as a "second" but as a "changed little Rosalind": the cruel Rosalind of the *Calender* has relented and married Colin.[27] But other difficulties aside, this difficulty, and the need for a special translation, would disappear if we were to accept Rosalind as Elizabeth Regina. Being compared to a Queen would be a compliment to any Elizabethan lady—especially since the Queen in song and story was regarded as the supreme embodiment of beauty and virtue in womanhood.

Rosalind also appears in *Colin Clouts Come Home Againe*, published in 1595. When this poem appeared the Alençon episode was an old, unhappy, far-off thing, a battle of long ago that was still being fought when the *Calender* was printed, but a battle that actually was won by the English people, a battle in which a foreign schemer was defeated. And in the meantime, fifteen years later, through the fame of the *Calender* Colin Clout was no longer the voice of the people (as in Skelton) but had become the pastoral pseudonym for the poet Spenser.

In the final section of *Colin Clouts Come Home Againe* Spen-

---

[27] I admit that the context of Harvey's letter equally supports Banks' translation of "altera Rosalindula est": "little Rosalind has changed"—her love for Spenser having made her more friendly to Harvey. This interpretation is also acceptable to me—and I explain it thus: the little Queen has changed. Harvey is using a common metaphor, calling Spenser's first wife not Rosalind (i.e., *the* Queen), but "a little Queen."

ser applies to Rosalind such praise that it would be difficult to conceive this praise being directed, in a court poem, to anyone except the Queen.[28] In fact, mere quotation of lines, without argument or elaboration, is really all that is necessary to demonstrate my contention. In the last fifty lines of the poem, Lucida, a beautiful lady, in a spirit of courtly banter mentions that some had criticized Rosalind for being "too cruel hard" and then proceeds to defend her.

> But who can tell what cause had that faire Mayd
> To use him so that used her so well:
> Or who with blame can justly her upbrayd,
> For loving not? for who can love compell?
> And sooth to say it is foolhardie thing
> Rashly to wyten creatures so divine,
> For demigods they be and first did spring
> From heaven, though graft in frailnesse feminine. (911–918)

Colin replies with a soaring panegyric to the "celestiall" Rosalind that concludes by turning the mournful strains of the Calender into an ingenious conceit.

[28] Raymond Jenkins, "Rosalind in Colin Clouts Come Home Againe," MLN, LXVII (1952), 1–5, interprets an earlier passage (ll. 466–79) as referring to Rosalind. He suggests that both passages refer to Spenser's second wife, Elizabeth Boyle; also that Rosalind of the Calender (probably Spenser's first wife) is not the same person as Rosalind of Colin. Charles E. Mounts, "Two Rosalinds in Colin Clouts Come Home Againe," NQ, New Series, II (1955), 283–84, agrees with Jenkins that lines 466–79 probably refer to Elizabeth Boyle, but suggests that the second passage (ll. 903–51) is a "tribute, under the veil of ambiguity," to Spenser's first wife, the dead Machabyas Chylde. The first passage could very well refer to my Rosalind, Queen Elizabeth; the issue, however, is not important to my argument. I would be inclined to agree with Mounts: the first passage, in which Rosalind is never mentioned by name, probably refers to Elizabeth Boyle. Spenser was perhaps shrewd enough to leave the matter ambiguous: if the Queen was able to read her praises in the first passage also, so much the better.

For she is not like as the other crew
Of shepheards daughters which emongst you bee,
But of divine regard and heavenly hew,
Excelling all that ever ye did see.
Not then to her that scorned thing so base,
But to my selfe the blame that lookt so hie:
So hie her thoughts as she her selfe have place,
And loath each lowly thing with loftie eie.
Yet so much grace let her vouchsafe to grant
To simple swaine, sith her I may not love:
Yet that I may her honour paravant,
And praise her worth, though far my wit above.
Such grace shall be some guerdon for the griefe,
And long affliction which I have endured:
Such grace sometimes shall give me some reliefe,
And ease of paine which cannot be recured.
And ye my fellow shepheards which do see
And heare the languours of my too long dying,
Unto the world for ever witnesse bee,
That hers I die, nought to the world denying,
This simple trophe of her great conquest. (931–51)

The poet himself can now laugh at the lugubrious notes of the
Calender—the "languours" of his "too long dying"—proportioned
not only to the twelve months of the year but even to the four
seasons of life itself in the December eclogue. But Spenser is
still willing to testify that he will die the faithful servant of his
Queen: in a sense the *Calender* is prophetically true. To restrict
myself to a single further remark on this passage, such a line as
"So hie her thoughts as she herself have place" could be addressed
only to the Queen.

   As in the *Faerie Queene* and the *Calender*, various aspects of
Elizabeth's virtues as Queen and woman are praised under dif-

ferent characters in *Colin Clouts Come Home Againe*; however, now nothing like the Alençon affair demanded protective mystification. As Cynthia particularly, Eliza is continually praised throughout the poem in much the same fashion as Rosalind.[29]

My conclusion, then, is that a great deal of evidence strongly suggests that Spenser's Rosalind is Queen Elizabeth and that Spenser was extremely bold in the *Shepheardes Calender* in mirroring England's sorrow at, and opposition to, the contemplated marriage of the Queen to Alençon in the story of Colin Clout, Rosalind, and Menalcas. Indeed, if we read the *Calender* closely, in relation to its historical background, we should realize that Spenser was as clear as the times allowed. The Gloss by E. K. was added so that the allegory would not be overlooked. In his Epistle to Harvey E. K. writes that he composed his glosses because otherwise he "knew many excellent and proper devises both in wordes and matter would passe in the speedy course of reading, either as unknowen, or as not marked." But like Falstaff in relation to the Lord Chief Justice, many of us have been troubled with "the disease of not listening, the malady of not marking." Hence E. K.'s efforts have been largely in vain, and we have missed Spenser's "great matter of argument."

---

[29] See especially ll. 332–68; 590–648. Sometimes (as in ll. 40–48) the Queen is praised but not named.

IV

Elizabeth as Dido

THE POETIC excellence of Spenser's lament for Dido in the
November eclogue of the *Shepheardes Calender* has long been
recognized, but the identity of the mysterious Dido has never
been satisfactorily established. In this chapter the case for Dido
as Queen Elizabeth will be again stated, but with additional
evidence and in a new light. This identification was originally
made by Mary Parmenter, who suggested that *November* portrays the figurative death of Elizabeth, who in 1579 was "dead"
to the Leicester-Sidney group by reason of her policy of marrying
the Duke of Alençon, brother of the French king.[1]

Although scholars have tended to accept Leicester as Lobbin,
the chief mourner of Dido, they have generally regarded all iden-

[1] Mary Parmenter, "Spenser's 'Twelve Aeglogues Proportionable to the
Twelve Monethes'," *ELH*, III (1936), 213–16. For two reasons Miss Parmenter's identification has never commended itself to scholars: (1) it was
not fully developed or supported by convincing evidence; (2) it was buried
in a long article mainly devoted to something else—the relationship of the
twelve eclogues of the *Calender* to the material in the old *Kalendar and
Compost of Shepherds*.

tifications of Dido as highly speculative and dubious. To review these identifications briefly: Malone and Higginson believe Dido to be an alleged illegitimate daughter of Leicester by Lady Sheffield; the girl was six to nine years old at the time of her supposed death. Buck and Moore Smith think Dido is Ambrosia Sidney, Philip's sister, who died at Ludlow in February, 1575, at the age of fourteen. And Judson suggests Susan Watts, the daughter of Thomas Watts, who, from the provisions of her father's will, would apparently have been well under eighteen at the time of her conjectured death shortly before 1579. Susan's connection with Spenser would be that Watts's widow had, sometime before 1582, married Bishop Young, Spenser's employer in 1578.[2]

In my judgment, the weakness of these identifications lies in the fact that Lady Sheffield's supposed daughter, Ambrosia Sidney, and Susan Watts were all young girls, whereas Spenser's Dido not only appears to be a mature person, but also is one that Spenser says (1. 78) he had already celebrated in verse. In addition, the superlatives that Spenser applies to Dido, the many consequences that follow her death, and the fact that Lobbin was her "lover and deere frende," would suggest someone historically much more important than any of these young girls. There are also individual difficulties in these identifications. It seems improbable that Spenser would have known Ambrosia Sidney, since his association with Philip Sidney began four years after her death. And we can't prove that Lady Sheffield's daughter ever existed—in addition to the fact that it would have been extremely tactless for Spenser to celebrate a young girl whose mother Leicester had recently repudiated as his mistress in order to marry the Countess of Essex. In regard to Susan Watts, we do not know the exact date when her mother married Bishop Young, or

[2] Var., pp. 402–404.

where or when Susan died; on such fragmentary evidence it seems unlikely that Spenser would have had her in mind.

The identification of Lobbin as Leicester is, I think, quite sound, since Leicester, the Queen and Court's "Sweet Robin," is clearly the Lobbin that Hobbinol refers to in *Colin Clouts Come Home Againe* (11. 735–38).

A major difficulty in accepting Elizabeth as Dido is connected with the problem of dating, for it has generally been supposed that Spenser completed the *Calender* too early in 1579 for the November eclogue to reflect Elizabeth's figurative death in terms of the Alençon marriage negotiations. I have already suggested that the April 10, 1579, date following E. K.'s Epistle to Harvey was probably a fiction. But in any case, even if it is a true date, Spenser would have had nearly eight months to rework certain eclogues or substitute new ones before handing the *Calender* to the printer in early December, 1579. My study of the composition of the various eclogues has convinced me that Spenser wrote *November*, or made significant changes in a possible earlier version, in the period from August to mid-November, 1579. However, if this late dating disturbs any scholar, I might point out that the Alençon marriage negotiations were creating apprehensions and eliciting protests in the first six months of 1579 also.[3] And I would add that the composition of this eclogue (and the Rosalind eclogues, too) can just as easily be put earlier in the year if my suggestion on dating raises unanswerable questions on speed in poetic composition, or on the extent a work of art can be reshaped for the allegorical accommodation of recent events.

Miss Parmenter presents enough evidence to indicate that Spenser occasionally used *death* and *dead* in a figurative sense. For instance, in the October eclogue, Piers says of Cuddie's songs,

[3] See Chapter II for a more complete account of these matters.

Now they in thee, and thou in sleepe art dead. (6)
And in *Colin Clouts Come Home Againe*, Hobbinol says that in Colin's absence

> ... all dead in dole did lie: ...
> But now both woods and fields, and floods revive,
> Sith thou art come, their cause of meriment,
> That us late dead, hast made againe alive. (22, 29–31)

On the basis of poetic practice, then, and the time-problem of composition, there should be no objection to accepting, in the November eclogue, the figurative death of Elizabeth's true self—the Virgin Queen who had preserved England and the Protestant religion from enemies at home and abroad. Elizabeth's alienation from those statesmen opposing the Alençon marriage could likewise be a figurative death, both to them and to her.

As I interpret *November*, however, Elizabeth's death was something decidedly more than a figure of speech—although also present no doubt would be the figurative sense suggested by Miss Parmenter. In the last five months of 1579 the group of English statesmen led by Leicester, Walsingham, and the Sidneys regarded the Alençon marriage as threatening the real and actual death of England, Elizabeth, and themselves. This point of view is frequently repeated in Stubbs' *Gaping Gulf* (as we have seen in Chapter II). It is also clearly stated in a letter, dated October 16, 1579, of Mendoza, the Spanish ambassador at London, to his king, referring to the situation at Court in the first two weeks of October. Mendoza wrote that all of Elizabeth's Council, except Burghley and Sussex, strongly opposed the French marriage. They thought that "for the security of her person, the tranquillity of her realm, and the preservation of the crown" the Queen should not marry Alençon.

> If she were to die, as might be feared if the French were to obtain control of her person, they would take possession

of the country, with the aid they would get from Scotland,[4] without the English being able to prevent it. . . . They said that, even if she did not desire to foresee the evil results which they placed before her, and insisted upon marrying Alençon, it was nevertheless their duty to cast themselves at her feet and die there as they believed she would die if she did this thing.

In his close analysis of the situation, Mendoza could see a number of interesting developments. Elizabeth was given to understand, Mendoza declared,

that when she proposed to marry, Parliament would urge her to declare an heir to the Crown, as the people did not wish, in the case of her death, to find themselves in the present position with their enemies within their own gates. She has been greatly alarmed by all this, as she has been given to understand that as soon as a successor is appointed they will upset her.

In another letter, dated November 11, 1579, Mendoza related that Elizabeth, the day before, had declared to her Councillors her determination to marry Alençon. If the marriage went through, Mendoza thought the Established Church would be crushed and a civil war would be inevitable. He wrote:

If this [the marriage] is put into execution it may undoubtedly be looked upon as a divine provision to reduce this country to the Catholic religion, and to punish it by means of an intestine war, to judge by present conditions, for having separated therefrom.[5]

It is against this background that we must consider November's eclogue. As one employed by Leicester, Spenser would necessarily be cautious in the light of recent events. Stubbs' loss

---

[4] At this time in late 1579, the danger from Scotland was more acute than usual, for Esmé Stuart, James's cousin, a French Catholic who was an agent of the Guises, had become the youthful king's chief favorite and political adviser. See Chapter VI.

[5] *C.S.P., Spanish*, 1568–79, pp. 702–704.

of his right hand for his publication of *The Gaping Gulf* and the Queen's edict against any further spoken or printed protest against the marriage made necessary either discreet silence or an exceedingly subtle procedure. In pointing out the consequences of the Alençon marriage, how could Spenser both protect himself and be understood at the same time? A dark conceit would be perhaps suitable, with enough hints for his readers to decipher his intentions.

In turning to the November eclogue and attempting to clarify its riddles in terms of the political events of the period, let us keep in mind, then, that the Alençon marriage was regarded by those associated with Leicester as a virtual death sentence to England, Elizabeth, and her staunchest English protectors. The evidence suggests that Spenser, in writing of the English Queen, adopted the following procedure.

First, in assuming the point of view towards the French marriage of the Leicester-Sidney group, Spenser chose to protect himself by writing an imitation of Marot's elegy on "the death of Loys the Frenche Queene." He chose the name Dido because Dido was a Queen whose real name was Elisa (or Elissa), as every reader of Virgil and Ovid would know. A good example of the currency of the Elisa-Dido equivalence is found in the title of the summary preceding Surrey's highly popular translation of Book IV of the *Aeneid*: "The occasion of the love between Elissa the Quene of Cartage, after called Dido, and the Troian lord Aeneas, briefly gathered out of Virgyll."[6] As McKerrow points out, the names of Elissa (or Dido) and Eliza were regarded as equivalent and interchangeable, and many writers of the time refer to the Queen as Elissa. For instance, Gabriel Harvey, Spenser's best friend, presented his *Gratulationes Valdinenses* to the

---

[6] *Surrey's Fourth Boke of Virgill*, Herbert Hartman, ed. (New York, 1933), p. 5.

Queen in the summer of 1578. In this work Harvey dramatizes
his being allowed to kiss the Queen's hand:

> Siste, Harveie, inquit, iam iamque videbis Elissam,
> Teque tuosque elegos iam iamque videbit Elissa.

And even when Virgil's Dido was being referred to, the equivalence of the names would call forth the praises of the English
Queen. In Marlowe's *Tragedy of Dido Queen of Carthage*
(probably written about 1586) occur these lines:

> Hear, hear, O, hear Iarbus plaining prayers,
> Whose hideous echoes make the welkin howl,
> And all the woods Eliza to resound.[7] (IV. ii. 8–10)

Readers of the *Calender* would recall that Spenser had celebrated
Elizabeth in the April eclogue as Elisa, and they would probably
not have much trouble in identifying Dido, the "mayden of
greate bloud." By protesting too much that the "personage [of
Dido] is secrete, and to me altogether unknowen, albe of him selfe
[Spenser] I often required the same," E. K. indicates that there
is more here than meets the eye and encourages readers to ferret
out the mystery that demanded such a persevering silence.

The eclogue has hardly begun when Colin startles us with a
strange bit of information: he tells Thenot, the other shepherd
of the eclogue, that it is no time for merriment:

> But nowe sadde Winter welked hath the day,
> And *Phoebus* weary of his yerely taske,
> Ystabled hath his steedes in lowlye laye,
> And taken up his ynne in *Fishes* haske. (13–16)

As Miss Parmenter explains, this putting of Phoebus in the
Fish's hask in November can be no real error, for Spenser, E. K.,
and most readers of the *Calender* would surely know—as did the

---

[7] See *The Life of Marlowe and the Tragedy of Dido Queen of Carthage*,
C. F. Tucker Brooke, ed. (London, 1930), p. 194. Tucker Brooke here
cites McKerrow and the quotation from Harvey.

engraver of the woodcuts before each eclogue—that Pisces is the proper sign of the zodiac for February, and Sagittarius for November. They would also know that the sign changes during the month, as marked in the most common almanacs. Yet E. K. nails the "error" to the mast when he writes: "the sonne, reigneth that is, in the sign Pisces all November. A haske is a wicker pad, wherein they use to carry fish." It does not seem likely, as Renwick has suggested, that Spenser wrote this eclogue originally for February, for the lines are particularly appropriate to November—the days of the month getting shorter, not longer.[8] But what does it all mean?

Recall that the sun is the monarch symbol to the Elizabethans; and that Alençon, a Catholic, was next in line to the French crown. Like the Kid of May's fable, caught in the Fox's bag, Elisa was in the Fish's hask—or basket or bag. The Fish is possibly a reference to Alençon, as heir to the French throne the "Dolphin" of France. Or it is perhaps a reference to Catholics in general: the Fish could symbolize Catholics because of their observance of fast days, which were especially abhorred by Puritans as a papist superstition; and on some old calendars, as Miss Parmenter observes, fast days were called "fish days" and indicated by writing in the word "fish." At any rate, however we interpret this reference to the Fish's hask, if Elizabeth married Alençon, the "Dolphin" and Catholics would have England and Elizabeth in their power.

Proceeding through *November*, we notice significant details which Spenser stresses and which do not appear in his source,

[8] Moore Smith and Miss Darbishire, in their reviews of Renwick's edition of the *Calender*, reject Renwick's theory, observing that the whole context of the Fish's-hask passage fits November much better than February. Var., p. 415.

Marot's elegy on the French Queen. Thenot remarks:

> For deade is Dido, dead alas and drent,
> Dido the greate shepehearde his daughter sheene. (37–38)

E. K. glosses the "greate shepehearde" as "some man of high degree, and not as some vainely suppose God Pan. The person both of the shepehearde and of Dido is unknowen and closely buried in the Authors conceipt." My guess is that E. K.'s gloss is meant to recall *April's* Elisa who is the daughter of Pan—Henry VIII—although it is here prudent to rebuke those who so "vainely suppose" and to reiterate the absolute and protective "no comment" of the author.

Notice the details and the implications of the second stanza on the death of Dido, all of which would be relevant to Elizabeth's "death" in terms of her marriage to Alençon.

> Shepheards, that by your flocks on Kentish downes abyde,
> Waile ye this wofull waste of natures warke:
> Waile we the wight, whose presence was our pryde:
> Waile we the wight, whose absence is our carke.
> The sonne of all the world is dimme and darke:
>   The earth now lacks her wonted light,
>   And all we dwell in deadly night,
>   O heavie herse. (63–70)

Most of these details would be highly appropriate to Elizabeth, but why are the shepherds "Kentish"? The Sidneys, of course, had their family seat at Penshurst, in Kent, but this would not quite explain the reference. My conjecture is that Spenser is referring to all those prominent members of the Court who opposed the Alençon match; and I would recall that except for the period from August 5 to mid-September, 1579, when Elizabeth made a short progress through Essex and Suffolk, the Court was in attendance at the royal palace of Greenwich, Kent, from July to the end of the year. All of the bitter meetings of the Privy

Council with the Queen in October and November were at Greenwich.

To an Englishman at this time, the "sonne of all the world" would certainly suggest Elizabeth, for it was an epithet that the poets of the time, with interesting variations, frequently applied to her. (For instance, she was also called the "Sunne of Christendome" and "Albion's shining Sun."[9]) In his letter to the Queen discussing the Alençon marriage, Philip Sidney applies the term *sun* to Elizabeth in a number of ways. He first contrasts Alençon and the English Queen thus:

> He of the Romish religion, and if he be a man, must nedes have that man-like propertye to desire that all men be of his mind: you the erector and deffendour of the contrary and the onely Sunne that dazeleth their eyes.

Sidney then twice refers to, and tries to allay, the Queen's fear that the English people are looking towards the "rising Sunne," i.e., her successor. Then Sidney asks:

> But in so lineal a monarchie where even the infants sucke the love of their rightfull Prince, who would leave the beames of so feare [i.e. fair] a Sunne for the dreadfull expectacion of a devided companie of starres?[10]

In the third stanza of the lament for Dido a reference is made to "the songs that *Colin* made in her prayse." This reference might suggest the beautiful lyric that Spenser wrote in honor of "fayre *Elisa*, Queene of shepheardes all," in the April eclogue. And in the next stanza on the riddle of the painful earth occurs the line:

> The braunch once dead, the budde eke needes must quaile.
>
> (91)

E. K. glosses "the braunch" thus: "He meaneth Dido, who being, as it were the mayne braunch now withered the buddes that

---

[9] Wilson, pp. 180, 187.
[10] "Letter," Feuillerat, ed., Works, III, 56–58.

is beautie (as he sayd afore) can nomore flourish"—a beautiful tribute peculiarly applicable to Elizabeth at this time in view of the political situation explained above.

In the following stanza there is possibly a tribute to Elisa's courtesy, hospitality, and pleasantness to all—even social inferiors and Colin Clout—put into pastoral terms. While the "old" Elisa was "alive," the Virgin Queen who had protected England and the Protestant faith and her true supporters, she

> For beauties prayse and pleasaunce had no pere:
> So well she couth the shepherds entertayne,
> With cakes and cracknells and such country chere,
> Ne would she scorne the simple shepheards swaine, . . .
> Als *Colin cloute* she would not once disdayne. (94–97, 101)

This last line could well allude to Spenser's "late beeing with hir Majestie," mentioned in Spenser's letter to Harvey of October 15, 1579.

In the Lobbin stanza there is a possible recounting of Leicester's grief, of Elisa's almost unlimited bounty to him, and of his present eclipse at Court, his position of leadership lost in part because of the machinations of his political enemies, the Queen's favor lost because of his discovered secret marriage to the Countess of Essex and his opposition to the French marriage.

> O thou greate shepheard *Lobbin*, how great is thy griefe,
> Where bene the nosegayes that she dight for thee:
> The colourd chaplets wrought with a chiefe,
> The knotted rushrings, and gilte Rosemaree?
> For shee deemed nothing too deere for thee.
>> Ah they bene all yclad in clay,
>> One bitter blast blewe all away.
>>> O heavie herse,
> Thereof nought remaynes but the memoree.
>>> O carefull verse. (113–22)

I am not sure what "bitter blast" is here being referred to, for Elizabeth directed a number of bitter blasts at Leicester during the last six months of 1579: in early July, when she discovered his secret marriage to the Countess of Essex; in late August, when, after Leicester was finally allowed to return to Court, Elizabeth had an angry private interview with him; in the first week of October, during the stormy five-day session while the Privy Council discussed the Alençon marriage; in mid-November, when Elizabeth excluded Leicester from the group of Councillors that arranged the terms of the marriage contract with Simier, Alençon's agent in the negotiations.

In a following stanza (11. 133–42) Spenser gives a characteristic Elizabethan twist to pastoral symbolism, when, except for the wolves, the "feeble flocks in field" and forest beasts all show their grief—

Now she is gon that safely did hem keepe.

Here we should recall that the pastoral wolves of evil nature symbolized to Spenser's age sowers of discord and sedition (usually Catholics).[11] In other words, all except traitors mourn for Elisa.

Many of the details applied to Dido in November had been earlier applied to Elisa in April. For instance, in April the water nymphs—"Ladyes of the lake"—carry to Elisa a garland of olive branches (11. 120–24) to symbolize the years of peace that Elizabeth has given to England; and the Muses come bearing "Bay braunches" (1. 104), which, as E. K. explains, are "the signe of honor and victory." Now consider these lines in November:

The water Nymphs, that wont with her to sing and daunce,
And for her girlond Olive braunches beare,
Now balefull boughes of Cypres doen advaunce:

[11] See, for instance, John Ferne, Blazon of Gentrie (London, 1586), Section II, 41.

The Muses, that were wont greene bayes to weare,
Now bringen bitter Eldre braunches seare. (143–47)
These correspondences might suggest that Dido is not only a
Queen, but the Queen already celebrated in the April eclogue.

The shift from sorrow to joy, in terms of eternal destiny, is of
course a convention of the pastoral elegy, but in addition it provides a certain grim irony that Elisa might not be able to appreciate fully:

Why then weepes Lobbin so without remorse?
 O Lobb, thy losse no longer lament,
 Dido nis dead, but into heaven hent.
  O happye herse. (167–70)

And in the next stanza *April's* goddess, i.e., Elizabeth (*April*, l.
97), whose Accession Day, November 17, was celebrated as if she
were indeed a saint on the church's calendar, is joyfully and perhaps ironically referred to thus:

She raignes a goddesse now emong the saintes,
 That whilome was the saynt of shepheards light:
 And is enstalled now in heavens hight.
  I see thee blessed soule, I see,
  Walke in *Elisian* fieldes so free. (175–79)

(The irony, of course, stems from the situation and from the
poetic device in relation to prophetic fact rather than from the
tone of the poet.) These verses have an added interest because
the Cambridge poets mourned Elizabeth at her death in 1603 in
Latin verses embodying similar sentiments. For instance, in
death, Elizabeth the earthly goddess and royal virgin has become
a goddess, a royal virgin in heaven,

 Quae fuit in terris Dea, Virgo, Regia Virgo
 Nunc est in coelis Regia, Virgo, Dea.[12]

---

[12] Quoted by Wilson, p. 383.

The phrase "Elisian fields" in Spenser's stanza is, I suspect, a perfectly normal Elizabethan pun that points to the Elisa that Dido represents. It too was employed in memorial verses, as in John Lane's *Elegy* on the death of the Queen, where Elizabeth is implored to live evermore now in the celestial sky:

> Raine ever there on that Elyzian greene:
> Eliza, well may be Elyziums Queene.[13]

Other details in the November eclogue can be analyzed in this same fashion, but I think by now it should be fairly clear that the mysterious Dido is most probably designed to embody the prophetic fears of the group around Leicester who were strongly opposing the French marriage—but with no apparent success, it would seem—in the black months of October and November, 1579.

The choice of November for the lament over the death of Dido was in itself a happy stroke, for November was the Queen's month, the month in which her triumphs over the enemies of England and of the Established Church were formally celebrated. In addition, November was the month whose teaching, in the old *Kalendar and Compost of Shepherds*, was of death and immortality, and hence could accommodate an elegy with ironic overtones which stated, in riddling fashion, the death of England and of Elizabeth, a death which seemed, in terms of the Alençon marriage, imminent in the last few months of 1579.

[13] Wilson, p. 377.

V

Leicester and Oxford as Oak and Briar

THE FABLE of the Oak and the Briar in the February eclogue of the *Shepheardes Calender* has provoked more varied interpretations than any other piece of poetry of similar length in Spenser. In this chapter I intend to interpret this fable as a reflection of persons and events that Spenser became well acquainted with in his employment at Leicester House in 1579. Specifically, I will venture to explain the political aspects of the fable and suggest that the Oak represents the Earl of Leicester, and the Briar, the Earl of Oxford, interpretations which, as far as I know, have never before been made. Second, I will go beyond this particular application and explain the "morall and generall" meaning of this fable, a meaning which E. K. stresses in the introduction to *February*.

All commentators, of course, agree that *February's* fable reflects the conflict between youth and age. But when it comes to a closer application or further meaning, there is no agreement.[1] Friedland emphasizes that Spenser's "amplification of the fable of the Oak and the Briar has no known model in English or foreign literature and is a fresh invention"; and he rejects as wholly unconvincing all the attempts at allegorical interpretation that have so far been made.[2] With Friedland I agree wholeheartedly, and here I hope to provide a more convincing explanation of this fable.

The fable of the Oak and Briar requires an analysis and interpretation before it can be understood or applied to contemporary events. In brief, there is the basic plot: the bragging and spiteful Briar complains of the aged Oak to the husbandman; the latter, in anger, cuts down the Oak; the winter storms then destroy the Briar, which now lacks the protection of the Oak. To my mind, the Oak—"a tree of state," "his honour decayed"—represents some powerful statesman of the period who was maligned and "cut down" (i.e., lost the Queen's favor and his position of influence) through misunderstanding, spite, and false complaints. The Briar is the upstart and younger courtier who brought about the elder statesman's downfall. And the husbandman is Queen Elizabeth, who listened to the unjust complaints and in anger proceeded to cut down her erstwhile favorite, the mighty "tree of state." What happens to the Briar finally is in a sense a prophecy: cut down or remove from royal favor statesmen of proven value, and misfortune (winter's storms) will afflict not only the state but especially those lesser, more ornamental figures, such as the dainty Briar, whose very existence must depend on the trees of state.

We do not know exactly when Spenser left the employ of

[1] For summary of scholarship, cf. Var., pp. 254, 261–62.
[2] Louis S. Friedland, "Spenser's Fable of 'The Oake and the Brere'," *Shakespeare Association Bulletin*, XVI (1941), 57.

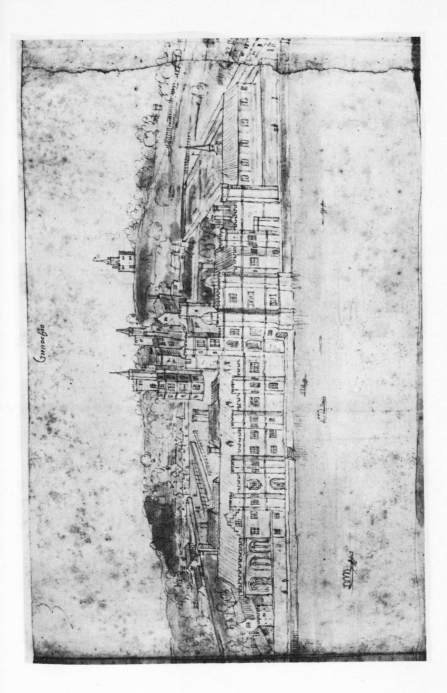

Grenoble

Plate 2: GREENWICH PALACE

Palace of Placentia, where the Queen was residing in late 1579. This is one of several drawings of Greenwich Palace by Anthony van der Wyngaerde in the Sutherland Collection, Ashmolean Museum, Oxford. It probably dates between 1558 and 1562- (A.M. Hind, *Engraving in England*, I, 30)

Young, bishop of Rochester, for that of Leicester. Padelford suggests the spring of 1579,[3] and this date, I think, would be generally acceptable. But as secretary to Young, a Court bishop, Spenser would be pretty well aware of the fortunes of Leicester's group and of the big events of the time, especially the furor over the Alençon marriage; hence it does not affect my subsequent arguments whether Spenser entered Leicester's service in the spring of 1579 or later. From Spenser's letter to Harvey dated October 5, 1579, we do know that Spenser had been at Leicester House long enough to become friendly with Philip Sidney and Edward Dyer, and that Leicester knew and trusted him well enough to consider sending him on a secret mission to the Continent.

It is fairly clear that the fable of the Oak and the Briar contains specific allegory and that the husbandman is Queen Elizabeth. In introducing the fable and attributing it to Chaucer, Thenot, the narrator, tells Cuddie that it has a pointed application: he knows "none fitter than this to applie." And the husbandman can be only the Queen. Going forth to survey his "trees of state," the husbandman is addressed by the Briar—who calls himself a "suppliant" and "poore vassal"—as "my liege Lord" and "my Soveraigne, Lord of creatures all." Such terms would be used only in reference to the Queen. For those who might be puzzled by the Queen's being called a husbandman, it should be mentioned that the term *husbandman* (or *husband*) was often used to represent Elizabeth in the literature of the period. For instance, in Anthony Munday's *Watchward to England* (1584) Elizabeth is called "the husband of the common weale, married to the Realme, and the same by ceremony of Ring as solemnly signified, as any other marriage."[4] It should also be noted that the

[3] Var., p. 612.
[4] Quoted by Wilson, p. 218. His notes to this page refer to like sentiments in many other writers of the period.

engraver of the woodcut before this eclogue, who was certainly aware of the allegory, depicted the husbandman as feminine in every way—dress, stature, and manner of holding the axe.[5]

Leicester's fall from the Queen's favor in 1579 would well qualify him for the Oak of *February's* fable. Since his fall from favor was so intimately bound up with the Alençon courtship, and since it has been given in such detail in Chapter II, there is no need to repeat it here. As we have seen, it was precipitated by Elizabeth's discovery, in early July, 1579, of Leicester's marriage to the Countess of Essex.

Before equating Leicester with the Oak, I wish to make a few observations. Tillyard has pointed out that in the accepted concept of the chain of being there is a vast difference in virtue within each class and that every class has a primate. The oak is king of trees, as the sun is king of stars, the dolphin of fish, the eagle of birds, and the rose of flowers—to mention those primates used by Spenser in the *Calender.*[6] Furthermore, as Friedland has pointed out, the oak became a stock metaphor and was commonly used for figurative purposes.[7] The oak was also a personal symbol of Leicester, as well as of other important people at Leicester House who had tied their political fortunes to his.

The Elizabethans had quick minds, were inveterate punsters, and would perhaps notice that the Latin word for oak, *robur*, resembled *Robert*, Leicester's first name. Now this resemblance was the actual basis of Leicester's use of the oak as a personal

[5] It is unfortunate that Herford and Renwick omit the woodcuts before each eclogue in their editions of the *Calender*. The woodcuts are significant, but have apparently never been closely studied as an aid to ferreting out the allegory.

[6] E. M. W. Tillyard, *Elizabethan World Picture* (London, 1948), pp. 25–27. The cedar, of course, was sometimes given first place among the trees.

[7] Friedland, p. 53.

symbol. Sometime during his fifteen months' imprisonment under the sentence of death (July, 1553, to October, 1554) as an aftermath of the Lady Jane Grey affair, Robert Dudley cut into the stone of the Tower of London oak leaves and acorns to represent himself—just because *robur*, an oak, echoed *Robert*.[8] And from the time of Elizabeth's accession, Robert Dudley was the Queen's *robur*—the oak on whom she depended both as her favorite courtier and as a "tree of state."

One of the better known equations of the Oak with Leicester occurred during the entertainment of the Queen at Kenilworth in 1575. In 1576 George Gascoigne (who was commended as a poet by E. K. in a gloss to the November eclogue) brought out his *Princely Pleasures at Kenilworth Castle*, a work that Spenser undoubtedly knew. In the final masque Gascoigne, as Sylvanus, discourses on the theme of Leicester's ardent devotion to the Queen. In a pastoral setting, a great Oak rises over a Bramble Briar. The Oak, according to Sylvanus, represents Constancy or Leicester, and the Briar "that busy elf, Contention."[9]

Do we find any personal touches pertaining to Leicester in Spenser's depiction of the Oak? Such, I think, there are. Leicester, tall and well proportioned, by early 1579 had been the Queen's favorite courtier for over twenty years, and had served the Queen and his country with great distinction—and reward. Now let us consider these lines about the Oak and make a personal application:

[8] Frederick Chamberlin, *Elizabeth and Leycester* (New York, 1939), p. 81. The Bear and the Ragged Staff, referred to in *October*, 1. 47 (and in E. K.'s gloss on this line), was more properly the coat-of-arms of the oldest living brother, Ambrose, Earl of Warwick. It too was cut on the walls of the Tower. Chamberlin, p. 80, gives a reproduction of the carving. On the sprig of oak as a personal device of Leicester, see also Milton Waldman, *Elizabeth and Leicester* (London, 1946), p. 58.

[9] Louis S. Friedland, "A Source of Spenser's 'The Oak and the Briar'," *PQ*, XXXIII (1954), 222–24.

The bodie bigge, and mightely pight,
Throughly rooted, and of wonderous hight:
Whilome had bene the King of the field,
And mochell mast to the husband did yielde. (106–109)

Leicester "whilome" had certainly been "King of the field," but his enemies—and historians—might be inclined to debate the value of his contributions ("mochell mast") to Elizabethan England. In possible references to Leicester's height, E. K. has a gloss on "trees of state," pointing out that these are "taller trees fitte for timber wood." Or we can consider lines like the following, recalling that the angry Queen for a time (in July and August, 1579) refused to allow Leicester to function as a Privy Councillor, or to explain his position to regain her favor.

Anger nould let him [husbandman] speake to the tree,
Enaunter his rage mought cooled bee. (199–200)

There are, of course, the following puzzling lines on the Oak:

For it had bene an auncient tree,
Sacred with many a mysteree,
And often crost with the priestes crewe,
And often halowed with holy water dewe.
But sike fancies weren foolerie,
And broughten this Oake to this miserye.
And nought mought they quitten him from decay. (207–13)

Although this passage has misled many scholars, it has, I feel, no real significance. It is merely a little dust thrown in the eyes of the readers to protect Spenser from the dangers of plain speaking. As the fable makes clear, it was the insistent and lying complaints of the Briar, plus the wrath of the husbandman, that brought about the Oak's downfall. For those, however, who would stress this passage, I would point out, following Higginson, that whoever the Oak represents was undermined and brought to decay by Catholic practices. This was the exact position of Leicester in

Januarye.

Februarie.

Plate 3: January and February

Woodcuts before the January and February eclogues. Both reflect the allegory. In *January's* woodcut, Colin Clout (the English people) looks toward a royal castle—the abode of Rosalind (the Queen). In *February's* woodcut, the Husbandman who represents the Queen (note the female figure) cuts down the Oak (the Earl of Leicester).

late 1579 when viewed through Protestant eyes horrified at the apparent success of Simier, Alençon, and the pro-Catholic group at Court (at least pro-Catholic to the extent that, for whatever reasons, it advocated the French marriage).

Now let us turn to the Briar. Both internal and external evidence point to Edward de Vere, the seventeenth Earl of Oxford and Burghley's scapegrace son-in-law, as the Briar in *February's* fable. In the crucial period from March to December, 1579, Oxford became the special favorite of the Queen, and said only what pleased her; no one was more ostentatiously in favor of the French marriage. Oxford was much in the company of Simier, and later of Alençon's suite during the few days of the Prince's visit to London in mid-August. Most probably Oxford was the one who informed Simier of Leicester's marriage, information which precipitated Leicester's fall from favor in early July.

In one of the more sensational incidents relating to the Alençon marriage, Oxford, in the presence of the French commissioners, in late August called Philip Sidney a "puppy" and arrogantly ordered him and his friends from a tennis court at Whitehall. Sidney gave Oxford the lie direct, and then after a few words of "sharp accent" abruptly strode out. He waited a full day for Oxford's challenge, and finally sent a gentleman of worth to awaken Oxford "from his trance." Oxford then sent the challenge. The Council intervened, but was unable to compose the quarrel and referred it to the Queen. She pointed out Oxford's superior rank, but Sidney boldly told her that difference in degree between an earl and a gentleman should not countenance wrongs or insults. On the Queen's command, however, the duel did not take place.[10]

In addition, Oxford, who had secretly become a Catholic on

[10] Wallace, pp. 214–15.

his return from Italy in 1576,[11] was one of the leaders of the pro-Catholic faction at court. The group at Leicester House probably did not know that he was a Catholic, but his Catholic sympathies were apparent, as well as his opposition to the "war party." This group, led by Leicester, Walsingham, and Philip Sidney, were advocating a league of Protestant princes and open opposition to Spain both in the Low Countries and on the high seas.

Oxford, eighteen years younger than Leicester, would fittingly represent youth in conflict with age. Internal evidence also suggests Oxford as the Briar, for the fable is filled with significant touches that exceed fabular verisimilitude. The most obvious are that the Briar is a braggart, spiteful, short of stature, "embellisht with blossomes fayre," and endowed with a "Sinamon smell." In regard to Oxford all of these details are palpable hits.

Oxford was without doubt the best-known lying braggart at Court during this period. After his two-week unauthorized trip to Flanders in July, 1574, during which he may have visited the Spanish lines, Oxford told fantastic stories about how the Duke of Alva had made him General over the armies of the Low Countries, and how he had led a picked group of Spaniards that captured bridges and entrenchments with horrible slaughter to the enemy. When Thomas Bedingfield came with a mandate from the Queen for Oxford to return to England, both he and his horse—so the story went—were terrified by the heaps of dead bodies. But the Italian trip produced even better stories in which Oxford was the hero amid great difficulties and against great odds, though here his triumphs were more as a statesman than as a military leader. B. M. Ward, Oxford's overly sympathetic biographer who would make him another, but a superior, Sir

[11] B. M. Ward, *The Seventeenth Earl of Oxford* (London, 1928), p. 207. On the whole, the facts that Ward assembles on Oxford contradict his consistently favorable interpretations of his subject.

Philip Sidney, excuses these stories as amusing inventions of a high-spirited youth who was exhilarated by wine and company.[12] But, sad to relate, Oxford had such a reputation as a liar that when (in December, 1580,) observing the trend of the times, he disavowed Catholicism and dramatically informed the Queen that Lord Henry Howard, Charles Arundel, and Francis South-well—his closest friends—were traitors and Catholics, he was not believed; he was thrown into the Tower for a while, and the Queen would not allow him at court for two and a half years.[13]

Oxford's spitefulness and vengeful nature were evidenced in a number of ways: his brutal treatment of his wife after his Italian trip, when he entertained the notion that he was not the father of his child; his alleged attempts to dissipate his fortune in order to spite Burghley; and his attempts to assassinate servants and political enemies. In 1567 Burghley confessed to his diary: "I did my best to have the jury find the death of the poor man whom he [Oxford] killed in my house, se defendendo." In 1573 three of Lord Oxford's men tried to kill two former associates. The latter, in writing a letter to Burghley and seeking his protection, named Oxford as the instigator of the attempt on their

[12] Ward, pp. 94–100, 128.
[13] Ward, pp. 208–33. A complicating factor, if not the chief one, in Oxford's lengthy disgrace, was that he was named as the father of an illegitimate child (March, 1581) by Anne Vavasour, who accused Oxford of having seduced her. Lord Howard, Charles Arundel, and Francis South-well (whom Oxford charged with plotting against the government) were relatives of Anne and friends of her family. The Queen imprisoned Oxford for this affair and took a new interest in Oxford's confession of Catholic activities and his charges against his former friends. After Anne's condition was discovered, Oxford's earlier confession looked like a move of self-protection in a personal quarrel. Josephine W. Bennett, "Oxford and Endymion," PMLA, LVII (1942), 354–58, gives a good account of this quarrel and Oxford's disgrace. See also E. K. Chambers, Sir Henry Lee (Oxford, 1936), pp. 150–63.

For some strange reason all mention of this scandal is omitted by B. M. Ward, Oxford's chief biographer.

lives. Oxford was also charged with reluctantly abandoning "a safe plan" of assassinating Philip Sidney in an aftermath of the tennis-court quarrel.[14]

The Briar's "blossomes fayre" and "Sinamon smell" also suggest Oxford. Oxford was the most prominent example at Court of the perfumed dandy. Returning in 1576 from his Italian trip with luxurious articles of dress, Oxford won for himself the dubious honor of introducing into England embroidered gloves, scented leathern jerkins, sweet bags, and expensive perfumes. He ingratiated himself with the Queen by presenting her with perfumed gloves trimmed with four tufts or roses of colored silk. The Queen was so pleased with these gloves that she was pictured with them upon her hands, and for many years after the perfume was called "the Earl of Oxford's perfume."[15] Spenser was possibly referring to these gloves in these words of the Briar:

Seest, how fresh my flowers bene spredde,
Dyed in Lilly white, and Cremsin redde,
With leaves engrained in lusty greene,
Colours mete to clothe a mayden Queene. (129–32)[16]

As Great Chamberlain, Oxford had precedence over all the other earls of England, but his position was purely an ornamental

[14] Ward, pp. 91, 113–26; and DNB article on Oxford.
[15] Stow, Annals, p. 868. Quoted by Ward, p. 129.
[16] It should be remembered, however, that such flowery adornments would be appropriate to the Briar as a member of the wild-rose family; they would also suggest the fashionable young lover, such as Chaucer's Squire, or, as in this case, perhaps the Earl of Oxford. Like Chaucer's Squire, Oxford was proficient in making songs, jousting, and dancing. He was, indeed, the most graceful dancer in Elizabeth's Court and was often called upon to perform. In late 1578 and in 1579 Oxford, at the Queen's request, sometimes displayed his dancing skill before the French delegation arranging the Alençon marriage. (If Leicester, however, asked Oxford to entertain the Frenchmen with his dancing, Oxford would refuse.) See M. A. S. Hume, The Courtships of Queen Elizabeth (London, 1898), p. 195.

one of no real importance. The only duties it required were those in connection with royal processions and coronations.[17] Spenser is possibly alluding to Oxford's rank when the Briar asks the husbandman:

Was I not planted of thine owne hand,
To be the primrose of all thy land? (165–66)

E. K. then glosses "primrose" as "the chiefe and worthiest." And in his complaint about the Oak, the Briar declares:

Untimely my flowres forced to fall,
That bene the honour of your Coronall— (177–78)

which is another possible reference to Oxford. But the fable is full of ambiguous personal allusions. When we are told that the Oak "with his nuts larded many swine," we might recall that Oxford's crest contained a Blue Boar and see more than one level of meaning here. And when we recall that the sun is the monarch symbol, we might see something more in the Briar's complaint that the Oak's shade robs him of the "swete sonnes sight." It was, of course, a common complaint against all the Queen's favorites, especially against Leicester, that they prevented access to the sovereign. And after the Oak is felled, the Briar standing, in all his arrogance and vanity, "like a Lord alone," might be a refence to the attitude of Oxford and the Queen on the tennis-court quarrel with Sidney: a lord stands apart, and has privileges denied to mere gentlemen.

Like the Briar, Oxford was short in stature. He was even shorter than the Queen, who was by no means a tall woman. In his biography of Oxford, Ward devotes a full chapter in the appendix to prove that he was a little fellow. These lines of the Briar could allude to the contrast between Oxford and the tall Leicester:

[17] Ward, pp. 53, 149.

Ah my Soveraigne, Lord of creatures all,
Thou placer of plants both humble and tall. (163–64)

Even the nightingale singing in the Briar's branches would probably be significant, for *nightingale* was a term quite often applied to frivolous, foppish, or effeminate characters. In earlier French and English poetry the nightingale also symbolized wanton or courtly love, a point on which the profligate Oxford would be exceeding vulnerable.[18]

The general figurative use of the Briar to represent troubles, difficulties, or vexations would also fittingly describe Oxford's relationship to the group around Leicester in 1579. In addition, religious writers and preachers of this period sometimes followed the Book of Judges (9:6–15) in making the Bramble or Briar the symbol of one covetous of power and dominion, an interpretation of Oxford that would certainly be held by the Leicester-Sidney group in 1579.[19]

Other writers of the period often caricatured Oxford as an effeminate fop in foreign clothes.[20] Perhaps Gabriel Harvey's attitude towards Oxford (since Harvey was Spenser's closest friend) would be to the point here. Harvey was at times ironic in his bombastic praise of Oxford in his *Gratulationes Valdinenses* of 1578, especially when he exhorts him to cease being a dilettante and to become a soldier.

[18] For instance, see *NED* and such works as the *Owl and the Nightingale* and Marie de France's *Lai of the Nightingale*. Lydgate in "A Sayinge of the Nyghtyngale" (pp. 16–19 in Lydgate's *Two Nightingale Poems*) interprets the Nightingale as a sign of "fleshy love."

[19] Bishop Young, Spenser's employer in 1578, made a reference to this biblical parable in a sermon given on March 2, 1575. See P. W. Long, "Spenser and the Bishop of Rochester," *PMLA*, XXXI (1916), 727. French Fogle has informed me that references to this parable also occur in the sermons of Richard Sibbes, a prominent Puritan preacher of the early seventeenth century.

[20] Ward, pp. 189–94.

Aprill.

October.

Plate 4: APRIL AND OCTOBER

Woodcuts before the April and October eclogues. In April's woodcut we see the Queen,
surrounded by the Muses and ladies of the
Court, who carry musical instruments, bay
branches (symbols of honor and victory) and
olive branches (symbols of peace and concord).
In October's woodcut we see the royal palace
behind Piers and Cuddie, Court bishop and
Court poet respectively.

O thou hero worthy of renown, throw away the insignificant pen, throw away bloodless books, and writings that serve no useful purpose; now must the sword be brought into play, now is the time for thee to sharpen the spear and to handle great engines of war.[21]

In his *Speculum Tuscanismi* Harvey gives a portrait of the Italianate Courtier which Ward calls an obvious but nonmalicious caricature of Oxford. On the publication of the Spenser-Harvey letters in the summer of 1580 this satire got Harvey into trouble. Incited by Lyly, Oxford had Harvey apprehended and haled before the Privy Council on charges of libellous writing. Before matters went too far, Oxford thought it was wiser to accept Harvey's denial of any attempt to satirize him than to admit that he saw a portrait of himself in the caricature.[22] In the *Speculum*, besides the vanity, arrogance and villainy of the Italianate dandy, Harvey stresses his foppish posture, gestures, and apparel; his "valorous words" and "womanish works"; Harvey then ironically describes him as a "mirror for gallants" and a "primrose of honour," and is especially ironic in his extended portrayal of the fop's pretensions to statecraft.[23] As we have already seen, many of these same details are either directly reflected or implicit in Spenser's depiction of the Briar.

My study of this fable has, I hope, made it strongly probable that Spenser intended to hint particularly at Leicester and Oxford in the fable of the Oak and the Briar. But in regard to the Oak, I think that Spenser had more than Leicester in mind. The problem of the maligned, misinterpreted, and supplanted "tree of state" had wider implications and a more general application,

---

[21] As translated from the Latin by Ward, p. 157.

[22] An interesting treatment of this episode is given by Warren B. Austin, "William Withie's Notebook: Lampoons on John Lyly and Gabriel Harvey," *RES*, XXIII (1947), 297–309.

[23] Harvey's *Speculum* can be found in the Oxford *Spenser*, p. 625.

especially to one associated with the group at Leicester House. As E. K. tells us in the introduction to *February*, this eclogue is "rather morall and generall then bent to any secrete or particular purpose." However much this admission may be regarded as a protective device, Spenser as a poet would be inclined to particularize a general abuse, as I have tried to demonstrate. But Spenser, I feel sure, through E. K.'s phrase "morall and generall" meant to call attention to other oaks, specifically Walsingham and Sir Henry Sidney, who in late 1579 were felled through spite and lying complaints, their long years of service to the State completely forgotten. The specific details of the fable itself, however, fit only Leicester and Oxford.

Walsingham, always a statesman and never a courtier, opposed the French marriage just as strenuously as Leicester. Rumor from Paris had it that he was instrumental in the publication of Stubbs' *Gaping Gulf*. His efforts to thwart the marriage tripped him up in early November, when the Queen rated him a protector of heretics and banished him from court. With Leicester he was allowed to return to court in early January, 1580, when the Queen lost her enthusiasm for the marriage.[24] But when the *Calender* appeared he was banished, and his political future was most uncertain.

Perhaps an even better example of a neglected and maligned statesman—whom Spenser certainly knew at Leicester House in 1579, if not earlier—was Sir Henry Sidney, who was recalled from Ireland in February, 1578, after many years of loyal but unappreciated service as Lord Deputy.[25] To the group at Leicester House Sir Henry was the perfect example of the devoted public

[24] Read, II, 27–28.
[25] Either because of his close political affiliation with his brother-in-law Leicester, or for other reasons, Sir Henry also used the Oak as a symbol. For instance, when Philip was born, Sir Henry planted an oak tree, later called "Sir Philip Sidney's Oak," to commemorate the event. See Wallace,

servant whose labors and loyalty were called into question because of the malicious complaints of his political enemies, the chief of whom was Thomas Butler, the tenth Earl of Ormonde.[26] In the last half of 1577 and during all of 1578, Philip Sidney was much occupied at court in defending his father's reputation and actions; often during this period, according to Wallace, Philip was "utterly depressed by Elizabeth's failure to show adequate appreciation of his father's services."

When Sir Henry finally arrived at Court in late 1578, he was received coolly by the Queen, and was considered a "*servus inutilis*" (as he later wrote Walsingham) because he had somewhat exceeded a supposed commission "in spending her Majesty's treasure," though in reality he had squandered his own patrimony.[27] Sir Henry Sidney, then, a prominent figure at Leicester House in 1579 and an outstanding example of the Queen's ingratitude to her statesmen, could be represented by the Oak

---

p. 19. Ben Jonson refers to this Oak in his well-known lines:

> That taller tree, which of a nut was set,
> At his great birth, where all the Muses met.

Edward Dyer (Leicester's chief lieutenant and closest of friends to Philip and Sir Henry Sidney, and the one at Leicester House with whom Spenser appeared to be most friendly) also used the Oak as a symbol. In September, 1575, on the Queen's visit to Woodstock, Dyer (who had languished for four years under the Queen's displeasure), as the mournful minstrel of the Oak, made a dramatic appeal to Elizabeth and was returned to royal favor. See R. M. Sargent, *At the Court of Queen Elizabeth: The Life and Lyrics of Sir Edward Dyer* (London, 1935), pp. 30–34.

[26] Ormonde for years had kept Ireland in a turmoil in his feud with the Desmonds, but he had the ear of Elizabeth and could do no wrong. Because of Ormonde's insistence that he be free from all taxes, in which demand he was supported by the Queen, discontent and mutiny spread among the lesser landowners. Walsingham had warned Sir Henry that no one could govern Ireland successfully without counting Ormonde among his friends, but Sir Henry, holding to his policy of firm dealing and uniform justice, insisted on levying the tax on all impartially. See Wallace, pp. 190–201.

[27] *Ibid.*

and would certainly be included in any "morall and generall" application of *February's* fable.

We should also recall Elizabeth's threat in late 1579 to "pack" the Privy Council with influential Catholics in order to gain support for her romantic objective, marriage to Alençon. Like Sidney in his famous "Letter," Spenser in this fable was probably appealing to Elizabeth to retain and support her trusted Councillors, Leicester, Walsingham, Knollys. As we have already seen in Chapter II, Sidney in his letter to the Queen had pointed out that her fortunes were inextricably entwined with those of her Protestant advisors, who hold the "principall offices and strengthes" in the realm. They are men "renowned all over Christendome for their well tempred mindes, having sett the uttmost of their ambition in your favour and the study of their sowles in your safety." The very last point that Sidney makes is for Elizabeth to respect and rely on her present Council. "Lett those in whome you finde truste and to whome you have committed trust in your weighty affaires be held up in the eyes of your subjectes."[28]

It is highly probable, then, that the fable of the Oak and the Briar has a particular as well as a more general application. In general, and apart from the conflict between youth and age, the fable would be an attack on the Queen's policy of capricious ingratitude towards elder statesmen, especially such men as Walsingham and Henry Sidney, who merited generous recognition of their services to Queen and country. In particular, and in terms of its highly specific details, the fable was a defense of Leicester and an attack on the Earl of Oxford.

[28] "Letter," pp. 52, 56, 60.

VI

Aubigny and King James as Fox and Kid

IN AN excellent study of a few years ago, Mary Parmenter, in a short paragraph, made an interesting suggestion as to the meaning of the fable of the Fox and the Kid in the May eclogue of the *Shepheardes Calender*: the Kid is the youthful King James of Scotland, who in the fall of 1579 was completely captivated by his French cousin, Esmé Stuart, Duc d'Aubigny, the Papist Fox. Queen Elizabeth is the woeful Goat, the Kid's mother, who, politically speaking, maintained a policy of careful motherliness over James in the 1570's. Miss Parmenter then remarked: "Anyone familiar with the records can see how pertinent and amusing the whole application is. But it is one which would take up too much space to work out here."[1] In attempting to ferret out Spenser's intentions in this fable, I have concluded that Miss Parmenter was substantially correct in her suggestion, and in this chapter

[1] Parmenter, p. 205. See first note to Chapter IV.

I will attempt to furnish the necessary proof. The only change I would make is in the identity of the Goat: here I think Spenser had in mind George Buchanan, James's tutor, rather than the English Queen.

The mysterious E. K., in a gloss to this eclogue, makes it clear that the fable has a special meaning. He writes: "By the Kidde may be understoode the simple sorte of the faythfull and true Christians. By hys dame, Christ, that hath alreadie with carefull watchewords (as heere doth the gote) warned his little ones, to beware of such doubling deceit. By the Foxe, the false and faithlesse Papistes, to whom is no credit to be given, nor felowshippe to be used." But is there another level of allegory in this fable? Most critics and editors, it is true, do not try to go beyond E. K.'s explanation. Higginson, however, seeks a further application. To him the Kid's dead father is Christ, the Kid is the Puritans, the Goat is the true Church, and the Fox the Anglicans. Then, as a secondary meaning, Higginson suggests that the Fox is Lord Burghley, and the Kid, the young Earl of Essex.[2]

Higginson's suggestions have not commended themselves to scholars. In his study of Spenser's fables, Friedland takes up Higginson's contentions and refutes them point by point. Friedland also notices Miss Parmenter's suggestion, but feels that Spenser was not in a position to have sufficient knowledge of Scottish affairs in late 1579 for her suggestion to be of value.[3] Nor has any one else, as far as I know, argued for or accepted Miss Parmenter's unsupported suggestion. I will try to show that Spenser was in a position to know the situation in Scotland. But before presenting Spenser's opportunities for such knowledge of Scottish

[2] James J. Higginson, *Spenser's Shepherd's Calender in Relation to Contemporary Affairs* (New York, 1912), pp. 86, 89–98.
[3] Louis S. Friedland, "Spenser As a Fabulist," *Shakespeare Association Bulletin*, XII (1937), 137–41.

affairs, I will give a short account of the pertinent incidents.

On March 8, 1579, the regency of the Earl of Morton was ended by a coalition of his political enemies, and the twelve-year-old James was set up as active ruler. But by June, as a result of a second coup d'état, Morton was back in power as chief councillor, and his old enemies, Argyle and Athole, were preparing for war. As it was decidedly to the best interests of England to avert a struggle, Queen Elizabeth, through the efforts of her Scottish ambassador, Robert Bowes, finally managed to bring the warring parties to terms. With Morton still in power Elizabeth felt secure, for his policies were in a sense hers. They included not only friendship with Elizabeth but opposition to all foreign intrigue, retention of the imprisoned Mary Stuart, and maintenance of the Protestant religion.

Suddenly the picture changed. On September 8, 1579, Esmé Stuart, Seigneur d'Aubigny, James's French cousin, landed in Scotland, coming at the instigation of the Guises and as their agent. In less than a month the Catholic Aubigny became a factor to be reckoned with in political affairs. Handsome, cultured, and courtly, he was one of the most adroit schemers of his time. He completely captivated the young king, and within a few months silenced the Protestant ministers—who at first shouted fulminations from their pulpits at this Catholic newcomer—by a pretended conversion to the Protestant faith. In the Parliament which convened in Edinburgh in late October, 1579, James let it be understood that Aubigny was to receive the Earldom of Lennox, as well as the rich abbacy of Arbroath. The Protestant lords, of course, regarded Aubigny as a subtle flatterer, but as yet were not prepared to intervene.[4] Aubigny's subsequent success, culmi-

---

[4] The above material on Aubigny and James can be found in Read, *Walsingham*, II, 30, 145–57; and in Clara and Hardy Steeholm, *James I of England* (New York, 1938), pp. 58–71.

nating in the disgrace and death of Morton, and the final over-reaching himself which brought about his own downfall, occurred after the publication of the *Calender*; I will therefore omit this part of the fascinating story from my study.[5]

As foreign secretary, Walsingham was informed by his agents of political developments affecting England and anticipated trouble.[6] In late August, 1579, Paulet, English ambassador to France, wrote Walsingham that Aubigny was about to take ship for Scotland and that he had conferred with the Archbishop of Glasgow, Mary Stuart's representative in France, before setting out.[7] Captain Errington was immediately dispatched to Scotland to keep an eye on Aubigny. As early as October 10, 1579, Errington wrote Walsingham that Aubigny was high in favor with James and likely to receive the Lennox title in reversion. In another letter written a few days later, Errington declared that Aubigny would be the most powerful person in the Scottish court if he changed his religion, and that Aubigny's closest friends had intimated that such a change was imminent. In this same letter Errington wrote that Alençon's coming to England in late August was well known in Scotland, and that there was much murmuring against Elizabeth's French-Catholic suitor. Other letters of Errington written in October, 1579, as well as one from Robert Bowes, the English ambassador in Scotland, contain much information about Aubigny's rapid political progress.[8] By the end of October, then, at the latest, the group at Leicester House knew the broad outlines of what was happening in Scotland.

Another probable indirect source of information about Scotland for Spenser was George Buchanan, James's tutor, who, as

[5] For these developments, see Read, II, 164–92.
[6] In his three-volume study, Read gives ample evidence of Walsingham's alertness and political sagacity.
[7] *C.S.P., Foreign*, 1579–80, p. 50.
[8] *C.S.P., Scottish*, 1574–81, pp. 355–57.

Phillips brought out in his excellent article on Buchanan and the Sidney circle, could be considered a member *in absentia* of the Leicester-Sidney group.[9] Buchanan could also be considered almost an English agent, for in late 1578 he assisted Robert Bowes in the latter's attempts to reconcile the warring Scottish lords, and he received a one-hundred-pound pension from Bowes for his helpfulness and for his readiness in seeing things from an English point of view.[10] Buchanan was in constant communication with the group around Leicester in 1579. From Thomas Randolph and Daniel Rogers especially he received news of the interests and activities of the Leicester-Sidney group; in turn he sent them his views on matters in Scotland and England. In his letters to Rogers, Buchanan clearly wrote for the whole general group to which Rogers belonged, and was especially concerned about the danger of the proposed Alençon marriage both to England and to his friends at Leicester House.[11] Although there is no mention of Aubigny in Buchanan's surviving letter to Rogers in the period from early October to mid-November, in earlier and later letters Buchanan often discussed the political situation in Scotland. Hence it is probable that he also kept the Leicester group informed about Aubigny. And as we know from the Spenser-Harvey letters, Spenser was friendly with Rogers, Buchanan's devoted correspondent. In the letter of April, 1580, Harvey forbids Spenser to show his "patcheries and fragments" to anyone except Philip Sidney, Dyer, and Rogers.

It would, then, be almost impossible for Spenser not to know what was happening in Scotland in late 1579, situated as he was at Leicester House, the friend of Sidney, Dyer, and Rogers. And

[9] James E. Phillips, "George Buchanan and the Sidney Circle," *Huntington Library Quarterly*, XII (1948), 23–55.

[10] Steeholm, *James*, p. 64.

[11] Phillips, pp. 24–31. Some of the time in late 1579 the more important members of this group were at Greenwich rather than at Leicester House.

when we consider that the news of Aubigny's success in Scotland was in no sense confidential, but news of a general character which it was to the advantage of Walsingham to disseminate and of every patriotic Englishman to know, it is highly probable that Spenser knew the whole story, and knew it early in the fall of 1579. The way the progress of the Alençon negotiations filtered down to all levels of England's citizenry and provoked a storm of protest indicates that English suspicion and fear of French intrigue were not restricted to just a few top-level statesmen.[12]

If we grant, then, that Spenser was in a good position to know Scottish affairs, the question arises whether Spenser had time to incorporate the Aubigny-James story in the fable of the May eclogue. The answer again is yes. Since the *Shepheardes Calender* was not licensed until December 5, 1579, events which occurred in October, or perhaps through early November, could have been reflected in the *Calender*.[13]

If we grant, then, that it was possible for Spenser to refer to Aubigny in the fable of the Fox and the Kid, there remains the task of proving that he actually did so. What evidence in the fable or the gloss would lead one to suspect that the Fox represents Aubigny; the Kid, James; and the Goat, George Buchanan? Surely Spenser or E. K. would give some hints if Spenser wished the action of the fable to point toward happenings in Scotland. Such hints, I believe, were provided. But before indicating and explaining these hints, I will first briefly review the fable of the Fox and the Kid as Piers relates it in the May eclogue.

Before leaving home "for good reason," the Goat warns her offspring the Kid, whose father was dead, to beware of the treacherous Fox and to keep the door locked. Disguised as a peddler, the Fox comes to the door, claims relationship to the

[12] See, for instance, Read, *Walsingham*, II, 21n.
[13] The problem of dating has been briefly discussed in Chapter I.

Kid, and succeeds in captivating him with the toys taken from his pack. The enamored Kid then opens the door, is further enthralled by additional trifles, and while reaching in the bag for a remaining bell, he is popped in and carried away. When the Goat returns, she realizes with grief:

Such end had the Kidde, for he nould warned be
Of craft, coloured with simplicitie:
And of such end perdie does all hem remayne,
That of such falsers freendship bene fayne. (302–305)

It is of course difficult to separate fabular verisimilitude from touches which the author hopes will be given a particular application; it is also too much to expect that the author will so change his fable that every detail will fit the contemporary incident or personalities that are being presented. In fact, it was better not to do the latter: the reader's intelligence must be complimented; and more important, in cases of satire the author must protect himself from the dangers of plain-speaking. But if there is a pointed application, it should be indicated by the alterations the author chose to make in the fable itself.

Friedland has shown that the fable of the Fox and the Kid, like the fable of the Oak and the Briar in *February*, is developed "with many an original touch in both narrative and style."[14] This originality, in the genre of the fable at least, should alert us for possible contemporary allusion. E. K. also makes it clear that this fable is not straight out of Aesop: "the catastrophe and end" are far different.

One good reason for thinking that Spenser is referring to Scottish affairs in his transformed fable is the use in its first lines of the Scottish form *gate* for *goat*.[15] E. K. does not let us miss the

[14] "Spenser As a Fabulist," p. 96.
[15] See John W. Draper, "The Glosses to Spenser's *Shepheardes Calender*," *JEGP*, XVIII (1919), 563.

significance of this, for he explains: "Northernly spoken to turne O into A." Other expressions used, such as "sperre the yate" (which E. K. glosses as "shut the door"), are also peculiarly Scottish, as well as northern English, a point which has been apparently overlooked; however, as Draper has pointed out, in most cases it is difficult to distinguish the various northern forms from each other.[16] Hence editors and critics call these words northern English and let the matter rest.

It is my belief that Spenser was doing the same kind of thing here that he did in the September eclogue. There, to indicate the identity of Diggon Davie—Richard Davies, bishop of the Welsh diocese of St. David's—Spenser has both Hobbinol (Harvey) and Diggon, in the first four lines of the eclogue, use a term so characteristic of the Welsh dialect of the times (use of her for he or him) that none of his contemporaries could possibly mistake it.[17] Then in the first gloss of September E. K. informs us that "the Dialecte and phrase of speache in this Dialogue seemeth to differ from the comon. The Cause whereof is supposed to be, by occasion of the party herein meant. . . ." In fact, I believe that deciphering the personal and political allegory of the eclogues goes a long way toward explaining Spenser's use of dialectal expressions in the Calender. As early as 1715 Hughes pointed out that the language of May and September was more obsolete than that of the other eclogues.[18] Other scholars such as Herford and Padelford have noticed the same phenomenon,[19] but very little attempt has been made to find an understandable reason for this procedure. Failure to do so has led to such pronouncements as Dr. Johnson's on the "studied barbarity" of the first

[16] Ibid., pp. 560–63.
[17] See later chapter on Bishop Davies.
[18] See Var., p. 290.
[19] Ibid., pp. 617, 627.

The Fox and the Kid 85

four lines of *September*, and—because of the use of such forms as *gate* for *goat*—Greg's on the "wanton confusion of dialectal forms" in the *Calender*.[20] E. K. was no doubt trying to forestall such misjudgments when he warned in the Epistle to Harvey:

> But if any will rashly blame such his purpose in choyce of old and unwonted words, him may I more justly blame and condemne, or of witlesse headinesse in judging, or of heedelesse hardiness in condemning, for not marking the compasse of hys bent, he wil judge of the length of his cast.

E. K. furnishes other clues. He glosses *orphane* thus: "A youngling or pupill, that needeth a Tutour and governour." In his study of the language of the *Calender*, McElderry was somewhat puzzled at the glossing of this word, which could hardly be considered archaic.[21] But who was this orphan, presumably Scottish, that required both a tutor and governor? A contemporary reader would most probably think of the youthful King James of Scotland and his tutor Buchanan, and recall the political significance of the word *governor*—it was used to designate the keeper of the young king's person and the castle at Stirling—and the many quarrels among the Scottish nobles over who was to be the governor of James.[22] And when the Papist Fox tells the Kid:

> And if that my Grandsire me sayd, be true,
> Sicker I am very sybbe to you: (268–69)

this reader would recall that Aubigny was in truth a nephew of James's grandfather. And when the Fox captivates the Kid with his bag of trifles and toys, especially the newell (*newell* is prob-

[20] *Ibid.*, pp. 575, 619.
[21] Bruce Robert McElderry, Jr., "Archaism and Innovation in Spenser's Poetic Diction," *PMLA*, XLVII (1932), 153.
[22] The most noteworthy fracas, of course, was the successful attack (on April 26, 1578) of the young Earl of Mar on Stirling Castle and the seizure of the young king. Mar had been persuaded by Morton that not his uncle, Alexander Erskine, but he himself, as heir of the House of Erskine, should be governor of James. See Steeholm, *James*, pp. 60–61; and Read, *Walsingham*, II, 148.

ably a French loan word and is glossed by E. K. as "a newe thing"), those cognizant of what was happening in Scotland at this time (and I would include here the group at Leicester House in close touch with Walsingham and Daniel Rogers) would perhaps think of Aubigny's captivation of James by French toys and fashions as well as by a fascinating personality.[23] Many other details in the fable as well, such as the adolescent sprouting of the Kid's beard, and the reference to the murder of the Kid's father—Fortune having spited him

> And cutte of hys days with untimely woe,
>
> Betraying him into the traines of hys foe— (200–201)

would also fit the thirteen-year-old James, whose father, Lord Darnley, had been so dealt with.

In a metaphoric, fabular sense, what happened to the Kid in relation to the Fox—at least to English eyes fearful of France's regaining its old and dangerous influence in Scotland—was exactly what happened at this time to James in relation to Aubigny: James was already "in the bag"! In a biography of James, Clara and Hardy Steeholm write of the period from September 30 to October 17, 1579, when James, awaiting the celebration being prepared for him by the citizens of Edinburgh, remained outside the city gates until the ceremonies were ready to start: "In the meantime he [James] hunted with d'Aubigny, he hawked with d'Aubigny, he played 'tinnis,' he rode out and dined in great halls, with d'Aubigny forever by his side."[24] Because of the progress of the marriage negotiations between Elizabeth and Alençon at this time, no one in England was more antagonistic to French and Catholic political success, or more interested in calling attention to its dangers, than was the Leicester-Walsingham group,

---

[23] Steeholm, *James*, pp. 65, 80. Draper, p. 565, suggests that *newell* is a French loan word. So does the *NED*.

[24] *Ibid.*, p. 67.

with which, as we have seen, Spenser was associated. And to this group, even if it were judged that James was as yet not entirely in Aubigny's power, the tragedy the Kid experienced might equally well be James's future fate.

Another interesting fact is that Bowes used the same figure of the peddler to represent Aubigny and his chief assistant Henry Keir in his letter to Walsingham of October 22, 1579. Bowes wrote: "D'Aubigny and he [Keir] are both suspected and spoken against by the ministers of the church and also by them so narrowly awaited as they cannot open their pack in any corner but their wares will be seen and published in the pulpit."[25]

A number of reasons, other than the use of the Scottish form for *goat*, suggest that Spenser had George Buchanan, James's tutor, in mind as the Goat of the fable who warned the Kid so thoroughly but in vain against the Papist Fox. As tutor, Buchanan might be considered to have James in his primary care; and like the Goat in relation to the Kid, Buchanan was mainly responsible for properly developing the young king's mind, and molding his character. Phillips has shown the great admiration that the group at Leicester House had for Buchanan, one of the leading Latin stylists of his time and Scotland's foremost scholar.[26] Not only was Buchanan famous in the world of humane letters, but Protestant Christianity paid him tribute as one who was rearing James as a good Protestant king in the precepts of the reformed faith and with a proper knowledge of the iniquities of Rome. For instance, Rudolph Gualter wrote a letter to Buchanan, dated from Zurich, March 8, 1580. In it he said: "I therefore esteem the most serene king of Scotland as fortunate and happy, in having obtained, in so corrupt an age, such an instructor, who is able to imbue his youthful mind with most

[25] *C.S.P., Scottish*, 1574–81, p. 357.
[26] Phillips, pp. 36–55.

wholesome precepts, and implant in him the seeds of truly royal
virtues."[27] Philip DuPlessis-Mornay and Hubert Languet, Sidney's Continental friends, wrote in a similar fashion about Buchanan's influence on James.[28]

Thomas Randolph was so inspired by reading *De Jure Regni*,
Buchanan's famous treatise on the limitations of kingly power,
that he wrote on March 15, 1579, to Peter Young, Buchanan's
colleague: "I thought the Kinge your Maister more happie that
had Buchanan to his Maister, then Alexander the Great, that
had Aristotell his Instructor."[29] On the same day, Randolph
wrote also to Buchanan to commend his tutorship: by it "shall
your Fame remayne immortall."[30]

The interest of the Leicester circle in Buchanan and James was
no doubt in part political, for as early as 1579 Leicester and his
group regarded James as the most likely successor to Elizabeth
and thought his education under Buchanan extremely important.[31] In October, 1579, for instance, Philip Sidney wrote Buchanan: "God prosper him [James] and mak him lerne be you
that gudeness is the greittest gritnes."[32] But there was also an
interest in Buchanan's political theories. Since 1576 Daniel
Rogers had been circulating a manuscript copy of Buchanan's
De Jure Regni; after this work was published in Edinburgh in
January, 1579, Rogers immediately began to arrange for a London
edition; in August, 1579, he wrote to Buchanan for a copy of the

[27] *Zurich Letters*, Rev. Hastings Robinson for Parker Society, ed. (Cambridge, 1846), p. 534.
[28] See Phillips, p. 37.
[29] George Buchanan, *Opera Omnia*, 2 vols., Pieter Burman, ed. (Leyden,
1725), II, 746.
[30] *Ibid.*, II, 755.
[31] See Phillips, p. 36.
[32] Day of month not given. *Warrender Papers*, Scottish History Society,
Ser. 3, XVII (1931), I, 146.

Edinburgh edition to check against his manuscript copy.[33] The
Goat's absence from home "for good reason" in the fable might
be a cryptic reference to Buchanan's temporary relinquishing of
his duties as tutor in 1579 in order to see the *De Jure Regni*
through the press.

A general objection that might be advanced against my interpretation of the fable of May is the lack of more complete identifying details. Why the mystery? Surely every true Englishman
of the period would be fearful of and condemn Aubigny's influence over the youthful James. Elizabeth, Burghley, Sussex,
Leicester, Walsingham, all would be of one mind in regard to
this development. True enough. But Spenser was, I think, slyly
adverting to other things also. The French Catholic Aubigny
could not be trusted, but neither could any other French Catholic—and this meant Alençon, also, the French duke Elizabeth
was so determined to marry in late 1579. On this point there was
a sharp difference of opinion between Elizabeth, Burghley, and
Sussex on one hand, and the whole group at Leicester House, on
the other. Palinode, to whom this fable is related, knowing full
well that Alençon rather than Aubigny was the real object of
attack, meaningfully remarks:

Truly *Piers*, thou are beside thy wit,
Furthest from the marke, weening it to hit. (306–307)

E. K. was hitting home and meant to include Alençon when he
wrote that the Fox represented "the false and faithlesse Papistes,
to whom is no credit to be given, nor felowshippe to be used."
Like John Field in the dedication to Leicester of his translation
of Mornay's *A Treatise of the Church* (see Chapter II), E. K.
was proceeding safely, attacking Catholicism in general rather
than Alençon in particular. Spenser did not wish to be too specific

[33] Phillips, pp. 41–42. All of the material in the above three paragraphs
was noted by Phillips, pp. 33–38.

in pointing to Aubigny, nor did he wish to take any unnecessary risks in making an open attack on Alençon. Remembering the fate of Stubbs, he counted on being understood without jeopardizing his right hand. Besides, as Friedland wrote in his study of Spenser as a fabulist, "how better may one clothe one's thought, at once hiding and revealing it, than by use of the fable?"[34]

On what, then, does my case rest in interpreting the fable of the Fox and the Kid as an allegory of James, Buchanan, Aubigny and Alençon. It rests primarily on the following facts: (1) Spenser, employed at Leicester House and friendly with Sidney, Dyer, and Rogers, had many opportunities for knowledge of Scottish affairs; (2) Spenser had sufficient time to incorporate a treatment of these affairs in the *Calender*; (3) to point the allegory, Spenser used Scottish dialectal words and E. K. contributed telltale glosses; (4) the many close parallels between the historical incident involved and the details in the fable itself are too striking to be accidental.

In concluding this first section, on the political allegory, I wish to point out the implications of my study thus far. First, the knowledge of the political allegory gives us Spenser's main intention not only in the fables of the Fox and the Kid and the Oak and the Briar but also in such central eclogues as those dealing with Rosalind and Dido; second, it has a decided relevance to Spenser's language, and much ink used in the study of Spenser's dialectal terms could have been saved, had Spenser's allegory first been determined; third, against the prevailing interpretation, that the *Calender* was completed before Spenser's employment by Leicester, it furnishes us important evidence on the composition of the *Calender*; fourth, it tells us that the *Calender* (like

[34] "Spenser As a Fabulist," p. 87.

drama to Hamlet) was the abstract and brief chronicle of the period, revealing to the age and body of the time its form and pressure; finally, it indicates that late 1579 was an exciting period for Spenser, living and working at Leicester House, and associating not only with such talented poets as Dyer and Sidney, but also with such influential political leaders as Walsingham and Leicester. Most probably with the knowledge and encouragement of this particular group, Spenser was expressing in the *Calender* a mutual concern over Scottish affairs and the Alençon marriage, and he brought out the *Calender* at this particular time largely because of these events.

THE
SEES OF ENGLAND
AND WALES
AS RE-ARRANGED
IN 1541
AND
1555

THE HEAVY LINE SHOWS THE BOUNDARIES OF THE NEW SEES FOUND
BY HENRY VIII IN 1541 AND RECOGNISED BY POPE PAUL IV IN 15
THE STIPPLE MARKS THE AREA OF THE SEE OF WESTMINSTER, i.e., MIDDLESEX, FOUND
BY HENRY VIII IN 1541 AND SUPPRESSED BY EDWARD VI IN 1550

Plate 5: MAP OF ENGLISH AND WELSH EPISCOPAL SEES AS
REARRANGED IN 1541 AND 1555.

Religious Allegory

VII

The Religious Situation of 1579

THE RELIGIOUS situation in England in 1579 was so desperate that it is almost impossible to give, in a short chapter, a true picture of the deplorable conditions that prevailed. Most of these conditions, it is true, were centuries old; but it is equally true that they were far worse than they had ever been in the past primarily because of the religious settlement of 1559, a settlement that, except for the Queen and her Council, apparently pleased very few. At the accession of Elizabeth, according to a recent student of the English Reformation, a large proportion of the people, thoroughly bewildered by the many religious changes enforced by the power of the State in the last thirty years, were totally without any religious conviction; they were skeptical, indifferent about religion as dogmatic truth, and only the coercive power of the government made them attend church.[1] These, as well as those who were genuinely Catholic in their religious attitude,

[1] Philip Hughes, *The Reformation in England*, 3 vols. (London, 1950–1954), II, 187, 303; III, 51, 60, 66, 97, 106. This study makes use of important primary sources and is carefully documented.

would be naturally either apathetic or hostile to the new arrangements. The Protestant minority who favored the Reform were
bitterly disappointed that the government's new religion contained so little of what they had hoped for—a church formed on
the model now operating in Geneva and Zurich.

But the real trouble with the Church was that its leadership
was now political and lay. The Church itself had little control
over matters ecclesiastical. The Church, in effect, was an arm of
the State, and the new laws of religious conformity and royal
supremacy were largely tests of political loyalty.[2] The bishops and
the lesser clergy were in a sense ecclesiastical police who tried to
ensure obedience to the Queen's religious tests of temporal loyalty, tests that the cynical and indifferent found no difficulty in
taking but which did little to develop a religious spirit in the
people.

Since five sixths of all the benefices in the realm were controlled by the Crown or lay patrons,[3] the higher clergy to a much
smaller extent than in pre-Reformation days controlled the personnel of the lower ranks. As a result the incompetent, the corrupt, the ignorant could not be easily rejected, disciplined, or
deprived through ecclesiastical supervision. The Settlement of
1559, then, not only delivered the administration of the Church
and the personnel of the clergy into the hands of laymen—the
Queen's chief ministers—but "took away from the bishops, themselves the nominees of the State, their power of deciding upon
the qualifications of the ministry."[4]

[2] Roland G. Usher, The Reconstruction of the English Church, 2 vols.
(New York and London, 1910), I, 5. This is a thoroughly documented,
impartial study of ecclesiastical problems during the Elizabethan age.
[3] Usher, I, 95. In the realm as a whole the lay patrons controlled 60 per
cent of the benefices; in the province of Canterbury, about 70 per cent.
The Crown, then, would control about 23 per cent of the livings; the
Church, about 17 per cent.
[4] Usher, I, 96.

The clergy of the late 1570's were apparently a bad lot. Approximately one third of them were former Catholic priests whose enthusiasm for the Establishment would be suspect;[5] these parochial clergy were uneducated, lacking in zeal for the government's notion of what constituted true religion, and no doubt hoping for the day when the Old Faith would be either tolerated or returned. According to the views of the leading Reformers, this group was in need of conversion and could not be expected to show any fervor for the new ways.[6]

The clergy ordained since 1559, if we can believe contemporary reports, were just as bad, if not worse. Because of the poverty of the livings, few competent or learned men would consider the Church as a profession. The great cry of the bishops was for better livings so that fit men could be recruited into the ministry. But the lay patrons and leading members of the Privy Council who gained profit and power from the present arrangements, and had no regard for the Church as against this profit and power, would not relinquish their strangle hold on the Church. The Queen, then, her chief Councillors, her favorite courtiers, and the lay patrons pillaged the Church properties and revenues in a

[5] Many of these, however, had received what little religious training they had in earlier "heretical" regimes (i.e., under Henry VIII and Edward VI), and their Catholicism might be no more than a sentimental preference for the Mass and certain Catholic customs. (A large percentage of these, because of the pulpit campaigns and other propaganda against the Roman Supremacy, would be anti-Pope.) At the accession of Elizabeth about 7,000 of these parochial clergy changed over from the Catholicism of Mary to the Protestantism of Elizabeth as easily as twenty-five years earlier they had rejected the Papal Supremacy alone. Hughes, III, 38.

[6] Hughes, III, 133. The correspondence of the bishops and the *Homilies* furnish evidence of the opposition to the Settlement. *Ibid.*, III, 104, 122f. The Reformers admitted they were a mere handful in number. For instance, the noted Reformer, Thomas Lever, complained that of the conforming clergy only about 1 per cent (70 to 80) were able or willing to preach the new doctrines. *Ibid.*, III, 41, 55.

merciless fashion, not only through impropriations, simoniacal pacts, and fraudulent leases, but through outright robbery achieved through threats and intimidation.[7] Corrupt men who would agree to return a portion of the benefice were appointed to livings; likewise lay patrons often presented their cooks, servants, grooms, or other candidates who would regard the appointments to ecclesiastical preferments as a means to augment their regular income, for the average preferment was not enough to support an honest or learned man, or encourage him to fit himself for the ministry through education.[8] Writing in 1577 (just two years before the publication of the Shepheardes Calender), parson William Harrison gives a bleak picture of the general contempt of the ministry, the manifold ecclesiastical abuses, and the graft of all kinds that prevailed.[9]

In 1585 Whitgift declared that of the nearly 9,000 benefices in the realm, not 600 were adequate to support a learned man. Out of 8,803 benefices, 4,543 were rated at less than ten pounds each. Of these, 2,973 were valued at less than five pounds, a sum so small that their holders were not obliged to pay first fruits. "Of all the benefices three fourths were rated at less than twenty pounds, and nearly ninety per cent were under twenty-six."[10] With conditions such as these, little wonder it was difficult to attract a capable clergy. Even the sculls in the kitchen and the grooms in the stable, as Whitgift once bitterly remarked, were better provided for.

As an illustration of the prevailing clerical ignorance, we may

[7] The inequitable Exchange Act of 1559 was also responsible for the loss of valuable Church properties. The early bishops-elect, Parker, Cox, Grindal, Scory, Barlow, called this act a sacrilege and offered the Queen a thousand marks each annually if she would veto it. She refused. Hughes, III, 20–21.

[8] Usher, I, 219–20.

[9] Elizabethan England, pp. 74–82. Quoted by Hughes, III, 135.

[10] Strype, Whitgift, I, 536. Quoted by Usher, I, 219.

cite the records of the clergy in Lincoln and Leicester, two of the most thoroughly evangelized counties of England. In 1576 Thomas Cooper, bishop of Lincoln, discovered on a visitation that of the 215 clergy of Lincolnshire ordained since 1559 only 36 possessed a university degree, and only 51 out of the 396 clergy of the shire were licensed to preach. Of the 69 at work in Leicestershire who had been ordained by the new bishops, 11 had a university degree, 48 were judged "insufficient," and only 10 out of the total of 112 clergy were licensed to preach.[11] But even the possession of a university degree was no guarantee of learning, for at the university "many men attended no lectures at all, read little,[12] spent much time out in the country earning money as itinerant preachers and schoolmasters, and the degrees were sometimes granted without proper examinations."[13] As Whitgift wrote

[11] Hughes, III, 138–39.

[12] In 1572, Spenser's third year at Cambridge, only 177 books remained of a once magnificent library. Most of these were badly mangled from the zeal of certain Reformers to eliminate everything that recalled the Catholic past. Hughes, II, 157.

[13] Usher, I, 208. The two universities, of course, were in the same situation as the Church. Fellowships were awarded, not on merit, but on the strength of letters from influential courtiers or orders from the Queen. In 1578 Cambridge complained about this interference of the Court: one result was that the "scholars did neither follow their studies in hope of preferment for their diligence and proficiency; nor much regard their superiors, as hoping for favour from them: but chiefly from courtiers." John Strype, *Annals of the Reformation* (Oxford, 1824), II. ii, 199.

These appointees, if they were not disposed to continue their studies, sold their fellowships to the highest bidder. In 1576 Whitgift attempted to put a stop to this buying and selling of university scholarships and fellowships "whereby not learning and merit were regarded so much as men's purses." John Strype, *Life and Acts of John Whitgift* (Oxford, 1822), I, 148–49.

In the Parliamentary session of 1577 a bill was introduced "for the purpose of repressing the buying and selling of fellowships, scholarships, and all offices of emolument" at the two universities. Without opposition it passed both Lords and Commons. On the advice of Burghley, Elizabeth refused her assent to the bill, which would have "prevented many a hand-

Burghley in 1589, "the university gives degrees and honours to the unlearned and the Church is filled with ignorant ministers being for the most part poor scholars."[14]

And the bishops were not allowed to disturb this state of ignorance. Through clerical conferences on the Scriptures called "prophesyings," which Grindal and other bishops permitted or encouraged in their dioceses in order to develop a zealous and informed ministry, the wrath of the Queen was provoked. Furious at this attempt to develop a religious life apart from political direction, Elizabeth in late 1576 ordered Grindal to suppress the prophesyings and reiterated her conviction that it was good for the Church and the State to have few preachers. Putting principle before prudence, Grindal politely but firmly defied the Queen, refused to transmit her orders, and was consequently suspended from the exercise of his ecclesiastical jurisdiction and sequestered. One result of this suspension was that the Church was rapidly drifting towards administrative chaos in the three years before the *Calender* appeared.[15]

Other ancient evils were pluralism and non-residence: the holding of more than one benefice and the consequent inability of being in two or more places at once. Most of the bishops and the cathedral clergy were pluralists. For instance, the Welsh bishops (one of whom is celebrated in the September eclogue) and Young, bishop of Rochester, Spenser's employer in 1578,

---

some gratuity from finding its way into their [the courtiers'] pockets." James Bass Mullinger, *The University of Cambridge*, 3 vols. (Cambridge, 1884), II, 268–69.

Spenser would undoubtedly regard these abuses in the university just as seriously as he did those in the Church.

[14] Strype, *Whitgift*, I, 610.

[15] P. M. Dawley, *John Whitgift and the English Reformation* (New York, 1954), p. 154: "The resulting disorganization brought the English Church into its darkest days."

derived a large part of their income from benefices held *in commendam*.[16] But pluralism was a necessary evil—the only means in fact by which the Church could attract and retain learned and competent men. The bishops knew that except for pluralities the Church would have been in a much worse state than it was; consequently, the best of them, although aware of certain abuses involved, condoned or even defended pluralism.[17] A typical defense was that of Whitgift (in spite of his integrity and ascetic character, a great pluralist) in his letter to Cox, bishop of Ely, in 1575: ". . . except it might be lawful for men to join more livings together you should have a beggarly clergy, which will be the decay of learning, religion, and in time the Church also; for there would not be many meet livings for learned men besides a few bishoprics."[18] Unless the livings were improved, pluralism was inevitable, and those in power showed no real interest in any improvement that would restrict their power to control and pillage the Church.

Many benefices, of course, were held by important personages. For instance, Philip Sidney held many benefices, and it seems that his main sources of income were his church preferments, the first of which was bestowed on him when he was nine years old.[19] And even Spenser, in 1586, while busily serving as clerk of the Munster Council, augmented his income by holding the prebend of Effin.[20]

The poverty of the livings of those serving as active clergymen was further aggravated by royal taxation. First fruits and tenths were rigorously collected on all benefices rated at more than ten

---

[16] Usher, I, 210.
[17] Usher, I, 220.
[18] Strype, *Whitgift*, I, 146. On Whitgift as a pluralist see Dawley, p. 85.
[19] Wallace, pp. 28–34.
[20] Judson, *Spenser*, p. 119. Spenser, of course, would be against pluralism only when the pluralist or his appointee was incompetent or disreputable.

pounds per year. Parson Harrison wrote that of a benefice paying twenty pounds, the incumbent was lucky if he retained two thirds of it after the ordinary payments to the Queen.[21]

Bishops, too, suffered the same financial woes, with the Puritans calling attention to their alleged wealth and encouraging the Queen and her courtiers to still further plundering. The bishops were forced by their patrons to surrender episcopal property or pensions as the price of appointment or continued favor. And other royal impositions fell heavily on them. Benevolences and subsidies were exacted from them for almost every military venture. To illustrate: Thomas Cooper, in 1587 (now bishop of Winchester), "paid 2,217 pounds to the State out of an income of 2,773, of which 133 was for a benevolence to the Queen, and 200 for regular pensions to the Earl of Leicester and Sir Francis Walsingham." And in the seven years Bancroft was bishop of London, he paid 1,600 pounds as first fruits and tenths, 972 for subsidies, and 900 for his ambassadorial journey to Emden, a total of 3,472 pounds, or one half of his entire income during his episcopate.[22]

And the yearly expenses of the bishops were exceptionally heavy. For instance, Bishop Young, Spenser's Roffyn, calculated that out of his yearly income of 340 pounds "he must spend at least 250 to supply meat and drink for his household, and complained that the remaining 90 pounds would go but a short way towards his taxes, wearing apparel for himself and family, his son's schooling, the repair of his houses, the expenses of his stable, to say nothing of the entertainment he was supposed to be ready to offer to recusants, political prisoners and noblemen, and the gifts and rewards expected of him by the throng of needy clergy and courtiers."[23]

[21] Usher, I, 224.
[22] Usher, I, 225.
[23] Usher, I, 223.

Many of the bishops, driven by necessity or greed, allowed their palaces and buildings to fall into ruin either because they would not, or could not afford to keep them up. Still others sold the stands of timber on their land so that their successors could hardly find kindling wood to start their fires. And others connived to pay their patrons handsomely for all preferments, to the detriment of the bishopric and their successors. For instance, Barnes, elevated to the bishopric of Carlisle in 1570 and promoted to Durham in 1577 through the favor of his patron Burghley, showed his gratitude on both occasions by surrendering a large number of episcopal manors to the Crown.[24] Still others leased out lands belonging to their sees for a long term of years at a very low rental, if a considerable sum of money were paid down in cash. Consequently their successors found much of their income virtually destroyed by these fraudulent leases.[25]

Certain patrons forced the helpless clergy to make over to them, as a condition of presentation, part of the tithes or of the land, not for a time but forever. And even though all such agreements were contrary to ecclesiastical law, the prospective incumbent had either to accept the existing arrangement or be passed over for someone who would.[26]

[24] F. O. White, *Lives of Elizabethan Bishops* (London, 1898), pp. 183–85.

[25] Usher, I, 226.

[26] Usher, I, 227. In the preface to Bullinger's *Decades* (translated into English and published in 1577), the publisher holds the corrupt patrons, not the bishops, responsible for the scarcity of a competent clergy. "For patrons nowadays search not the universities for a most fit pastor; but they post up and down the country for a most gainful chapman: he that hath the biggest purse, to pay largely, not he that hath the best gifts, to preach learnedly is presented.

"The bishops bare great blame for this matter; and they admit, they say, unworthy men. See the craft of Satan, falsely to charge the worthiest pillars of the Church with the ruin of the Church; to the end that all church-robbers and caterpillars of the Lord's vineyard may lie unespied. There is

Another point to remember was that the purchasing power of money had enormously declined, for prices were more than double what they had been at the beginning of the Reformation, when the various benefices were rated as to ecclesiastical income. Where in 1539 ten pounds could fairly support a learned divine, in 1579 and afterwards it took double that amount.[27] Also the original values of the benefices were calculated for a celibate clergy: hence the support of wife and children was an added burden to those who availed themselves of the new privilege. But the notion of clerical marriage was repugnant at first, at least to those accustomed to the old system, and in 1579 about one half of the clergy were unmarried. The Queen strongly discountenanced clerical marriage, and the provisions made to supervise it early in the Queen's reign would suggest that many of the clergy found it difficult to find suitable mates.[28]

---

nothing that procureth the bishops of our time more trouble and displeasure, than that they zealously withstand the covetousness of patrons, in rejecting their insufficient clerks." Strype, Annals, II. ii, 146.

And the influence of the Court was just as harmful as that of the lay patrons. After his appointment to the bishopric of Worcester in 1577, Whitgift was much troubled because the prebends of his cathedral were not under his control, but in the Queen's; as a result he did not have assistants that were learned or agreeable to him, or that he could trust in his encounters with Puritans and Catholics. In February, 1579, Whitgift wrote Burghley, seeking to remedy this situation. By special favor of the Queen, Whitgift was then allowed to bestow the prebends of that church while he retained the bishopric. Strype, Whitgift, I, 175.

[27] Usher, I, 235–37.

[28] The prospective wife had to be passed on by the diocesan bishop and two justices of the peace; also the permission of the lady's kinsmen was required. These conditions were considered "degrading." See White, p. 42, who quotes Sander (Anglican Schism, Lewis, ed., p. 379) to the effect that most of the early Elizabethan clergy married women of "tarnished reputations." The old prejudices, of course, wore away in time. But Elizabeth refused to allow the statute of Edward VI legalizing clerical marriage to be re-enacted; hence many regarded the offspring of these unions as illegitimate. See Hughes, III, 164.

Of the 9,000 or so benefices in the provinces of Canterbury and York, 3,849 were impropriate, that is, the revenues were paid to the laity instead of the clergymen who did the work and should have received them according to pre-Reformation practice. Hence, these clergy received but a small portion of the tithes paid by the people; the rest went to the legal owners, who bought and sold the livings as they saw fit. These impropriations yearly cost the Church 126,000 pounds, according to Hooker's estimate. (Whitgift, however, estimated the sum as 100,000 pounds.) When we consider that the total income of all the bishoprics was 23,000 pounds, we can gauge the loss.

Three thousand, eight hundred and twenty-eight of the livings were termed "appropriate," i.e., the income went to some other clergyman than the one who served the parish. These benefices, of course, supported the higher clergy, the bishops, deans, or rectors whose income was largely dependent on this necessary aid.[29]

The Puritans blatantly protested against this state of affairs—

Bishops were forbidden to have their wives with them in their palaces, and married clergy were not allowed to have their wives with them in colleges or cathedral closes.

A prominent objection to clerical marriage was that it inhibited hospitality and charity; and at their deaths the well-beneficed clergy no longer left their wealth to found colleges and hospitals but to their wives and children.

[29] Usher, I, 232–33. In 1575 an attempt was made to introduce a bill that would restrict churchmen to a single benefice but would leave undisturbed the financial advantages that the lay patrons and the Crown had in the impropriations. Bishops and other leading churchmen were very concerned about the effects of the bill on the Church. At the time Whitgift wrote to Bishop Cox that clerical pluralism was "to be reproved in such as had no care in doing their duties, not in such as labored and were diligent. And that it was better and more for the profit of the Church that some had many [benefices], than other some one." Strype, *Whitgift*, I, 144–46. This, I think, would also be Spenser's view on clerics holding more than one benefice.

of appropriations, pluralities, and non-residence—but their criticism was not exactly honest, since they themselves were usually backed by powerful patrons who provided them with livings worth three to five times that of the ordinary parish rector,[30] and often with a captive audience that was usually too ignorant or indifferent to care whether the minister was breaking the law by "purifying" the government's brand of religion.

Another factor in the general poverty of the clergy was the new teaching of the Reformers that a man could acquire salvation by faith alone: hence such good works as the prompt and honest payments of tithes could be ignored in conscience if not by law. And both Catholic and Puritan were not much interested in supporting a Church (or its clergy) which, in their eyes, fell far short of that true Church of Christ found in the Scriptures as well as in certain places on the European continent.[31]

The abuses, then, in the Established Church were many, but we should not be inclined to blame the bishops, for the best of them, or at least those honored in the *Calender*, did all they could to eliminate these abuses. The Queen and her Council, the lay patrons, and the politico-ecclesiastical Settlement of 1559 must be held mainly responsible for failure to correct these evils. The unfit and the ignorant were inducted into the Church and maintained there by the patrons, politicians, and the Court.[32] As Whitgift wrote to Burghley in 1586, the Court—and he had such men as Leicester in mind—was the main source of all this wicked-

[30] Usher, I, 275.

[31] Usher, I, 234.

[32] The proper education of the parochial clergy was a problem that the medieval Church had never solved; in spite of the great success of Calvin at Geneva, and William Allen at Douay in meeting this problem, the English Reformers never solved it either. Hughes, II, 235–36. The "prophesyings" (which the Queen forbade in 1577) would have been, however, a promising start in developing an informed zealous clergy.

ness: the very fountain from which "are sprung all the evil bishops and deans now living in England."[33] White comes to the same conclusion, laying the blame for most of these church evils at the feet of the Supreme Governor herself. In relation to the Elizabethan bishops he calls her a "cruel despot tyrannizing over a helpless set of men" and emphasizes her heartlessness, spite, and unprincipled greed.[34]

PURITANS

From the very beginning of the Settlement of 1559 many of the leading Reformers were displeased, and in directing their attack against the bishops—many of them their fellow Marian exiles—they called for the elimination of many retained popish practices and for agreement in rites as well as doctrine with the Swiss churches. A good many of the first Elizabethan bishops considered themselves faithful sons of Calvin, and it was only after a period of soul-searching and consultation with such foreign religious leaders as Gualter, Bullinger, and Peter Martyr that they came to terms with such things as clerical dress, vestments, the Prayer Book, and the authority of the Queen over Christ's Church, all crucial points with the Reformers. In order to shut out possible "wolves or antichrists," the foreign advisors suggested that scruples should be put away and these things should be considered indifferent or temporary necessary evils. But the more ardent brethren would not make such compromises and

---

[33] Quoted by Hughes, III, 145. "And yet," Whitgift asks, "where is greater zeal pretended?" Whitgift discreetly asks Burghley to burn the letter.

[34] White, p. vii. Dawley, p. 108, also emphasizes the constant plundering of the Church by the Crown: "Elizabeth systematically bled the Church, . . . translated her bishops frequently in order to enjoy a steady income of first fruits and taxes," and on appointing or translating her bishops would appropriate episcopal manors or force long leases of episcopal properties at terms highly disadvantageous to the Church.

pressed for further changes. In the Convocation of 1563, by a single vote in the Lower House (59 to 58) the party of further reform was defeated in its attempt to eliminate the remnants of Catholicism and to draw closer to the Primitive Church. But the Queen was unalterably opposed to any further change, sensing immediately that the "Primitive" party was calling into question her religious supremacy. And even though the Queen's chief ministers were personally favorable to the cause of the Reformers, they too saw that their own political power, as against the Church's, was at stake, and had no wish to lessen this power.[35]

The early Parliaments, particularly those of 1566 and 1571, against the Queen's wishes took up religious issues, and with difficulty were restrained from dealing with what the Queen considered her royal prerogative. But the Queen was adamant, and would not modify her order to Archbishop Parker (in 1565) insisting on strict conformity: as a condition of ecclesiastical appointment all must promise to wear the prescribed clerical apparel and observe the approved rites and ceremonies.

But the divisions within the Church and the resentment against the bishops only increased. The criticism of the Establishment continued to such an extent that it brought about the expulsion of Cartwright, the Puritan leader, from Cambridge in 1570, and the Admonition Controversy, which began in 1572 and carried on until 1577[36]—the two most sensational events of relig-

[35] My summary account of the Puritans in this section has been taken largely from D. J. McGinn, *The Admonition Controversy* (New Brunswick, N. J., 1949), pp. 3–142. A more complete treatment can be found in T. W. Knappen's *Tudor Puritanism* (Chicago, 1939), William Haller's *The Rise of Puritanism* (New York, 1938), and A. F. Scott Pearson's *Thomas Cartwright and Elizabethan Puritanism* (London, 1925). Hughes, III, 146–87, has an excellent short account of these matters.

[36] In effect, of course, it carried on long afterwards, for the Puritan contributions to the controversy were reprinted many times after 1577 and kept the people stirred up.

ious controversy in the decade before the appearance of the *Calender.*

From 1566 to 1572 there had been a modest war of pamphlets between the Puritans (as they were beginning to be called) and the Anglicans (defenders of the Establishment) in which the main issues of the controversy were clarified. The Puritans continued their attack on vestments and wished to purge the Church of its popish rites and ceremonies, stressed that the Scriptures set forth the complete plan for Christ's Church, and hinted that the Queen was subordinate to the authority of the Church. The Anglicans, however, still regarded vestments as indifferent, and while endorsing the view that the Scriptures contained all doctrine essential to salvation, held that the details of policy could be determined by the Church itself and could change according to conditions.

With the publication of the *Admonition to the Parliament* (probably written by the Puritan ministers John Field and Thomas Wilcox) in the summer of 1572, a new hostility to, and virulence against, the Establishment appeared. The time had come, the Puritans felt, to reorganize the Church according to the Presbyterian plan, and they would do away with the whole episcopal system of deans, bishops, and archbishops, and even remove the Queen herself from the headship of the Church. Soon the great champions of Puritanism and of the Established Order, Thomas Cartwright and John Whitgift, appeared in the controversy.

These two had earlier had their differences at the University of Cambridge, where Cartwright, after his election in 1569 to the Lady Margaret Professorship of Divinity, had begun his life's work of condemning as contrary to Scripture the constitution and hierarchy of the Church of England. The forces of orthodoxy immediately went to work. William Chaderton denounced Cartwright to Burghley, as did Grindal, just appointed archbishop of York; and Whitgift, the vice-chancellor, acting with the heads of the colleges, expelled Cartwright from his professorship. Two years later Whitgift, discovering that Cartwright had broken his oath to take orders within seven years after receiving his Master's degree, dismissed him from the university.

In the ensuing paper war between Puritans and Anglicans, Whitgift contributed two weighty pamphlets, and Cartwright three. Whitgift, consulting with Archbishop Parker and Bishop Cox, brought out in late 1572 *An Answere to a Certen Libel Intituled an Admonition to the Parliament*. Shortly before, Cartwright or someone else,[37] feeling the first *Admonition* to be somewhat sketchy, had brought out *A Second Admonition to the Parliament*. In April, 1573, Cartwright contributed *A Replye to an Answere Made of M. Doctor Whitgifte Agaynste the Admonition to Parliament*. Then in February, 1574, Whitgift brought out his *Defense of the Answere*; Cartwright's rejoinders were *The Second Replie of Thomas Cartwright* in 1575 and *The Rest of the Second Replie* in 1577, both books printed abroad.

In his attempt to replace the Episcopalian system with the Presbyterian form of church government, Cartwright appealed to the authority of the "Primitive Church," and found there and in the Scriptures no warrant for the present positions of bishops. For the Elizabethan Book of Common Prayer, with its Catholic remnants, he would substitute the Genevan Prayer Book. Furthermore, in religious matters the Queen would be subservient to the elders of the new Church. And what the Puritans regarded as the tyranny and intolerance of the bishops would be succeeded by, if Cartwright and his party had their way, all the severities of the Mosaic law. The death penalty would be meted out to all

---

[37] Pearson, p. 73, thinks either Anthony Gilby or Christopher Goodman wrote the *Second Admonition*.

who refused to attend church, to blasphemers, adulterers, and heretics, as well as to murderers.

Professor D. J. McGinn, who has recently made a thorough study of the Admonition controversy, gives all the honors to Whitgift for his intellectual incisiveness, scholarly procedure, clear writing, careful logic, tolerance, and charity. On the other hand, McGinn finds Cartwright guilty of loose logic, ambiguity and evasiveness, careless scholarship, and poor writing; he agrees with Pearson, Cartwright's biographer, that Cartwright rationalizes the Primitive Church into existence, and went to the Scriptures only to justify beliefs already held.[38]

But however we judge this controversy, at least we can now see that with the *Admonition to Parliament* of 1572 clear-cut divisions had been set up between Puritan and Anglican. To the Puritans, the bishops were now their enemies; and all the bad language hitherto used to describe the "superstitions" and "corruptions" of Catholicism was now turned against the Established Church.

Most of the Puritan clergy, at least in 1579, still remained in the Established Church. There, protected to a certain degree by influential noblemen with Puritan leanings, they carried on their work. It is difficult to discover how numerous they were, but in a listing made for the years 1582–1590 there were 162 Puritan ministers. Ten years or so later (1600 to 1610) their number increased, according to a careful study made by Usher, to somewhat less than 350.[39] But they were strong in the city of London and in Cambridge, and in the late 1570's their cause was popular. Ten years later, principally through the efforts of Whitgift, Ban-

[38] Pp. 86–107
[39] Usher, I, 251–52. They were, then, slightly fewer in number than the Catholic missionaries from Douay, 216 of whom had been sent into England between 1574 and 1585. Four hundred thirty-eight in all were sent in before 1603; of these, 98 were put to death. Hughes, III, 293.

croft, and an improved Court of High Commission, the tide of public opinion had changed against them in favor of the bishops. The Puritan clergy were active and zealous, but studies made of their academic status indicate that, as a body, they were not remarkable for learning, and proportionately had no more able or learned men than could be found in the ranks of the conforming clergy.[40] Moreover, the Puritan doctrine of the "inner light," by which even the most ignorant man could interpret Scripture, led to a certain hostility to education and to an intellectual decline. J. B. Mullinger, the historian of the University of Cambridge, declares that at St. John's College, where Puritans were the strongest, there was a considerable decline in learning and morality after 1560.[41]

CATHOLICS

The Catholics of England, according to many historians, in 1579 still outnumbered the Protestants.[42] From 1559 to 1574, however, they were leaderless,[43] and, on the whole, slowly drifting away from the faith of their fathers. But in 1574, with the arrival in England of the first missionary priests from the English Seminary at Douay, a new spirit was evident among English Catholics. By the end of 1579 a hundred missionary priests had made

[40] Usher, I, 251.
[41] St. John's College (London, 1901), p. 55. See also McGinn, p. 556.
[42] Hughes, III, 49, cites Pollard, Black, and Usher, who hold that the majority of English were Catholic in 1559; he further cites (III, 239) Froude and Conyers Read, who believe that the majority were still Catholic years later. Hughes, however (III, 51, 60, 97), suggests that a large percentage of the English by 1559 had lost all religious conviction because of the religious upheaval of the prior thirty years and that very few people under thirty-five years of age had any religion.
[43] The Marian bishops had been deprived and imprisoned, and most of the diocesan officials and university clergy (some 300 of the latter) had fled abroad. Hughes, III, 247.
The best treatment of the Catholics in these years (1559–1579) is that of Hughes, III, 239–305, whom I largely follow in this section.

their way into England and their influence was beginning to be felt. Nominal Catholics, having been reconciled to their faith by the hundreds, were staying away from the services of the State Church, and were being encouraged to be openly and plainly Catholic. The missionary priests, who knew they were facing death in their attempts to administer the Catholic sacraments, were zealous and highly trained for their work. Usher—certainly an unprejudiced witness—in stressing their purity of purpose and nobility of aims declares: "As for the rank and file, it is likely that the enthusiasm and piety of the Seminarists burned with a purer and more unselfish piety than did that of either the Puritans or the Churchmen. . . . There is visible, too, among the Catholic clergy, little of that taint of worldly baseness, the seeking of the place with the largest stipend, which the rank and file of Puritans and Churchmen preeminently display."[44]

The success of these seminary priests in the years 1574–1580 was, of course, linked with political problems of all kinds. One was the fact that Mary Stuart, Queen of Scots, was a Catholic and still very much alive. If anything happened to Elizabeth, or if the Catholic party grew too strong and found leaders, the Queen's Protestant ministers might well be tumbled from power; or if Elizabeth married Alençon, as seemed likely in late 1579, still further concessions must be granted the Catholics, which in time might make them dangerous to the group in power. Also Elizabeth for the moment seemed to be growing tolerant of Catholicism: since February, 1578, no Catholics had been sent to their deaths for religious reasons. And because of the Alençon marriage negotiations (and also because the prisons were full) orders had been issued moderating the persecution of Catholics. Furthermore, Catholic books, written by the exiled Catholic scholars, were flooding into England and were being secretly sold.

[44] Usher, I, 149.

Twenty thousand of these books, it has been estimated, made their way into England at this time (i.e., between 1565–1580) and were incalculable aids to the Catholic cause.[45]

The Puritan frenzy over the Alençon marriage in 1579, and the consequent heightening of the anti-Catholic propaganda, suggest the fear of certain prominent members of the Privy Council over the success of the Douay mission and the need of extraordinary measures to counter it. Some of the books of the Puritan writers which appeared in 1579, although perhaps exaggerated expressions of the growth of Catholicism, bear witness to the Protestant fear of a Catholic triumph. For instance that arch-Puritan, John Field, in his dedication to Leicester of his translation of Mornay's *A Treatise of the Church*, mentions the great increase of Catholics. In his dramatic appeal to Leicester to save the Church of England, Field prays that "wicked heritikes may be confuted and abandoned, which (alas) encrease and grow to infinite nombers daily amongst us." And although Field would include Anabaptists and members of the Family of Love among these "heritikes," he had Catholics mainly in mind.[46]

Another book appearing in 1579 (also dedicated to Leicester), which shows the temper of the times and sheds light on some of E. K.'s glosses in the *Calender*, is *Newes out of Powles Churchyarde* by Edward Hake. In his sixth satire this Puritan lawyer identifies the corrupt clergy with Roman Catholics, as does E. K. in his Arguments before the ecclesiastical eclogues. Hake is also indignant at those Catholics who hypocritically pretend to be "true professors." With their wealth they buy themselves immunity or procure pluralities and prebends for "popish jacks" who prove to be indifferent pastors and keep "true preachers from

---

[45] Hughes, III, 114, 296.
[46] Quoted by Rosenberg, p. 248.

obtaining livings."[47] Hake, in Puritan fashion, was probably calling all non-Puritans Catholic: the frenzy of the times provided him a convenient stick with which to beat Anglicans.[48]

The great increase in the number of Catholics can also be witnessed from Catholic sources. For instance, Mendoza, the Spanish ambassador, writing to his king in late December, 1579, declares that a hundred seminary priests had entered England during the last twelve months,[49] and that their zeal and competence were daily increasing the number of reclaimed Catholics and converts. Very few of the Marian priests who were genuinely Catholic remained, and most of these were in prison. In the last three months, he writes, five Protestant preachers have been converted to Catholicism.[50]

At least we can be sure that the group around Leicester and Walsingham (to which Spenser belonged in late 1579) regarded the revival of Catholicism with great alarm: Catholicism was not only "idolatrous" and "superstitious" but its growing strength threatened their positions of power at the head of Elizabeth's government as well as the dominance of Protestantism in England itself. For these reasons they encouraged the anti-Catholic

[47] Quoted by Rosenberg, pp. 281–82.

[48] The Catholic gentry, of course, often offered benefices to Catholic sympathizers, but the Puritans were much more successful in providing for their own, principally because most of the influential and powerful were Puritan in sympathy. In these years also *Papist* (and its many variants, both noun and adjective) was a common term of abuse for someone less Puritan than the one using it.

[49] His figure was high. About 50 had entered England in 1579, and 52 had entered in the four-year period 1574–1578.

[50] *C.S.P., Spanish*, 1568–1579, pp. 710–11.

On their way to the Continent on business many Englishmen, out of curiosity, visited the seminary at Douay and were reconciled to the Catholic faith—over 500 by September, 1578. Hughes, III, 295.

propaganda that, however intense in late 1579, grew still more
fierce in the next few years.[51]

[51] Christopher Hill, *Economic Problems of the Church* (Oxford, 1956),
gives an excellent account of the ills of the English Church (from Archbishop Whitgift to the Long Parliament). Since this book appeared after I
had finished my chapters on the religious allegory in the *Calender*, I have
not referred to it in my notes. I can recommend it highly, however, for in
some of its chapters it clarifies and supplements information given in
Usher's classic study.

VIII

Spenser and the Religious Problems of His Time

BEFORE DEALING with the religious allegory in the *Shepheardes Calender*, it would perhaps be well to clarify Spenser's position in terms of the problems of the Established Church and the conflict between Anglican, Puritan, and Catholic. Fortunately a recent study powerfully demonstrates that Spenser was a faithful, if conservative, son of the English Church; when Spenser, in a few points, departs from orthodox Anglican doctrine, it is never in the direction of Calvinism but rather towards Catholicism.[1] And although it is true that Spenser had a hatred of Roman Catholicism as a political force and sometimes indulged in the common Protestant abuse of the Pope, his attitude toward doctrinal Catholicism—the religious views traditionally ascribed to good works, the ascetic ideals represented by monasticism, grace

[1] Virgil K. Whitaker, *The Religious Basis of Spenser's Poetry* (Stanford, Cal., 1950).

117

as a reality in the soul, the Real Presence in the Eucharist, the Bible's not being open to every man (but to be interpreted by experts)[2]—was far removed from that of the ardent Puritan of the sixteenth century.

It is now rather clear that with such teachers as Peter Baro, a critic of certain central doctrines of Calvinism who often quoted with approval the Church Fathers and the Schoolmen, the University of Cambridge was not entirely Puritan. Indeed, at Cambridge about the same time as Spenser there were such future stalwart defenders of the Establishment against Puritanism as Bancroft, Samuel Harsnett, and Launcelot Andrews.[3] And Spenser, we can be quite sure, would have been on the side of Whitgift in the latter's controversy with Cartwright at Cambridge. In letters to Spenser, Gabriel Harvey reveals himself as strongly anti-Calvinistic, and is wittily ironic in his satiric references to Puritanism, references which would imply that he and Spenser saw eye to eye in these matters.[4]

In poetry which Spenser wrote about the same time as the Calender, he is clearly anti-Puritan. For instance, in Mother Hubberds Tale Spenser presents a typically ignorant, lazy clergyman who embodies Calvinistic concepts of grace, the sacraments, and of Christ as the sole shepherd or priest. In lines of burning satire Spenser unfavorably contrasts this specimen with the celibate Catholic priests of an earlier period who dress simply in wool or hair garments and are admirably active with their daily masses, prayers and religious exercises, remembrances of the dead, and almsdeeds. In the new order of things the clergy wear fine silks, have their "lovely Lasses or Bright shining brides" lying at their

---

[2] On all these characteristic Catholic beliefs, which were often attacked by the leading Reformers, Spenser, to the Catholic reader, seems surprisingly orthodox. See Whitaker, pp. 8, 24, 25, 46, 50, 53.

[3] Whitaker, pp. 60–63.

[4] Whitaker, pp. 63–68.

sides, and are no longer required to fast. Likewise they are no longer tied to voluntary chasity and have the Puritan "Gospell of free libertie."[5]

In another passage in this same episode, the Fox and Ape ask this clergyman how to obtain a benefice. Since these lines have a bearing on Spenser's summary treatment of the same abuses in the *Calender*, I will paraphrase them here, since they are plain, clear-cut, and—although the irony has tripped some scholars— unclouded by pastoral conventions.

To procure a benefice the Ape and the Fox are told to apply to a nobleman or to some "other great one in the worldes eye" who has a "zealous disposition." They should then assume a "godly zeale" and "walke in sober gravitee"; or they should go to Court and in ways offensive to human dignity toady to the great ones there. But usually the benefice requires that the courtier be given a "fee," or "benevolence," or the first year's income from the benefice. Even obtaining a bishopric requires the same simoniacal proceeding. But the best way to insure success is to sue the lay patron (where no inquiry is made about one's learning), and a reasonable deal can be worked out: if the living is worth forty pounds annually, all the Fox and the Ape would have to do would be to relinquish twenty pounds to the patron's youngest son. Then the patron will do all that is required: he will force the bishop both to admit them to the benefice and to maintain them there. This is the approved way for the ignorant to proceed. The learned and competent have another way (presumably when the living is controlled by the Church itself), yet many even here must accept benefices in "peeces riven."

[5] Ll. 431–78. Whitaker, pp. 17 f., accurately analyzes this passage. In his *View of the Present State of Ireland* Spenser contrasts the zeal of the igno- rant, impoverished Irish Catholic clergy with the indolence of the Protes- tant clergy and tolerantly holds Catholic baptism to be valid. Whitaker, p. 28.

The Fox and Ape follow this prudential advice, get their livings, and act in scandalous fashion until the diocesan bishop is going to call them to account before him on a Visitation. They realize that they must now scamper, so they sell their benefices to a neighboring clergyman for a few pence and make their getaway.[6]

As we can see, the chief abuses flow from the political and lay control of church livings: an inevitable situation since, as we have seen in the last chapter, five sixths of all livings were controlled by lay patrons and the Crown. The lay patrons and the powerful courtiers were chiefly responsible for the corrupt or incompetent clergy foisted upon the Church and for the attendant simoniacal pacts. The revenues that properly should go to the clergy, particularly the fit and the honest, were thus drained away. To a much lesser degree the Church was responsible: evil bishops and deans trafficked in the livings under their control. And the ignorant, poverty-stricken lesser clergy would sometimes relinquish their livings for a price to their associates. Spenser also apparently glances at influential noblemen with Puritan leanings. These great ones with zealous dispositions are sometimes favorable to those who put on a godly zeal and walk in sober gravity. In all these ways the Church is filled with ignorant, corrupt, disobedient, and sometimes Puritanic clergy. Spenser, too, frowns on a married clergy; like the Queen he prefers the celibacy of an earlier period.

We can now consider the three eclogues of the *Shepheardes Calender* in which Spenser delineates ecclesiastical abuses. These eclogues are a little more difficult to interpret than *Mother Hubberds Tale* because Spenser makes use of pastoral conventions (which must be rightly interpreted), often makes rapid, summary, or oblique references to evils in the Catholic Church past and present and to these same evils in the Established Church,

[6] Ll. 486–574.

and indulges in irony or banter, giving the speaking characters of these eclogues arguments which are meant to provoke responses from other characters but which must not be taken seriously. In addition, the glosser, E. K., exhibits a slightly different tone of Protestantism; his glosses often complicate matters by making references and attacking things in terms of the anti-Catholic propaganda elicited by the Alençon marriage controversy of late 1579. Furthermore, E. K. and Spenser are not in perfect agreement, principally because certain eclogues were probably written a year or so before the glosses and reflect a different climate of political and religious opinion. Hence I will now analyze the three ecclesiastical eclogues, interpreting their tone as well as their content in terms of the religious history of the times.

In *May*, the first ecclesiastical eclogue, Palinode does not represent the Catholic pastor, as E. K. tells us in his introductory argument. The context makes it clear that Palinode is the common pastoral opponent who provokes Piers and gives him a chance to speak on ecclesiastical problems. If Palinode were Catholic, he and Piers (the Protestant pastor, according to E. K.) would not be on such friendly terms. Out "of felowship" Piers tells Palinode the fable of the Fox and the Kid. Palinode is impressed by this fable and asks to borrow it for Sir John (the local clerical ignoramus) to repeat in church on the next holyday; he is also in perfect agreement with the meaning of the fable (which he would not be were he Catholic): "But and if Foxes bene so crafty, as so,/ Much needeth all shepheards hem to knowe." Then he and Piers go home together in a friendly fashion.

Much of *May*, then, is good-natured banter. To begin the eclogue, Palinode points out that it is the merry month of May when young folk dress in gaudy green, whereas Piers and Palinode are attired in dull grey. Nature, too, is decked in beauty and color. The young people joyfully go forth to the wood bringing back green branches and gay flowers to decorate the churches, thereby pleasing "holy Saints." Piers replies that such activities are suitable for young people but not for "men of elder witt." Hence the May games are a question of decorum or propriety, and not of morality, as strict Protestants would have it.

Palinode zestfully reports that this very morning he saw a group of shepherds go forth merrily to the woods, dancing and shouting and led by one playing a hornpipe. They returned with their music and songs, with May encrowned, and Lady Flora as his queen, accompanied by a fair flock of fairies and a band of lovely nymphs. Palinode wishes he had been there, and enviously contemplates their great fun.

Piers, in a sense, then goes off on a tangent, attacking clergy who neglect their flocks and spend their time in "wanton merryment." These clergy are hired for little pay by those (the lay patrons and the unworthy clerical pluralists) who are interested in the fleece rather than the flock.

> Thilke same bene shepeheards for the Devils stedde,
> That playen, while their flockes be unfedde.
> Well is it seene, theyr sheepe bene not their owne,
> That letten them runne at random alone.
> But they bene hyred for little pay
> Of other, that caren as little as they,
> What fallen the flocke, so they han the fleece,
> And get all the gayne, paying but a peece. (43–50)

Both the patrons, these pluralists, and their ill-paid, idle appointees will one day have to account to God.

Chaffingly, Palinode accuses Piers of envious spite, and expresses a *carpe-diem* philosophy; at their ease and leisure shepherds should enjoy the good things God provides, for when they are dead these pleasures are forever lost.

Piers then declares (quoting Algrind or Grindal) that the

clergy should not live like laymen: they are set apart and should live simply; they should not be concerned in piling up wealth for their children. Such wealth is ruinous spiritually for both the clergy and their heirs. God will take care of these children if they walk in His ways.[7] So it was in the Primitive Church. But "tract of time and long prosperitie" put an end to this simplicity:

> That not content with loyall obeysaunce,
> Some gan to gape for greedie governaunce,
> And match them selve with mighty potentates,
> Lovers of Lordship, and troublers of states:
> Tho gan shepheards swaines to looke a loft,
> And leave to live hard, and learne to ligge soft. (120–25)

This ambition and high living has allowed wolves (heretics of all kinds) to creep in and destroy both shepherds and their flocks. Although E. K. tells us that Piers is here referring to the Pope and his anti-Christian prelates, and not to the English bishops (plagued of late by the Puritans who would deny episcopacy to the great unrest and hindrance of the Church), it is clear that Spenser primarily has in mind, or at least would certainly include, those English bishops whose lives exemplify ambition, luxury, and neglect of their flocks.

Palinode banteringly declares that Piers is being unreasonable and reasserts his *carpe-diem* attitude. The clergy are not too prudent in attacking each other and laying their faults before the world to the delight of their foes. Tolerance is needed.

> Let none mislike of that may not be mended:
> So conteck soone by concord mought be ended. (162–63)

But Piers refuses to tolerate evil or those clergy who "the right

---

[7] These verses about a married clergy (and their tendency to be over-solicitous about their children's material welfare) should indicate that Spenser has the clergy of the Established Church in mind, not the Catholic clergy.

way forsake." They are his enemies and he can have no more concord with them than light with darkness, or the Fox with the Kid—the fable which he now tells Palinode. And the rest we have related in introducing this eclogue.

It is clear, I think, that Piers in May largely represents Spenser's point of view, and that Palinode is a paper antagonist who takes a position designed to give Piers a chance to express himself strongly on church evils. The May-games business is mere foolery (as Piers recognizes), and E. K.'s argument on the irreconcilability of Catholic and Protestant relates not to the eclogue proper but to the fable of the Fox and the Kid and the political allegory that lies immediately behind it.

The July eclogue, which deals with a few ecclesiastical issues, is again largely amiable banter between Morrell and Thomalin: mountain goatherd and lowland shepherd who represent, respectively, ambition and humility. For the sake of argument, Morrell is "imagined to bee" a proud and ambitious pastor. But there is no real disagreement between the two, who gradually work up to a mutual sympathy for Archbishop Grindal, the unfortunate victim of the Queen's wrath because of his refusal to suppress the prophesyings.

Morrell points out that many hills are sacred because of saints and that Christ Himself visited Mount Olivet. Thomalin agrees, praises Christ, and reverences those hills where dwelt holy saints who furnish examples of the good life.[8] Thomalin then goes on to note (as Algrind often remarked) that such an early shepherd as Abel was meek and humble; also the twelve sons of Jacob,

---

[8] The veneration of saints was not a strong point with Puritans, who constantly fought to have saints' days removed from calendars. Examples of the good life, likewise, would have no efficacy in a Puritan world where heaven and hell are not influenced by good works but are predestined.

unlike the lustful Paris, were meek, mild, and zealous. So too, declared Algrind, were Moses and Aaron.

But nowadays things have changed with shepherds:
> They bene yclad in purple and pall,
>> so hath theyr god them blist,
> They reigne and rulen over all,
>> and lord it, as they list. (173–76)

E. K. indicates that Popish prelates are here referred to; and Thomalin mentions Palinode's late visit to Rome ("if such be Rome") where Palinode saw many abuses: amid the impoverished sheep the shepherds (higher clergy) lead idle, luxurious lives. Thomalin then concludes, no doubt ironically,
> Sike syrlye shepheardes han we none,
>> they keepen all the path.

Morrell agrees that
> Here is a great deale of good matter
>> lost for lacke of telling,

and suggests that harm may come from meddling, and that Thomalin shall not be thanked for looking too closely into shepherd's (bishop's) wealth.[9] Morrell asks who is the oft-mentioned Algrind.

Thomalin relates the fable of the Eagle's dropping a shellfish on Algrind's head. Algrind now "lyes in lingring payne," and from what has happened to him Thomalin has been taught "to love the lowe degree." Morrell concludes by expressing sympathy for Algrind: his misfortune will be lessened in time. Both then say farewell in friendly fashion.

[9] In February, 1585, Puritans introduced a bill into Parliament directed in part against pluralities, and a commission was suggested to ascertain the wealth of bishops. The bishops, of course, were against this move, but so was the Council, for the commission would "have revealed the iniquitous church robberies perpetrated by and for Elizabeth's greatest ministers and statesmen." White, p. 231.

The emblems of the eclogue point the drama: Thomalin's, that virtue resides in the mean; Morrell's, that perfect virtue resides in supremacy. But the latter emblem is ironic in the fact that Archbishop Grindal, the primate of the English Church, the one who ostensibly has supremacy, does not possess felicity, but, stripped of many of his ecclesiastical powers and sequestered, figuratively lies in lingering pain. Another interesting point is that Thomalin's account of the simplicity of early religion or the early church is largely taken from the "Catholic" Mantuan. This reference, then, should not suggest that Spenser went back to the Primitive Church, like the Puritans, for no man of his time had more regard for the order and discipline of the English Church as established by law or was less of a "primitive." His primitivism, that of the golden age, did not have a religious basis, even though in his poetry, for telling contrast, he occasionally presented admirable clerical examples of a Catholic past. Also, the parenthetical qualification about Rome in regard to Palinode's late visit there might suggest that not Roman dioceses but ones much closer to home were those really being referred to.

The September eclogue gives the *Calender's* fullest and most precise account of ecclesiastical evils. And although these evils are particularized as taking place in Wales, the same ones were just as evident in the various English dioceses; and the fable of the eclogue deals with the success of Young, bishop of Rochester, in unmasking a subtle heretic who was winning converts to his doctrines.

September opens with the bantering use of a characteristic Welsh term (*her* for *he* or *him*) by both Hobbinol in his greeting to Diggon Davie and by the latter in his reply. Hobbinol is shocked to see Diggon in "so poore a plight" and anxiously asks about his fair flock. The disconsolate Diggon begs Hobbinol to "gall not" his "old griefe." Since Hobbinol has not seen Diggon for nine months, he encourages Diggon to unburden his sorrows.

Diggon announces that his sheep are wasted and that in the far country where he has been (Wales) the clergy are dishonest, idle, proud and avaricious, cheat each other, and with their associates and patrons traffic improperly in church livings. Encouraged to speak further, Diggon explains that his sheep "Bene all served with pyne and penuree" and that he himself has been "Driven for neede to come home agayne." In other words Diggon's diocese has been pillaged in a merciless fashion of its revenues and properties by the holders of the royal impropriations and by the Queen's favorites, and the flock is spiritually dying.

To Hobbinol's easy and almost mock consolation of the tried estate, Diggon further rehearses the idleness, disobedience, avarice, and contentiousness of the clergy of his Welsh diocese who have, in effect, become disciples of the Devil and do his work. Hobbinol encourages greater clarity.

Diggon, speaking plainly, declares that the best of his clergy are a bad lot: their scandalous behavior provokes damning judgments about their doctrine and faith. Some people assert that the world, because of the ignorance and corruption of the clergy, is much worse than in pre-Reformation days; others, that the clergy have only contempt for their calling and scorn for their charges; still others, that the clergy, in a worldly fashion, are overly concerned with adorning their wives and enriching their children: in their avarice and selfishness, hospitality, that pre-eminent custom of the higher clergy that nearly had the status of a legal obligation, is entirely disregarded. Still others—who shoot closest to the mark—say that powerful courtiers (Bulls of Basan) plunder church properties.[10]

[10] This passage (11. 104–129) might well have been quoted in full, for it gives the best brief picture in the *Calender* of the religious evils of the time.

Hobbinol, with mock consternation, is aghast at this plain
speaking and counsels silence on this matter, for "Such ill, as is
forced, mought nedes be endured." He then asks about the sheep.
In reply, Diggon declares that the people under these pastors are
equally corrupt, wilful, and disobedient; many have succumbed
to Wolves, or false religious prophets.

Again, in a bantering fashion, Hobbinol declares that since
the time of the Saxon King Edgar there have been no wolves in
England[11] (literally but not figuratively true), but many foxes
—which would probably suggest less open adherents to Catholicism. Diggon ignores this chaff and asserts that wolves in subtle
fashion, disguised in sheep's clothing (i.e., pretending to be of the
true flock), are abroad. Hobbinol, still speaking ambiguously,
asserts that there are large bandogs (i.e., pursuivants) to appre-
hend these wolves.

Diggon agrees, but says that careful shepherds (bishops) are
needed to discern these wolves, and asks permission to tell an
incident in which Roffyn (Bishop Young) figured not long ago.
Hobbinol praises Roffyn, Colin Clout's former master, as a meek,
wise, charitable, and careful tender of his flocks, one whose life is
in harmony with his priestly vocation. Then Diggon tells the
fable in which Roffyn uncovers a clerical hypocrite.

Hobbinol next asks how one should cope with such wolves.
Only through constant vigilance, replies Diggon. Hobbinol,
again relapsing into banter, declares that such vigilance is too
difficult. Diggon then cries out,

> What shall I doe? What way shall I wend,
> My piteous plight and losse to amend?

and seeks Hobbinol's counsel. The eclogue concludes with Hob-

[11] This was a point of pride to Englishmen: on his continental tour
Philip Sidney occasionally mentioned that there were no wolves in
England.

binol offering his heartfelt sympathy, his hospitality, and hopes
for a "fayrer Fortune" for Diggon.

E. K. tells us in the Argument before *September* that the eclogue deals with ecclesiastical abuses in a far country (Wales)
and with the "loose living of Popish prelates" there. "Popish" is
of course a figure of speech that would take on meaning principally in terms of the anti-Catholic propaganda of 1579.[12] Most of
the Welsh bishops—especially Hughes, bishop of St. Asaph—
and their clergy were a disgrace to the Established Church, but
they were not Catholic. (However, it should be pointed out that
the western and northern sections of England were the least
receptive to the new religion of 1559, and that the people of
Wales, where they were not thoroughly indifferent to all religion,
still preferred Catholicism.) The Welsh dioceses were the poor-
est in England, and the miserable livings offered no encouragement to a zealous or educated clergy; hence it is little wonder
that the clergy were avaricious, indifferent—and few in number.
An interesting point in the eclogue is the play on the literal and
figurative meaning of the word *wolf*. Even E. K. enters the game
when in a gloss he mentions that since the time of the Saxon
King no wolves have been found in England "unlesse they were
brought from other countryes," most probably a cryptic reference
to the invasion of the Douay missionary priests and of the apostles
of Anabaptism and the Family of Love from the Continent.[13]

[12] Instead of attacking Alençon directly, which was dangerous, there was
an indiscriminate attack on Catholics in general. E. K. engages in this
tactic, but his attack does not harmonize with the contents of the ecclesiastical eclogues, which were probably written (except for the appended
fables) in 1578 before the Alençon controversy started. It is likely that
Spenser did not have time in late 1579 to make all necessary changes to
accommodate this anti-Catholic propaganda. (For this tactic, see Rosenberg, p. 232.)
[13] Would Spenser regard Puritans as "wolves" (i.e., heretical) together
with Catholics, Anabaptists, and members of the Family of Love? (Tech-

It would be difficult to place in their order of importance these evils mentioned in the three ecclesiastical eclogues. First, however, I would place the forcing of ignorant and corrupt clergy on the Church through the evils of the patronage system; second, the plundering of church properties by the Queen's favorites; third, the simony and other kinds of graft encouraged by the patronage system; fourth, the loss of converts to Catholicism and to some of the newer, more radical sects because of the indifference and low standards of the clergy; fifth, clerical marriage, which, though perhaps not wrong in itself, inhibits hospitality and encourages worldliness. Too much attention is thereby paid to wives and children, a concern which should be given rather to the flock.

The personal ecclesiastical allegory of the *Calender* deals, of course, largely with what Spenser would consider the good bishops of his time. But at the back of Spenser's mind, in terms of all these abuses—and an indifference towards trying to eliminate them—would be the bad bishops. In the light of the abuses that Spenser reflects, a study of the ecclesiastical history of the early Elizabethan period, especially the ten-year period from 1570 to 1580, suggests those bishops that Spenser would regard as bad, as well as those he would consider admirable. But in his judgments

---

nically, of course, according to English law, Catholics were not heretics; but after a second or third refusal to conform they could be charged with treason and so executed, whereas Anabaptists, as "genuine" heretics, could be burned. Hughes, III, 31) Spenser might very well regard Puritanism as "heretical" as Catholicism, but his close association with the group around Leicester in 1579 would make this a difficult assumption, since the most important members of this group were clearly sympathetic to Puritans and often helped and protected them. Spenser's dislike of Puritanism is, of course, obvious enough in his poetry. (See Whitaker, *passim*, for Spenser's animus against Puritanism.) Certainly a few years after the *Calender* appeared many Anglicans less conservative than Spenser held Puritanism equivalent to Anabaptism. See Knappen, *Tudor Puritanism*, p. 497.

of the bishops Spenser would perhaps be influenced by a number of somewhat extrinsic factors: whether they were good scholars; whether they were unmarried; whether they were friends of Bishop Young and Archbishop Grindal; or (in 1579) whether they were friends of Leicester and the Sidneys. (Bishops who will be treated later in the chapters on the religious allegory will be here passed over.)

Spenser, secretary of Bishop Young—a long-time and close friend to Archbishop Grindal—I feel sure would both know something of the records and reputations of the following bishops and thoroughly disapprove of their conduct.[14]

Edwin Sandys, archbishop of York, 1577–1588 (earlier bishop of Worcester, 1559–1570, and London, 1570–1577), was spiteful and contentious, and carried on a long feud with the honest and learned Hutton, Dean of York (and close friend of Grindal's). Sandys was a spoliator, who robbed the Church for his self-enrichment (especially at Worcester) and impoverished his successors by granting fraudulent leases of the estates of his sees to his family and dependents. He caused trouble for Grindal at London and York over dilapidations; and in letters to his patron Burghley, Sandys attacked Grindal for the latter's heroic stand against the Queen in the matter of the prophesyings.[15]

John Scory, bishop of Hereford, 1559–1585 (earlier Edwardian bishop of Rochester and Chichester), was interested only in amassing a fortune. He was guilty of all kinds of scandalous be-

[14] Most of the following material (for the sake of convenience) has been taken from White, who has a chapter on each of the Elizabethan bishops. These chapters are somewhat uneven in merit and information (as are also the sections on these bishops in *DNB*).

[15] White, pp. 97–108. In one letter to Burghley, Sandys berates Grindal for his "wilfulness, and contending with the regal majesty, and obstinacy for not yielding to that which your honours [of the Privy Council] set down." Strype, *Annals*, II. ii, 110–111.

Grindal and Sandys were boyhood friends and fellow townsmen.

havior—maladministration, simony, and extortion. He sold benefices, also the stands of timber on his episcopal estates, and gave
three sinecure prebends of the collegiate church of Bromyard to
his wife.[16] His record was so bad that Sir John Harrington suggested that if he were in the line of apostolic succession it was
as successor to Judas.[17]

Edmund Scambler, bishop of Peterborough, 1561–1584, neglected the spiritual needs of his diocese, was interested in "the
fleece" rather than the flock, and used his Visitations chiefly for
the rich harvest of fees he collected on these occasions. He alien-
ated some of the best manors of the see to his patron Burghley in
1584, and, presumably by way of reward, was shortly afterwards
translated to Norwich.[18]

Richard Barnes, bishop of Durham, 1577–1587 (earlier bishop
of Nottingham, 1567–1570, and Carlisle, 1570–1577), was harsh,
greedy, despotic, and neglected the spiritual wants of his diocese.
Because of his character, Grindal had opposed him in 1567 when,
through the efforts of Burghley and Sussex, he was elevated
to Nottingham. Grindal, though suspended, also strongly opposed his election to the bishopric of Durham in 1577. Barnes
has been charged with bribery and corruption and alienation of
episcopal manors to his patrons and the Crown. And of all the
bishops, Barnes most strongly opposed Grindal's stand on the
prophesyings.[19]

William Hughes, bishop of St. Asaph, 1573–1600, was grasping
and avaricious, utterly neglected hospitality and charity, allowed
the cathedral to fall into a grievous state of dilapidation, and was
perhaps the greatest pluralist of the Elizabethan period, holding

[16] White, pp. 16–19.
[17] *Nugae Antiquae*, II, 178. Quoted by Dawley, p. 102.
[18] White, pp. 158–61.
[19] White, pp. 72, 181–85.

sixteen benefices himself, nine of which were sinecures. He sold benefices that were within his gift, paid but a starvation pittance to the incumbents out of the impropriate livings, fraudulently leased out episcopal manors for long terms to his family, pocketed monies paid for penances, and so that he could overcharge, in violation of the canons, would not allow a table of fees to be placed in his Consistory Court. "His clergy he squeezed dry at the Visitations, not only by rigidly exacting the customary fees, but making them defray the cost of the diet of himself and his attendants."[20] Like Scory, he died rich.

John May, bishop of Carlisle, 1577–1598, was covetous and tyrannous, and appointed corrupt and incompetent clergy. Grindal vigorously opposed his election to Carlisle. Earlier, when he was archdeacon of York, May was so offensively meddlesome that Dean Hutton cynically urged the government to make him bishop of Carlisle so that the Council of the North would be rid of him.[21]

These were apparently the worst. Gilbert Berkeley, bishop of Bath and Wells, 1560–1581, was on the whole a just administrator except when his imperious and avaricious wife "made him swerve from the path of rectitude." And although he was often forced by the Queen to cede episcopal property to her favorites, "he reluctantly yielded."[22] Edmund Freake, bishop of Norwich, 1574–1584 (earlier bishop of Rochester, 1572–1575, and later of Worcester, 1584–1591), was scholarly and fairly honest, but he and his diocese reportedly suffered from the despotic sway of his wife. And finally, to cut this list short, Richard Curteis, bishop of Chichester, 1570–1582, reputed by some to be dishonest and a drinker, was over-zealous in his proceedings against Catholics in

[20] White, pp. 196–98.
[21] White, pp. 249–50.
[22] White, p. 137.

his Visitation of 1577. They retaliated with thirty-eight articles of accusation to the Privy Council; among them he was called a "licenser of May games"—which might throw light on Palinode's colorful defense of May games in the opening lines of the May eclogue.[23]

Because of the abuse they received from the Puritans, the Elizabethan bishops have, on the whole, been rather harshly, and sometimes unjustly evaluated.[24] Even such a careful scholar as W. P. M. Kennedy suggests that the good and decent bishops were exceptional in the first thirty years of Elizabeth's reign.[25] But there were good bishops who did the best they could, fought bravely against ecclesiastical abuses, and encouraged learning and scholarship. Spenser, I suggest, would undoubtedly admire such scholars and lovers of learning as Parker, archbishop of Canterbury, 1559–1575; Guest, bishop of Salisbury, 1571–1577 (earlier bishop of Rochester, 1560–1571); Whitgift, bishop of Worcester, 1577–1583 (later archbishop of Canterbury, 1583–1604); Cheney, bishop of Gloucester, 1562–1579; Cox, bishop of Ely, 1559–1581; and perhaps even Pilkington, bishop of Durham, 1561–1576, and Horne, bishop of Winchester, 1561–1580.[26]

Spenser would no doubt also approve those bishops who strenuously opposed episcopal spoliation: hence Parker, Grindal, Cox (who between 1574 and 1579 put up stiff resistance to the efforts of Christopher Hatton and Lord North to obtain properties belonging to his bishopric of Ely), Whitgift, Piers, Young, Davies, and Pilkington would all have been commended on this score.

[23] White, pp. 187, 193–96.
[24] As by Herbert Hall, Society in the Elizabethan Age (London, 1886), pp. 105, 170. See Hughes, III, 46.
[25] Elizabethan Episcopal Administration, 3 vols. (London, 1924), I, xxv, xxxix. Dawley, however (pp. 104 f.), stresses the "character, ability, and surprising accomplishment amid very difficult circumstances" of the bulk of the Elizabethan bishops.
[26] See chapters on these bishops in White.

Theological precision of views would probably not influence Spenser too much, for those bishops he honors allegorically were those who—besides being good bishops—were the most friendly with Bishop Young. After 1572 those Bishops who were earlier sympathetic to Puritans and their religious scruples (such as Grindal, Cox, Sandys, Horne, and Pilkington) [27] were horrified at, and plagued by, the seemingly revolutionary shift of the Puritan attack. After the *Admonition to Parliament* of 1572 all bishops were necessarily anti-Puritan.

Next to Bishop Young (who had a few Catholic sympathies), the Elizabethan bishop that Spenser in the late 1570's would be closest to theologically would probably be the kindly and cheerful Cheney of Gloucester, who rejected predestination, believed in the Real Presence in the Eucharist, and admired the Church Fathers. As far as I can determine Cheney was the only bishop at this time who did not accept the Calvinistic interpretation of the Eucharist, but Cheney was apparently more Lutheran than Catholic. [28] But under Peter Baro a determined group was being educated at Cambridge to reject the Calvinistic notion of election and reprobation, and Spenser would probably be among this number. Unfortunately, except for the slight evidence furnished by his poetry, we do not know Spenser's authorities in theological matters. But we do know that Gabriel Harvey, Spenser's closest friend, relied on authorities who were, except for Ramus, almost exclusively Lutheran and Catholic. Harvey, too, was a fierce defender of the wisdom and zeal of the "auncient Fathers

[27] See Dawley, pp. 72–73.
[28] See A. L. Rowse, *England of Elizabeth* (New York, 1951), p. 415; also White, p. 177. When the collector embezzled Cheney's rents he was unable to pay the Queen the subsidies and first fruits called for in 1576. Consequently, process was served on him and all his episcopal property was seized by the sheriff. He died in poverty in April, 1579.

and Doctors of the Church" against those who were inclined to scorn them in favor of Calvin and Beza.[29]

Which of the Queen's ministers or favorites would Spenser consider "Bulles of Basan," those powerful courtiers and statesmen who wrest church properties from the various bishoprics? Here Spenser's eyes would be perhaps blinded by his association in 1579 with Leicester and Philip Sidney: against the facts Spenser would no doubt think that Leicester's record was better than that of other members of the Privy Council. And because Burghley and Sir Nicholas Bacon (who died in 1579) were largely in charge of church affairs, Spenser may have felt that the responsibility for church evils was mainly theirs. Leicester, however, like Burghley and others, obtained much wealth from the Church through his power, personal influence with the Queen, and his appointees. In 1586 Whitgift expressed the opinion to his patron Burghley that almost all the evil bishops and deans in England were the nominees of Leicester.[30] It is almost inconceivable that Spenser in 1579 should be ignorant of Leicester's real character;[31] however, I think Spenser was inclined to see Leicester through

[29] Whitaker, pp. 66–67.
[30] Not true, of course, for many of the "bad" bishops, such as Sandys, Barnes, May, Hughes, etc., were appointed through Burghley's efforts.
[31] What was Leicester's "real character"? Historians are inclined to take extreme views. In a recent study, in the light of Puritan dedications to Leicester, Miss Rosenberg pictures him as a great pattern of virtue, patriotism, and religious sincerity—certainly not the common appraisal. Miss Rosenberg (p. 198) also condones the alienation of church property by Leicester and other powerful members of the nobility: "If they were jealous of the power and wealth of episcopacy, it was because they thought they could put that power and wealth to a better use for the nation. Their greed was for fame and glory rather than for gain." Spenser, I am sure, would not take this tolerant view of episcopal depredations, nor do I.
Leicester undoubtedly treated Spenser with generosity and kindness, and Spenser was loyal to his memory. Spenser was shocked at the remarkable absence of grief when Leicester died in 1588; in his *Ruines of Time* (1591) he rebukes those who seemingly have totally forgotten Leicester. Miss

Philip Sidney's eyes (which were in turn blinded by "great expectations"), and as a result he idealized Leicester as a great statesman and true patriot, forgetting—if he ever knew—other sides of Leicester's character. My reading in ecclesiastical history would suggest that there was very little to choose between the guilt of the various leading members of the Council in the matter of pillaging the Church. Those who had the most power, such as Burghley and Leicester (perhaps because we know more about them) seem to have been the worst, but Christopher Hatton was beginning to show a real talent in episcopal plundering. And always behind these men, working with them, encouraging them, and usually giving stern orders if the bishop was reluctant or conscientious, was the Queen herself.

But perhaps we should not expect Spenser to regard ecclesiastical abuses with the cool, impartial eye of the modern historian. And we can never be sure how much Spenser actually knew. At Cambridge between 1569 and 1576 Spenser would certainly be aware of all aspects of the conflict between Cartwright and Whitgift and the points of difference between Anglican and Puritan in the Admonition Controversy. He also would certainly be aware of the prevailing clerical ignorance and clerical ill-living and the various ecclesiastical abuses connected with the patronage system. And when Spenser became secretary to Bishop Young in 1578 his knowledge of church evils would have been extended, and he would certainly be inclined to take the part of the good bishops against all who were enemies of the Church and throve on abuses. And since Burghley was in charge of church affairs for

---

Rosenberg (p. 322) suggests that "the rejoicing over the defeat of the Armada shut off grief over Leicester's passing." But there are contrary views. Parson William Harrison (a staunch Protestant) declared that the general rejoicing at Leicester's death equalled that occasioned by the victory over Spain five weeks earlier. See Hughes, III, 381 n.

the Queen, Spenser would probably hold Burghley responsible for many of the problems of the Church. He would also probably blame Burghley (and the Queen too) for the extended suspension of Archbishop Grindal.

When Spenser entered the employ of Leicester (probably in the late spring of 1579), Spenser in a sense had joined a political party that was fighting for its life and presumed right to dominate, and his attitude towards Burghley and Sussex would undoubtedly be colored by all the irrationality, frenzy, and inconsistency engendered by partisan politics in the Alençon marriage negotiations of late 1579. Church evils would for a time probably take second place in Spenser's interests, and Leicester, Walsingham, and Philip Sidney would become his heroes, fighting courageously for Church, Country, and Queen—at least so they were convinced—against a formidable group of political enemies. Spenser may not have been aware of Leicester's malign influence over the Church (which, by the way, was much more in evidence after 1580), for Leicester's wealth and power had come from other sources too—from his many monopolies, patents, and stewardships.[32] (But so too had Burghley gained much of his wealth as master of the Court of Wards.)

My own feeling is that Spenser would have in mind, in the pillage of the Church, those lesser figures of the Court, the Queen's gentlemen pensioners and grooms of the royal Chamber, who had few other sources of income except what they could extort from the Church through the Queen's favor by open and unashamed appropriation or through legal trickery (such as the commissions of concealment, where the royal "concealers" would seek to divert church property to themselves or the Crown through "discovery" of invalid title or original grant to the

[32] Rosenberg, p. 23.

Church for "superstitious uses"). At least where Spenser is fairly specific in his allegory, the villain of the piece (in *September*, as we shall see) is a groom of her majesty's Privy Chamber, Edward Carey.

IX

Archbishop Grindal as Algrind

THE MOST obvious bit of religious allegory in the *Shepheardes Calender* is that of Archbishop Grindal as Algrind. And although this identification has never been questioned, it has led to various interpretations of Spenser's religious position, interpretations based in part on conflicting readings of Grindal's religious position.

The life of Edmund Grindal, archbishop of Canterbury, 1576-1583, furnishes an interesting reflection of the progress of the Reformation in England.[1] Born in St. Bees, Cumberland, in 1519, Grindal at the age of fifteen went up to Cambridge, where, after a brief period at Magdalene and Christ's College, he took his B.A. from Pembroke Hall in 1538; he then became a fellow of Pembroke and proceeded M.A. in 1541. In 1544 he was ordained under the Catholic rite. In 1547, after reading the works of the Swiss Reformer, Henry Bullinger, and undoubtedly also

---

[1] The following summary account of Grindal has been taken from White, pp. 62–78, and DNB. Any important additions will be documented.

influenced by his tutor at Pembroke, Nicholas Ridley, Grindal rejected the Catholic dogma of Transubstantiation (the belief that the substance of bread and wine is turned into the Body and Blood of Christ in the Eucharist). In 1549 Grindal argued against the Catholic doctrine of the Eucharist before the Royal Commissioners at Cambridge; shortly afterwards were published his *Disputation at Cambridge* and his *Fruitful Dialogue Between Custom and Verity*,[2] which contained his new views on the Eucharist.

Under Edward, Grindal's ecclesiastical promotion was rapid, and only the accession of Mary in 1553 prevented his being named to a bishopric. Grindal spent most of the next five years as a Marian exile in Strasbourg. During this period he made the acquaintance of many of the leading Swiss Reformers, assisted Foxe in compiling his "Book of Martyrs," and in a number of trips to Frankfurt helped Cox resolve the Prayer Book controversy in favor of the Edwardian version (as against the Genevan) in opposition to the more radical group led by Knox.[3]

When Grindal returned to England in early 1559 he was a thoroughgoing Calvinist in theology, and, in many respects, would be regarded as a Puritan. His scruples about wearing vestments, and his disapproval of many of the rites and ceremonies of the Established Church made him hesitate to accept a bishopric. Advised by his friends abroad, he chose to regard the vestments and ceremonies as indifferent, and accepted the bishopric of London in order to keep it from someone possibly inclined to Catholic ways. As bishop of London (1559-1570), Grindal was sympathetic to Puritans and was reluctant to enforce conformity against them. He often confessed that he too disliked the surplice

---

[2] This dialogue is in the *Remains of Archbishop Grindal*, Rev. W. Nicholson, ed., for the Parker Society (Cambridge, 1843), pp. 35–74.

[3] For this period of his life, see Garrett, pp. 167–69.

and cope, and only conformed for "order's sake and obedience to the prince." Gentle and kindly by nature, he was often made miserable by the inflexibility of the London Puritans. Archbishop Parker encouraged his elevation to the archbishopric of York in 1570, for he thought Grindal was not "resolute and severe enough for the government of London" and its Puritans.[4]

At York (1570-1576), Grindal issued a new set of injunctions (instead of following Parker's for Canterbury) designed to reduce the existing ritual. He ordered the destruction and removal of all altars, rood-lofts, albs, censers, crucifixes, images, religious pictures, candlesticks, and holy-water fonts;[5] the communion bread was to be placed in the hand of the communicant; and the surpliced minister was to read the prayers from a desk outside the chancel, always facing the congregation. The task of rooting out Catholicism was much more congenial to Grindal than the repression of London's obstreperous Puritans,[6] yet even in this task his mild, gentle nature often revealed itself.

On the death of Parker, Grindal, strongly recommended by his old friend, Dean Alexander Nowell, and by Burghley, was named to Canterbury. His articles of inquiry on his first Visitation of the archdiocese reveal his old hatred of ritualism and his concern for the state of the Church. But almost immediately he was in trouble with the Queen and the Council for his refusal to suppress the clerical conferences on the Scriptures called prophesyings. These meetings, Grindal was convinced, were an excellent

[4] John Strype, *The History of the Life and Acts of . . . Edmund Grindal* (Oxford, 1821), p. 234.
[5] *Remains*, pp. 135, 140. Catholic prayerbooks, hymn-books, and saints' lives were to be "utterly defaced, rent and abolished"; the use of rosaries, the burning of candles, and the veneration of crosses, images, or religious pictures were strictly forbidden.
[6] In a letter to Secretary Cecil in 1570, Grindal reported that the Catholics were so numerous in York that "this seemeth to be, as it were, another church, rather than a member of the rest." *Remains*, p. 326.

way to educate the clergy and to promote religious zeal. But the Queen had other notions: she had no liking for such zeal, thought the prophesyings would encourage religious novelty and subversive political opinions, and absolutely forbade them.[7] In conscience Grindal could not accept the Queen's views, refused to suppress the prophesyings, and offered to resign if necessary. In early December, 1576, he wrote his extraordinary letter to the Queen explaining his position. The following June he was suspended from his ecclesiastical functions and sequestered; the suspension was never officially lifted since he steadfastly refused to change his mind on the matter. His punishment, however, was not too rigorous, and the year before his death, when he was ill and nearly blind, his suspension had "in effect" been lifted. He was also allowed to function in such necessary spiritual duties as the consecration of bishops.

We should remember, then, that for two and a half years before the *Calender's* appearance, Grindal was in official disgrace and in actual danger of deprivation. Only the opposition of Grindal's friends in the Council, and the inflexible determination of Bishop Whitgift (Grindal's friend and the Queen's nominee to replace him at Canterbury) not to succeed Grindal while the latter was alive, prevented deprivation.

We know so much about Grindal that we can easily define his religious position. Theologically he was a Calvinist. In his letters to the Swiss reformers Bullinger, Martyr, and Zanchy, as well as in his Injunctions to the clergy and the laity of York and Canterbury, he completely reveals his religious views. Holding the Calvinistic interpretation of the Eucharist, he regarded the Mass as an "accursed abomination and profanation of the Lord's Supper."[8] In this regard his orders for the destruction of altars and

[7] Strype, *Grindal*, p. 329.
[8] So he wrote to Bullinger in August, 1567. *The Zurich Letters*, p. 311.

the removal of the consecrated altar-stones (and putting them "to some common use"), and the placing of the communion bread in the hands of the communicant are revealing.[9] Grindal was also a stern enemy of Lutheranism, regarding it as a halfway point back to Catholicism.[10] In 1562, for instance, he defended the Calvinian theory of Predestination against Lutheran critics in Germany, trying to convict his opponents of bad logic.[11] He had the orthodox Protestant view of Purgatory; at York he ordered that no "superstitious ceremonies be observed or used which tend either to the maintenance of prayer for the dead or of popish Purgatory."[12] And his attitude towards the retained vestments and ceremonies of the Established Church would suggest that for the first ten years of Elizabeth's reign Grindal was fairly close to continental Protestantism.

Grindal, however, was constantly plagued by the Puritans in London, and about 1567 or so began to take an increasingly stiffer stand against them. For instance, in June, 1567, as a member of a group of commissioners examining seven Puritans caught in a raid on Plumber's Hall, Grindal had a difficult time with them, even after confessing his sorrow for having said Mass in the past, and stating his preference for not wearing a cope or surplice in St. Paul's. Hawkins, one of the Puritans, declared: "You have brought the gospel and sacraments into bondage to the ceremonies of antichrist, and you defend idolatry and papistry. There is no ordinance of Christ but you have mingled your own inventions withal." Grindal patiently inquired: "Will you be judged by the learned in Geneva? They are against you." Hawkins replied: "We will be judged by the Word of God, which will judge us on the

[9] *Remains*, pp. 124, 134.
[10] So he and Bishop Horne wrote to Bullinger and Gualter in February, 1567. *Zurich Letters*, p. 277.
[11] *Ibid.*, p. 142 (to Conrad Hubert).
[12] *Remains*, p. 136.

last day, therefore sufficient to judge now." [13] And so the encounter went, with the royal commissioners getting nowhere.

By the time Cartwright started his assault on the government, constitution, and Prayer Book of the Established Church in 1570, Grindal was in the foremost of those who criticized the Puritan leader, his "busy head . . . stuffed full of singularities," and insisted that even though Cartwright recanted he should no longer be allowed to teach at Cambridge. [14] And like the rest of the bishops, Grindal was horrified at the virulent pamphlets of the Admonition controversy attacking episcopacy and the constitution of the Church. [15]

Grindal's stand on the prophesyings (wherein he defied the Queen and her supreme religious authority) was largely a matter of conscience and not a conflict between Puritanism and the Establishment. Catholics, Anglicans, and Puritans all believed the clergy desperately needed more religious training: in fact, the ignorance, indifference, and venality of the clergy, as we have seen in the last two chapters, constituted the chief religious problem of the time. The prophesyings were a practical means of achieving a measure of clerical training and zeal. Grindal recognized the dangers of giving Puritans a possible forum and tried to set up adequate safeguards: the meetings would be strictly supervised by the bishop, the archdeacon, or his deputy; lay people and deprived or inhibited ministers would not be allowed to speak; and all mention of state policy or attacks on the rites of the Church were to be instantly silenced. [16] But Elizabeth would not budge in her decision. Many of the bishops, however, recognized the value of the forbidden exercises in improving the char-

[13] *Ibid.*, pp. 201–16, gives a full account of this examination.
[14] See his letter to Secretary Cecil of June 24, 1570. Strype, *Grindal*, p. 240; and *Remains*, pp. 323–24.
[15] Dawley, p. 93.
[16] Strype, *Grindal*, pp. 326–29.

acter and diminishing the ignorance of the Elizabethan clergy. Indeed, after 1570 none of the bishops would willingly lend themselves to anything that would directly strengthen Puritanism.

Grindal's long and eloquent letter to the Queen demonstrates, possibly better than any other act of his career, his religious principles, courage, and moral earnestness. In this letter Grindal defends the religious value of the prophesyings and argues strongly against the Queen's belief that few preachers are needed.[17] He begins by politely informing the Queen that she is wrong, as other Princes have been in the past, and cites scriptural instances of such mistakes and consequent royal change of mind in religious decisions. He next argues powerfully and learnedly on the necessity of having many preachers of the Gospel of Christ and demonstrates that such preaching makes loyal subjects. The reading of homilies is at best a poor substitute for preaching. He then explains the prophesyings, the regulations that govern them, sets forth their scriptural authority, and points out how profitable they are to the Church (listing nine bishops who have by letter stated their agreement with him about the value of the exercises).[18] Whatever abuses that exist can be reformed; that which is good can be retained. The exercises beat down Popery, improve preaching, and remove the "opinions of laymen touching the idleness of the clergy." Only "backward men in religion and contemners of learning do fret" against them.

Grindal then comes to the heart of the matter: ". . . I cannot with safe conscience, and without offense to the majesty of God, give my consent to the suppressing of the said exercises; much

---

[17] *Ibid.*, pp. 558–74.
[18] These nine bishops are: Aylmer (London), Horne (Winchester), Berkeley (Bath), Bentham (Lichfield), Cheney (Gloucester), Cooper (Lincoln), Curties (Chichester), Bradbridge (Exeter), and Davies (St. David's). The surprising omissions are Whitgift (Worcester), Young (Rochester), and Piers (Salisbury), all of whom were good friends of Grindal.

less can I send out any injunction for the utter and universal subversion of the same. . . . What should I win if I gained—I will not say a bishopric—but the whole world, and lose mine own soul?"

Grindal then bluntly requests the Queen to refer all matters "which touch religion, or the doctrine or discipline of the Church, unto the Bishops and Divines of your realm, according to the example of all godly Christian emperors and princes of all ages." These things should be determined "in a church, or a synod, not in a palace." In religious matters Elizabeth should not "pronounce too resolutely and peremptorily, *quasi ex authoritate*, as ye may do in civil and extern matters . . . It is the antichristian voice of the Pope: 'So I will have it; so I command; let my will stand for a reason.' "

In concluding Grindal untactfully reminds Elizabeth that she is a "mortal creature" with a "corruptible body which must return to the earth, God knows how soon"; and although she is a mighty Prince, "He which dwelleth in heaven is mightier."[19]

Elizabeth's anger over this letter is understandable. In early May, 1577, she sent letters to all the bishops, commanding them to suppress the prophesyings. If they failed, she wrote that she would "make some example of you, according to your deserts."[20] The Queen then ordered Grindal's suspension from his archepiscopal jurisdiction for six months and confinement to his palace at Lambeth. But since Grindal remained obdurate, his suspension, in spite of later appeals of Convocation and the bishops, was never fully lifted.

[19] Elizabeth tried hard to avoid all discussion of her death. Another untactful procedure on Grindal's part is his translation of the easy Latin of his quotations from the Vulgate, for the Queen was a good Latinist. And the use of the Vulgate, rather than of the Bishop's Bible or the Geneva Bible, is the most surprising thing of all.

[20] Strype, *Grindal*, pp. 574–76.

In the Shepheardes Calender Spenser shows his clear-cut admiration of Grindal, though this admiration need not indicate complete correspondence in religious views or even agreement on the value of the prophesyings. There were many varieties of religious opinion among those who subscribed to the Thirty-nine Articles and were willing to accept the laws of religious conformity and royal supremacy. And some of the good bishops (such as Whitgift, Young, and Piers), though somewhat suspicious of the prophesyings and the way they might be used by the Puritans,[21] nevertheless were friendly with Grindal, sympathized with his predicament, and thoroughly admired his character.

As secretary to Bishop Young in 1578, Spenser had probably met Grindal, who presided at Young's consecration (at Lambeth, March 16, 1578). Young had long been a good friend of Grindal and of Grindal's closest friends, Alexander Nowell, John Mullins, and Thomas Watts.[22] Many of Young's promotions were undoubtedly due in part to his close friendship with Grindal,[23] and Spenser could not help being influenced in Grindal's behalf by loyal friends as well as by Grindal's general reputation for scholarship, religious piety and zeal, and uncompromising principle. Let us now study the role that Grindal plays in the Calender as an authority on the good shepherd.

[21] In origin the prophesyings were Puritan. See Hughes, III, 182–83.

[22] For Young's relationship to this group, see A. C. Judson, A Biographical Sketch of John Young, Bishop of Rochester, Indiana University Studies, XXI (1934), 16–18; also his study of Thomas Watts, Archdeacon of Middlesex, Indiana University Publications, Humanities Series, No. 2, 1939, pp. 1–26.

From my study I would suggest that Nowell was Grindal's closest friend. Other close friends were Dean Hutton (of York), Whitgift, and (especially after 1576) William Redman, archdeacon of Canterbury, who was one of the executors of Grindal's will in 1583. Whitgift and Nowell were remembered in Grindal's will.

[23] For instance, through Grindal's efforts Young was named master of Pembroke Hall in July, 1567. Judson, Young, p. 6.

In May Piers quotes approvingly to Palinode Algrind's words on the ideal clergyman, who should not, like a layman, be concerned with laying up wealth for his children. This desire to leave children well provided for, although proper for laymen, has led to many abuses in the Church which will have dire spiritual consequences for those involved.

> But shepheards (as Algrind used to say,)
> Mought not live ylike, as men of the laye:
> With them it sits to care for their heire,
> Enaunter their heritage doe impaire:
> They must provide for meanes of maintenaunce,
> And to continue their wont countenaunce.
> But shepheard must walke another way,
> Sike worldly sovenance he must foresay.
> The sonne of his loines why should he regard
> To leave enriched with that he hath spard?
> Should not thilke God, that gave him that good,
> Eke cherish his child, if in his wayes he stood?
> For if he mislive in lewdnes and lust,
> Little bootes all the welth and the trust,
> 'That his father left by inheritaunce:
> All will be soone wasted with misgovernaunce.
> But through this, and other their miscreaunce,
> They maken many a wrong chevisaunce,
> Heaping up waves of welth and woe,
> The floddes whereof shall them overflowe. (75–94)

In *July* Grindal is twice quoted as an authority on the proper behavior of the clergy. Thomalin tells Morrell that he has heard "old Algrind often sayne" that such early shepherds as Abel and the twelve sons of Jacob, Moses and Aaron—unlike their modern counterparts—were characterized by humility, meekness, piety, mildness, courage, purity and simplicity of life, and loving care of their flocks.[24]

This last catalogue of virtues on the ideal clergyman has often been attributed to Grindal himself by students of English Reformation history. Indeed, ample evidence exists as to Grindal's character—evidence that would make almost inevitable Spenser's choice of Grindal as spokesman for the ideal shepherd, for Grindal possessed most of the ecclesiastical and human virtues, and labored hard to correct all the church abuses, that Spenser celebrates or adverts to in the *Calender*.

Grindal was widely respected for his learning and character. His work on the Bishop's Bible (which appeared in 1568) and on Foxe's "Book of Martyrs" would undoubtedly have been known to Spenser. In 1551 Ridley remarked on Grindal's "honesty, discretion, wisdom, and learning."[25] In dedicating a book to Grindal in 1575, Alexander Neville stressed his singular prudence, as well as his extraordinary affability, and his "most sweet and courteous manners."[26] In evaluating his character, his biographer, Strype, emphasizes Grindal's humility, mildness of disposition, kindness, and generosity.[27]

The fact that Grindal was unmarried would count in his favor in Spenser's eyes and make appropriate Algrind's declaration in *May* that clergy should not live like laymen and be concerned with piling up wealth for their heirs. Grindal in truth lived simply and was noted for his hospitality and relief of the poor. In his injunctions at York and Canterbury he ordered his clergy to be hospitable and charitable according to their means;[28] and in his own will he generously remembered all his servants, the poor of

[24] Ll. 125–68.
[25] *Remains*, p. ii.
[26] Strype, *Grindal*, p. 292.
[27] Pp. 436, 446–47.
[28] *Remains*, pp. 129, 165.

Canterbury, Lambeth, Croydon, and St. Bees, as well as Pembroke Hall and Christ's College, Cambridge.[29]

Grindal's concern for an educated, zealous ministry is well known. He carefully examined all candidates as to their learning and ability; and "such as were found unlearned he rejected, notwithstanding their presentations."[30] At York, the clergy were ordered to study one chapter of the Old Testament daily, and one of the New. They should have the New Testament in Latin also and confer the Latin and English.[31] In 1576 at Canterbury Grindal ordered the daily study of Scripture for all non-preachers, with periodic examinations by archdeacons. Candidates for the ministry were also required to give an account of their faith in Latin consonant with the Thirty-nine Articles. Only in case of necessity (and where stipends were small) were unlearned ministers admitted to cure of souls.[32]

Grindal continually fought episcopal spoliation. Before accepting the bishopric of London in 1559, Grindal protested the unjust exchange of episcopal properties for impropriate tithes.[33] Again, in 1573 Grindal interceded for his clergy who were oppressed by the "commissions of concealment" granted by the Queen to her gentlemen pensioners.[34] In his famous letter to the Queen in late 1576 Grindal bluntly declared: "This Church of England hath been by appropriations, and that not without sacrilege, spoiled of the livings, which at the first were appointed to the office of preaching and teaching. Which appropriations were first annexed

---

[29] *Ibid.*, pp. 458–63.
[30] Strype, *Grindal*, p. 273.
[31] *Remains*, p. 129.
[32] *Ibid.*, pp. 187–88.
[33] Strype, *Grindal*, p. 42. Through the Exchange Act of 1559 the various sees would not only lose valuable properties, but also all hope of restoring the impropriations and tithes to their rightful holders—the parish clergy who did the work.
[34] Letter to Burghley. Strype, *Grindal*, pp. 264–65.

to abbies; and after came to the crown; and now are dispersed to private men's possessions, without hope to reduce the same to the original institutions." Hence, in many parishes, "it is not possible to place able preachers, for want of convenient stipend."[35]

At Canterbury, as at York, Grindal was most anxious to uncover simoniacal pacts or fraudulent leases existing between corrupt patrons and clerical incumbents. An important Article of Inquiry was whether the clergy "have bought their benefices, or come to them by simony, fraud, or deceit, or by any colorable pact, or any other unlawful means whatsoever."[36] Grindal was also interested in detecting whether "any lay or temporal man, not being within orders or any child, . . . hath or enjoyeth any benefice or spiritual promotion."[37]

Grindal was also most careful in preserving the properties and incomes of his bishoprics. A prominent Article of Inquiry was whether his parsons and vicars had kept their houses and chancels in proper repair.[38] In May, 1578, Grindal prevented the Queen's agents from taking timber out of his woods, emphasizing that he neither sold it "for his own gain, nor used any more of it than was necessary for the reparation of houses and farms."[39] His exceeding care to keep up his episcopal manors and palaces did not, however, totally protect him, for Sandys, his old boyhood friend and successor at London and York, in 1576 caused trouble for him over dilapidations.[40] And trying to resign shortly before his death, Grindal petitioned Burghley (in February, 1583) that he

[35] Ibid., p. 565.
[36] Remains, p. 166 (see also pp. 178, 181).
[37] Ibid., p. 167. As we have already seen, Philip Sidney was breaking this regulation, as Spenser was later to break it in 1586 by holding the prebend of Effin. Judson, Spenser, p. 119.
[38] Remains, p. 165.
[39] Strype, Grindal, p. 357.
[40] Ibid., pp. 285, 364. Grindal was exceedingly angry over Sandys' action. It was adjudicated by Burghley after a year or two.

be not troubled over dilapidations as he has been in the past, and he seeks Burghley's assistance "if the case so require."[41]

Although Grindal disapproved of organs in church,[42] he liked music and patronized musicians.[43] As opposed to a growing tendency among Protestants, he also seemed to think that fasting had a certain religious value.[44] Like Piers in the early lines of the May eclogue, Grindal disapproved of the colorful festivities of May. At York, he had ordered that "no folks be suffered to dance" in the churchyard; also that ministers and churchwardens should not permit "summer lords and ladies," or any disguised persons at May games, or "any minstrals, morrice-dancers, or others at rushbearings, or at any other times, to come unreverently into any church or chapel or churchyard, and there dance or play any unseemly parts with scoffs, jests, wanton gestures, or ribald talk. . . ."[45] Grindal, as we have seen, also detested Lutheranism almost as much as he did Catholicism (whereas Harvey, and probably Spenser, too, admired the Lutheran religious writers).

Spenser and Grindal would, of course, be in perfect agreement in regard to church evils. But in other ways they would differ, for Spenser was not a Calvinist in his theology: Spenser believed in free will, in the Real Presence in the Eucharist, had no objections to altars or organs in church, had no pronounced hatred of ritualism, and did not overly emphasize the Bible (as against the traditional role of the Church). Spenser, too, I feel, had no real

[41] *Remains*, p. 399. Grindal, of course, knew that his good friend Whitgift was to succeed him.
[42] Writing to Bullinger and Gualter in February, 1567. *Zurich Letters*, p. 275.
[43] *DNB.*
[44] Strype, *Grindal*, p. 107.
[45] *Remains*, pp. 135, 141–42. (For a similar order at Canterbury, p. 175.) "Rushbearings" were bringing rushes to the church on feast days in honor of patron saints.

opposition to May games; and his preference for clerical celibacy was probably not shared by the unmarried Grindal.[46]

When Spenser entered Leicester's service in 1579, he would have found himself in another group where Grindal was greatly admired. Burghley, of course, was Grindal's great patron and friend, but in the crucial period of late 1576 to late 1579 Burghley strongly disagreed with Grindal's position on the prophesyings. Grindal had sent the famous letter to the Queen through Leicester, and when Burghley wrote a directive outlining the procedure of his expected submission, Grindal refused Burghley's counsel: "still esteeming himself not to have done amiss, he would not ask pardon, which supposed a fault." He also refused Burghley's invitation to appear before the Lords in Star-Chamber. In a letter carried by Sir Walter Mildmay, Grindal insisted on the "innocency of his doings."[47] In the words of Strype, Burghley "had no good mind" toward Grindal "at that time of his trouble" and so wrote to Bishop Barnes.[48] At this time, Leicester, Walsingham, and Knollys were particularly strong supporters of Grindal; Knollys even wrote a letter to Secretary Wilson declaring that if Grindal were deprived, "then up starts the pride and practice of the papists, and down declines the comfort and strength of her Majesty's safety."[49]

Spenser's sympathy for the sequestered Grindal is finally revealed in the transparent fable of the Eagle and the Shell-fish in the July eclogue—a fable short enough to be quoted in full. Morrell asks who is the oft-mentioned Algrind. Thomalin replies:

---

[46] Grindal's unmarried state was probably not a matter of principle. Many of Grindal's injunctions to his clergy (on hospitality, relief of the poor, etc.) could have been more easily followed by an unmarried clergy.

[47] Strype, *Grindal*, p. 350.

[48] *Ibid.*, p. vi. Barnes, of course, was hostile to Grindal.

[49] *Ibid.*, p. 354.

He is a shepheard great in gree,
  but hath bene long ypent.
One daye he sat upon a hyll,
  (as now thou wouldest me:
But I am taught by *Algrins* ill,
  to love the lowe degree.)
For sitting so with bared scalpe,
  an Eagle sored hye,
That weening hys whyte head was chalke,
  a shell fish downe let flye:
She weend the shell fishe to have broake,
  but therewith bruzd his brayne,
So now astonied with the stroke,
  he lyes in lingring payne. (215–28)

Morrell is sympathetic and hazards the hope that Grindal's misfortune will be gradually lessened.

Ah good *Algrin*, his hap was ill,
  but shall be better in time.

The meaning of this fable has been unnecessarily obfuscated through the explanations of scholars. For instance, Herford, thinking that Spenser did not wish to be too clear, advances this interpretation: "Elizabeth (the she-eagle) desiring to crush the Puritans (the shell-fish) sought to make Grindal, the newly appointed archbishop, the instrument of the blow. But Grindal, not being 'chalk,' declined to be used thus; whereupon the blow intended for the Puritans spent itself upon him."[50] Long thinks the Shell-fish represents, not the Puritans, but Bishop Young, because "a golden scallop dominates the arms of the Bishop of Rochester." He also points out that Grindal used the same fable in a sermon given in 1564 which Spenser, then twelve years old,

[50] Pp. 217–28 (as summarized in the Var., pp. 335–36).

might have heard.[51] "Spenser in effect declares that Elizabeth's command to suppress 'prophesyings' contemplated specifically a removal of abuses for which Young was responsible."[52]

Friedland, however, points out there is no sign of a scallop in the arms granted to Young on his becoming a bishop.[53] It might also be added that Young was not enthusiastic about the prophesyings (his name was not among the nine bishops listed by Grindal as favoring the exercises); hence the Queen could hardly hold him in any way responsible for them, nor is there any evidence that she did.

But all this unnecessarily complicates the fable. There is no need to drag in either Bishop Young, or the Puritans (as Herford does). The myth of the Eagle and the Shell-fish, as Friedland points out, is widely rooted in the folklore of many peoples. It appeared accompanied by a woodcut in a popular book of fables, Doni's *Morall Philosophie*, which Thomas North translated from the Italian in 1570. In the political context of 1579 Elizabethans would instantly recognize that the Eagle was Queen Elizabeth and the Shell-fish the order of suspension and sequestration against Grindal. In Elizabethan symbolism, the Eagle is, of course, the queen of birds, the primate of its species, and commonly represents the sovereign.[54] For instance, John Ferne wrote in 1586: "The Aegyptians when they would by a picture or

[51] *Remains*, p. 8. Thus: "Aeschulus the poet lying on sleep bareheaded near the sea, a great sea-fowl, thinking his head to be a stone whereon he might break the shell-fish which he carried, let it fall on his head, wherewith he was killed out of hand." (In most classical versions of the story, a tortoise is dropped.) In a gloss on the fable E. K. alludes to Aeschylus and the shell-fish.

[52] "Spenser and the Bishop of Rochester," pp. 734–35.

[53] "Spenser as a Fabulist," p. 144. For Young's episcopal arms, see Strype, *Annals*, II. ii, 184.

[54] Tillyard, *Elizabethan World Picture*, p. 27. Very often in Shakespeare, the eagle symbolizes the king.

emblem make a signification either of God, of the excellency of estate, of fortitude, of sharpness of wit, of victory, or of a Prince loving his countrey, they did always paint an Eagle."[55] Furthermore, scallop shells (as in the Knighthood of St. Michael) signify —one shell resembles another—equality and equal fraternity.[56] Hence the Shell-fish might suggest in the fable the blow or order that strips Grindal of his primacy or ecclesiastical supremacy and reduces him to mere equality with his fellows: in his punishment his ecclesiastical jurisdiction and powers as Primate of the English Church were taken away.

Unlike the time-problem involved in the other major fables of the *Calender*, the composition of the fable of the Eagle and the Shell-fish poses no real difficulty, for the event depicted took place in the past and no crowding of the licensing date (December 5, 1579) is necessary. According to the fable, however, Algrind has been "long ypent," so we may interpret this as we will (any period up to twenty-eight months).

Spenser's forthright advocacy of the cause of Archbishop Grindal would, of course, involve criticism of the religious policy of the Queen and her Lord Treasurer, as clear-cut (though perhaps not as dangerous) as Spenser's criticism of the royal policy in the Alençon marriage negotiations. (That he escaped punishment on both counts perhaps testifies to the mollifying and curative power of poetry.) In effect, Grindal was denying the royal supremacy in causes ecclesiastical as completely as ardent Puritans or Catholics, who held that the ministers of the Reformed Church, or the Pope, were superior to the Queen in religious matters.

[55] *Blazon of Gentrie*, Part 2, p. 21. Ferne then gives a long description of the symbolic qualities of the eagle.
[56] *Ibid.*, p. 125.

X

Bishop Young as Roffyn

IN THE September eclogue of the *Shepheardes Calender* Diggon Davie tells Hobbinol that more than good dogs (pursuivants) are required to track down wolves (teachers of religious heresy). Of first importance are "heedy shepheards to discerne their face." To illustrate this assertion he then refers to an incident that "Chaunced to Roffynn not long ygoe." In reply, Hobbinol characterizes Roffyn thus:

> He is so meeke, wise, and merciable,
> And with his word his worke is convenable.
> Colin Clout I wene be his selfe boye,
> (Ah for Colin he whilome my joye)
> Shepheards sich, God mought us many send,
> That doen so carefully theyr flocks tend. (174–79)

Even before the discovery of Spenser's secretaryship to Bishop Young, Craik, Palgrave, and Grosart, struck by the similarity of *Roffyn* to *Roffensis*, the Latin for *Rochester*, had suggested that the shepherd Roffyn, who detects and catches the wicked Wolf

158

in *September*, was the bishop of Rochester.[1] Then in 1908 Gollancz informed scholars of the brief inscription in a book (Turler's *Travailer*) presented to Gabriel Harvey by Spenser: "Ex dono Edmundi Spenseri Episcopi Roffensis Secretarii 1578."[2] In the wake of this announcement Padelford and Legouis, in particular, argued strongly for the identification of Roffyn with Dr. John Young, Spenser's employer in 1578.[3] In his study of Spenser's fables, Friedland concluded that this identification was soundly based and generally accepted.[4]

But in spite of agreement on the identification of Roffyn, scholars have not been too successful in explaining the full allegory of the fable of the Wolf in Sheep's Clothing. In fact, not much progress has been made since Craik in 1845 first suggested that Roffyn was probably Bishop Young, and that research into the ecclesiastical history of the time might uncover the meaning or literal fact hidden under the fable.[5] The purpose of this chapter, then, is, first, to follow Craik's suggestion and to further explain and clarify the specific allegory of the fable; second, to relate, as far as possible, the religious position of Bishop Young to that of Spenser.

So far, the most acceptable explanations[6] of *September's* fable are those of Padelford and Legouis: both suggest that the Wolf

[1] Grosart, *Spenser*, I, 63, and (for Palgrave) IV, liii–liv.
[2] *Proceedings of the British Academy*, 1907–1908, p. 103.
[3] F. M. Padelford, "Spenser and the Puritan Propaganda," *MP*, XI (1913), 100; E. Legouis, *Edmund Spenser* (Paris, 1923), pp. 41–42.
[4] "Spenser as a Fabulist," p. 149.
[5] *Spenser and His Poetry*, 3 vols. (London, 1845), I, 78.
[6] Some explanations can be immediately dismissed. For instance, Higginson suggested that Roffyn was Richard Cox, bishop of Ely, and the Wolf, Roger Lord North, who persecuted Cox and tried to alienate certain of his episcopal properties in the late 1570's. As we have already seen, Higginson apparently did not know of Spenser's employment by Young in 1578; he hence would not realize the significance of Hobbinol's statement in line 176 of *September*: "Colin Clout, I wene be his [Roffyn's] selfe boye."

probably represented Dr. Thomas Watson, the imprisoned Catholic bishop of Lincoln.[7] In February, 1579, Watson was transferred to Bishop Young at the request of the Bishop of Winchester, who had had Watson in his custody for five years.[8] The main difficulty with the equation of Watson with the Wolf is that the cultured and scholarly Watson, who remained steadfast in his faith through adversity and long imprisonment, was an open and avowed Catholic who had been effectively dealt with and silenced, whereas the Wolf in *September* appears to be a clerical hypocrite who has been recently detected. For this reason scholars have been slow in accepting Watson as the Wolf, even though, as Friedland admits, this interpretation is the most credible thus far advanced.

Explanations of the symbolism of the Wolf have appeared that are most helpful to a solution of this fable. Harold Stein has pointed out that in the controversial religious pamphlets of Spenser's time, particularly in William Turner's *The Hunting of the Fox and the Wolf*, printed in the first decade of Elizabeth's reign,[9] wolves and foxes are in general false prophets or those who teach false religious doctrine; in particular, "a fox is a person who seems to be or pretends to be a member of the Church of England, though at heart he has Romish beliefs, while a wolf is a Romanist in both belief and outward profession."[10] Friedland

Parmenter, p. 210, suggests that Ireland was the scene of Roffyn's exploit. But as Friedland points out (p. 151), the context suggests that the locale of the fable is surely England.

[7] See note 3 above. Padelford further suggests the dog Lowder is Young's Chancellor, Lloyd; Legouis thinks Lowder is Spenser himself.

[8] See Judson, *Young*, p. 19.

[9] This was a reprint of his *The Hunting of the Romish Wolf*, which was published in Emden in 1554.

[10] "Spenser and William Turner," *MLN*, LI (1936), 345–51. See also W. M. Carroll, *Animal Conventions in English Renaissance Non-Religious Prose, 1550–1600* (New York, 1954), pp. 70–71.

has fully indicated the Biblical inspiration of the tale of the wolf in sheep's clothing: Spenser would surely have known the sentence in Matt. 7:15: "Beware of false prophets, which come to you in sheep's clothing but inwardly are ravening wolves." Friedland declares: "Religious literature and pulpit oratory rang every possible change on the familiar theme, while secular writings, especially the pastoral in its various forms, were replete with references to wolves disguised in sheep's garb for the purpose of raven and betrayal."[11]

As we have already seen, one of the reasons scholars have not been able to pinpoint the allegory in various sections of the *Calender* is that they have not questioned the April 10, 1579, date following the postscript of E. K.'s Epistle to Harvey, or (if accepted as a true date) have not realized that Spenser had almost eight months to make additions or substitutions. And since other parts of the *Calender* were apparently written in the five-month period before December 5, 1579 (the licensing date), and since the other major fables (Oak and Briar, and Fox and Kid) deal with events of the last six months of 1579, we should study the ecclesiastical history of these months for a possible solution of the fable of the Wolf in Sheep's Clothing.

To fill in the existing picture, it should first be pointed out that Bishop Young in late 1579 apparently had in his custody, besides Bishop Watson, a Catholic cleric of the same name as himself, a Dr. John Young.[12] It is possible that this identity in names

[11] "Spenser as a Fabulist," p. 148.
[12] Catholic Record Society, *Miscellanea*, I (London, 1905), 61. In a listing of prisoners probably made up in early 1580, Young and Watson are cited as being in the custody of the Bishop of Rochester.
    The Catholic John Young (1514–80) was one of the best known scholars of the deprived Marian clergy. He was master of Pembroke Hall, Cambridge, from 1554 to July, 1559 (when he was deprived by Elizabeth and replaced by Grindal). He also served as vice-chancellor of Cambridge from 1553 to 1555. (In the latter year Bishop John Young—his probable

is referred to in the verses in *September* in which the Wolf had
learned to counterfeit Roffyn's voice so well that the dog Lowder
"his maister's voice did it weene"; however, the same objections
that might be raised against the identification of the Wolf and
Watson would apply also to the Catholic Young.

We should also keep in mind the earlier and wider significance
of the symbolism of the wolf which was still retained in heraldry:
besides a sower of heresy and sedition, the wolf also signified
craft, subtlety, greediness of mind, and an inordinate desire of
that which belongs to another.[13] In late 1579 this symbolism
would have significance in relation to Bishop Young in his efforts
on behalf of Chatham Hospital (within his diocese of Rochester),
when certain "concealers," with their pretense of concealment,
tried to obtain, through a suit then in the exchequer, some lands
from which Chatham Hospital derived its revenues. On October
20, 1579, Young wrote Burghley a strong letter of protest against
this attempt directed "to the utter spoil and undoing of certain
poor lazars, and other poor aged and impotent persons, there
resiant [sic] at this present: and not only of them, but of a great
number of other such like, as might stand in need of the like relief in time to come."[14] As Judson points out, Young was apparently successful in this appeal.[15] And since one of the main

custodian in late 1579—proceeded M. A. and subscribed the Roman
Catholic Articles.) Young spent most of his life in various prisons, with
occasional short periods of outside   custody. After leaving the custody of
Bishop Young in 1580, Young was probably removed to Wisbech prison,
where he died in October of that same year. *DNB.*

I have no evidence as to when Young was given over to the custody of
Bishop Young, but it was probably about the same time as Watson, for in
1578 Aylmer wrote Burghley suggesting that Watson, Young, and Abbot
Feckenham should be placed under the supervision of some bishop. Strype.
Aylmer, p. 25.

[13] See, for instance, Ferne, *The Blazon of Gentrie*, Part 2, p. 41.

[14] Strype, *Annals*, II. ii, 272.

[15] Young, p. 25.

themes of *September* is a denunciation of those who plunder the revenues and properties of the Church, this explanation of the fable is tempting. However, the immediate context of *September* in which the tale of the wolf in sheep's clothing appears, would suggest that the Wolf represented an influential false prophet, most probably a Catholic, who had hitherto successfully concealed his true position. We must look further.

In early October, 1579, a book appeared in which Bishop Young might be regarded as playing an important role in unmasking a false and dangerous Catholic. This, I think, Spenser was celebrating in *September's* fable. This book, by William Wilkerson, was entitled *A Confutation of Certain Articles Delivered unto the Familye of Love, with the Exposition of Theophilus, a Supposed Elder in the Sayd Familye, upon the Same Articles.* The title page also announced: " Hereunto are prefixed by the right reverend Father in God. J. Y. Bishop of Rochester certain notes collected out of their Gospell, and aunswered by the Fam."[16]

Young had somewhat earlier written these notes in Latin in the form of a review or critique of a book in Latin by H. N. called *Evangelium Regni* (or the *Gospel of the Kingdom*). Young's notes had been translated and interspersed with answers by a member of the Family of Love, and as such they form an eleven-page prefix to Wilkerson's work.[17] H. N., of course, was Henry Nicolas (or Niclaes), the famous Dutch Anabaptist mystic and founder of the Family of Love, who had written a number of books on his doctrines between 1540 and 1570, most of which

[16] The *Confutation* was dated London, 1579. The author's dedication to Bishop Cox was dated Cambridge, September 30, 1579. I consulted the Huntington Library copy.

[17] Strype, *Annals*, II. ii, 273–75, gives a good account of Young's notes.

had been translated into English.[18] William Wilkerson, the author of the *Confutation*, had been at Cambridge for six years with Spenser (he was at Queens College from 1568 to 1575, when he received his M.A.), and in late 1579 was acting as a schoolmaster at Cambridge.[19]

In his notes, Young thinks that H. N. is a Papist because he teaches no certain doctrine about Antichrist (whereas Young had no doubts that Antichrist was the Pope), calls Rome the communion of all Christians, and speaks reverently of popish orders and monks.

> But most plainly the author shews himself a friend to the Church of Rome, saying that many, through contention and discord, did cast off the Church of Rome; and did blaspheme her with her ministries; and of their own brains pretending the Scriptures have brought other ministries of religion. . . . Who doubteth that this is the voice and judgments of Papists against Protestants and true Christians.[20]

Young's excited revelation of H. N. as a Catholic can no doubt in large part be accounted for by the frenzy aroused against Catholics by the Alençon marriage negotiations and the success of the Douay mission in late 1579. The fact that H. N.'s books were

[18] *DNB*, "Henry Nicolas." By 1574 the Family of Love had gained a large number of English converts, and religious leaders of the Established Church were deeply concerned. John Rogers (brother of Daniel Rogers, who, as the Spenser-Harvey letters inform us, was a fairly close friend of Spenser in late 1579) had written two books against this "horrible secte of grosse and wicked heretiques" in 1578, and another book in 1579. In 1579, also, John Knewstubs (who was at Cambridge at the same time as Spenser, and in 1576 proceeded B. D. from St. John's) brought out his *Confutation of the Monstrous and Horrible Heresies Taught by H. N.* In 1580 Elizabeth sternly condemned the "damnable heresies" of the Family of Love (whose members Knollys called the "deified men"). Dawley, p. 158.

[19] *DNB*, "William Wilkerson."

[20] As quoted by Strype, *Annals*, II. ii, 275. Here I am using Strype's careful analysis of Young's notes.

condemned and prohibited by the Council of Trent and that his major doctrines bore little resemblance to those of Catholicism would not be particularly relevant.[21] Spenser probably knew Wilkerson, but even if he did not, his attention would doubtless have been called to the *Confutation* by the title page announcement of his revered former employer's notes.

Wilkerson's brief dedication to Bishop Cox is of especial interest in relation to *September's* fable. On the first page Wilkerson mentions that Solomon in his songs "resembled the Church of God unto a Vine, and the enemies thereof unto ravenous and greedy Foxes." On the next page he relates that in the days of Queen Mary and since

> Many false Christs arose, and while the watchmen slept, many lying seers and seducing prophets, under lambes skinnes, craftely crept into the sheepfold, privily whisperying perverse thinges, to seduce and beguile the simple. And though the word God (his name be praysed) have a clear and free passage amongst us, and the bloudly bandoges of the Romish Sinagogue be tyed up, that by them the Sheepe of Christ are in less daunger to be worryed.

On page five of the dedication Wilkerson concludes that "vigi-

[21] Strype, *Annals*, II. ii, 286–90, gives an interesting account of Henry Nicolas and his Family of Love. A belief of the Family that must have bothered Protestants was that "there were mysteries and great speculations in the Mass, and that it was a God-service."

Other doctrines of the Family, as cited by Strype, included the following: There is no Devil; the Bible is not the word of God but a signification thereof; the learned could not preach the Word truly, since it was revealed only to sucklings and babes; Adam did not sin, but the woman; a man should not get tired, for the Holy Ghost would not tarry in a body that was weary and irksome; and (the doctrine that evoked most horror) whoever had God's spirit could not sin.

That Young should think that H. N. was a Catholic was all the more amazing since he was one of the sanest and most scholarly of Elizabethan bishops, one who had himself been a conforming Catholic during the time of Queen Mary.

lant and watchfull eyes" are necessary to fight this heresy that has gained so many English converts.

In *September* are many parallels to—or perhaps even echoes of —statements in Wilkerson's dedication: Diggon, the main speaker of the eclogue, bemoans the wilful and disobedient sheep that have "bene of ravenous Wolves yrent" (11. 142–49); Hobbinol, Diggon's interlocutor, banteringly denies the presence of Wolves in England but will admit there are Foxes (11. 150–55); and the fable itself is an expanded version of the longer quotation given above from Wilkerson's dedication. Hobbinol also uses the term *Bandogs*, but in a different fashion: allegorically, Bandogs represent not Catholic priests but the English pursuivants who track them down. Diggon's main emphasis in the fable—alert and discerning shepherds, such as Roffyn, are needed to uncover false prophets (11. 167, 230–35)—recalls Wilkerson's emphasis on the need of "vigilant and watchfull eyes." The similarity of conventional imagery, or even of language, would, of course, be of less importance than the surrounding facts: two months before the *Calender* was licensed, Wilkerson, who had been at Cambridge with Spenser, brought out a book in which Bishop Young was praised on the title page and in the prefix was cited as having pointed out a dangerous false prophet of the period and as having unmasked him as a Catholic. About two months later Spenser in *September's* fable celebrates Bishop Young as the Argus-eyed and vigilant Roffyn who captured a Wolf "in his counterfeit cote," a Wolf that "with many a Lambe had glutted his gulfe." In other words, Bishop Young had uncovered a subtle heretic who had destroyed many souls by winning them to his creed.

What Spenser thought about H. N. and the Family of Love we do not know. In late 1579 he probably would have accepted Young's appraisal. In the feverish climate of opinion of late 1579,

Spenser, at the very center of the anti-Catholic propaganda insti-
gated by Leicester and his group, would not have been inclined to
tolerate a religious thinker, clearly unorthodox, who went out of
his way to praise ceremonies and beliefs of the Catholic Church
and to attack those of the Established Church. The times, indeed, did not permit a precise or judicious estimate of such a
religious thinker so demonstrably sympathetic to Rome. In a
less hectic period than the last six months of 1579, Spenser would
perhaps have agreed with John Rogers, who called the doctrines
of H. N. (whom Henry More later dubbed the "begodded man
of Amsterdam") "the drowsy dreams of a doting Dutchman."[22]
But as I have already indicated, I think that Spenser had undoubtedly read the dedication and Young's prefixed notes to
Wilkerson's *Confutation*, and that *September's* fable was primarily intended to celebrate Young's discernment in exposing
H. N., the author of the heretical *Evangelium Regni*, as a clever
and hypocritical Catholic.

In regard to specific persons and events I have no solution to
offer for the section of the fable dealing with the dog Lowder's
being so fooled by the disguised voice of the Wolf that he opened
the door of the sheepfold. Lowder was then seized by the Wolf
and would have been slain except for Roffyn's intervention
(11. 214–25). I might suggest that some officer or member of
Young's episcopal household was apparently led to consider the
doctrines of H. N. and was nearly converted to them. He was
deluded to the extent that he accepted H. N. as a true prophet or
religious authority; then Young providentially intervened and
saved him.[23]

[22] *DNB*, "Henry Nicholas."
[23] In his study of Young (p. 14) Judson endeavored to discover the members of Young's official family at Bromley (his episcopal residence), but
other than Hugh Lloyd, his chancellor, was not able to do so, since Young's
register does not contain this information.

In concluding my interpretation of the fable of the Wolf in Sheep's Clothing, I should like to emphasize that Spenser and his age were well aware of the different aspects of the symbolism of the Wolf and of the nature of allegory. Spenser's first readers would instinctively realize that *September's* fable was reflecting current events and that Roffyn's role would fit not only Bishop Young's recent published revelations about H. N., but also his equally recent attempts to thwart the "Wolves" who had designs on the revenues supporting Chatham Hospital.

The precise religious position of Bishop Young is much more difficult to determine than that of Archbishop Grindal. In a detailed account of Young, Professor Judson gives us much information about his life but very little information about his theological opinions, chiefly because the latter information is not available. The bulk of the evidence we have, though, would suggest that Young was a thoroughgoing Protestant who accepted the Elizabethan Settlement in its entirety and had little interest in further reform in the direction of continental Protestantism.

London-born in 1534, Young proceeded B. A. at Cambridge in 1552; in 1553 he was chosen fellow of Pembroke Hall (where he remained until 1563). In 1555 he received his M.A. from Pembroke, and in July of that year he subscribed the Roman Catholic Articles.

Young was apparently a conformist by temperament, for his life reveals no inner conflict in his shift to Protestantism when Elizabeth came to the throne in 1558. In 1562 he was ordained deacon at Ely, and in 1563 he proceeded B. D. From this time to his consecration to the bishopric of Rochester in March, 1578, Young received a number of preferments in or near London,[24]

[24] In August, 1563, he was appointed rector of St. Martin's, Ludgate (which position he held until 1566). In May, 1564, he received a prebend in St. Paul's (holding it until April, 1579). In May, 1566, Young was given

and was undoubtedly regarded as one of the most promising clergymen of the London area. For instance, in 1566 Young preached one of the Spital sermons during Easter week, and in March, 1567, he preached at St. Paul's Cross. In February, 1571, Archbishop Parker, commenting on Young's princely nature and pronunciation, appointed him to preach before the Queen. In the Convocation of 1572 Young preached a sermon before the assembled clergy at St. Paul's.

Recommended by Grindal (whose chaplain he was in 1564), Young was chosen master of Pembroke Hall, Cambridge, in July, 1567. Except for the year in which he was vice-chancellor of Cambridge (November, 1568, to November, 1569), Young largely governed Pembroke *in abscntia*. In his history of the University, Mullinger lists Young as one of the heads of colleges with Catholic sympathies.[25] What evidence Mullinger had for this charge I am unable to discover, for Young's many preferments, his steady progress up the *cursus honorum*, his occasional blasts at the Pope, and the religious position of his most intimate friends would lead me to question the assertion.[26]

---

a prebend in the church of Southwell, Nottinghamshire; in September, 1566, he was appointed rector of St. Magnus the Martyr, London Bridge (which he held until 1592). In April, 1573, he was installed as a prebendary of Westminster (a preferment he held until his death in 1604). Judson, *Young*, pp. 5–8. All of the information given in the rest of this chapter, unless otherwise noted, is from Judson's study of Young, pp. 3–41.

[25] II, 203. Other heads mentioned as having Catholic sympathies are Philip Baker (King's), Dr. Caius (Gonville), and Henry Harvey (Trinity). Mullinger is writing of the years 1567–1568.

[26] Ardent Puritans would consider pro-Catholic anyone who was satisfied with the Establishment and did not wish to make further concessions in the direction of Calvinism. And conditioned by seventeen years of ceaseless propaganda against papal supremacy, most Catholics (in a doctrinal sense) were perfectly satisfied with royal supremacy when Mary came to the throne in 1553. And the propaganda, of course, started anew under Elizabeth. Most of the English Catholics (who accepted the Pope as supreme in

During the year he was vice-chancellor, Young revealed his courage and independence in preserving the ancient privileges of the University, when the ecclesiastical commission directed him to investigate conditions in Corpus Christi College. Young resisted the order which infringed on his jurisdiction as vice-chancellor, supported one of the fellows (Thomas Stallar) who refused to appear before the commission, and also resisted the commission's search in the college for suspected Catholic books. Young's attitude (as revealed in a letter to Cecil of January 17, 1569) was that the university liberties must be kept unimpaired; that he was able to do all the commissioners could do; and that the responsibility was ultimately his. Besides, if the "wilful and obstinate Papists" at Corpus College "have refuge or succor at the commissioner's hands," he and the other heads "shall sustain reproach and infamy thereby," and the malefactors will be encouraged in their obstinacy.[27]

In 1573, as we know from the *Letter-Book of Gabriel Harvey*, Young showed great firmness in crushing opposition to Harvey's becoming Master of Arts. The fellows of Pembroke, obviously irritated by Harvey's intellectual independence, dislike of Calvinism,[28] and his general personality, refused to pass the grace necessary for his attaining the degree of Master of Arts. Young, then residing in London, first tried to settle things in Harvey's favor by letter, but to no avail. A hasty trip up to Cambridge produced

---

religious matters) rejected his authority in the political sphere, so mere verbal abuse of the pope would not infallibly reveal one's precise doctrinal position.

[27] Judson, *Young*, pp. 6–8. This incident, perhaps, might be the "evidence" for Mullinger's statement about Young's Catholic sympathies. (Grindal and Watts, good friends of Young, were members of this ecclesiastical commission.)

[28] These two points have not been sufficiently emphasized in explaining Harvey's difficulties at Cambridge. Thomas Neville, one of Harvey's bitterest opponents, was a strong Calvinist.

immediate results, however, and Harvey received the necessary votes. Shortly afterwards Harvey was hindered in his attempts to conduct the Greek lecture. Young again settled matters to Harvey's satisfaction.[29]

Hobbinol's characterization of Young as meek, wise, merciful, careful of his flock, and given to practicing what he preached, seems to be borne out by everything we know about him. Furthermore, he abhorred the Pope in proper Elizabethan fashion, was sound on vestments, and labored to reclaim both Catholic and Puritan. In his one published sermon (given before the Queen in March, 1576) Young makes an especial plea for humility. Perhaps in a confessional spirit, he briefly alludes to the "petie ambition which is to be found in us clergie men which piddel and scramble for benefices, prebends, deanries." He attacks pride of all kinds, but especially the pride of the lower classes who pass judgment on ecclesiastical and political matters. He seems to have Puritans particularly in mind when he asks: "What artificer, yea, servaunt, prentice, but he hath a common wealth, a Churche in his head, and nothing in his mouth, but the governement of the common wealth, and the governement of the Churche, specially the governement of the Churche."[30] But Young, it appears, tried to avoid theological arguments. For instance, in December, 1595, he was asked why he had not given his opinion on the Calvinistic Lambeth Articles at his last visit to Court. He replied that at that time he had not seen them. Now (hedging a bit) he confessed he had some doubts on the damnation of the non-elect, perhaps because he did not fully understand this proposition; "for the rest, he had no manner of scruple, as yet."[31]

[29] Judson, *Young*, pp. 8–12, gives an interesting account of these matters.
[30] As quoted by Judson, *Young*, pp. 35–36.
[31] Quoted by Judson, *Young*, p. 32.

Before his appointment to Rochester in 1578, as well as afterwards, Young was well beneficed. In his first year as bishop, Young was listed as receiving 280 pounds from the bishopric, and 160 pounds from two benefices and two prebends.[32] His income receded somewhat in the next seventeen years, for in 1595 Young wrote a sharp letter to Burghley answering critics whose word Burghley had apparently accepted in accusing Young of covetousness and lack of hospitality. Burghley had also questioned his right to hold livings in commendam. Young gave a full account of his revenues and expenses, pointing out that there had to be other sources of income since his bishopric yielded only 220 pounds a year. With the 120 pounds from his commendams (340 pounds in all), he could barely subsist, for his yearly bill for food alone amounted to 250 pounds. In the letter Young incidentally remarked on the prodigality and epicurism of other clergymen in contrast to his own frugality enforced by straitened financial circumstances.[33]

Another approach to Young's religious views is the religious position of some of his closest friends and associates. This theology through association is perhaps not too reliable, though, for Young does not seem to have been as inclined to the views of the Swiss and German reformers as were his close friends Archbishop Grindal, Alexander Nowell (Dean of St. Paul's), John Mullins (archdeacon of London), and Thomas Watts (archdeacon of Middlesex). All of these friends were Marian exiles. Watts, Nowell, and Mullins lived in the same house at Frankfurt, and the first two signed the "New Discipline" in 1557, in which the

---

[32] Ibid., p. 14. (Strype, Annals, II. ii, 184, furnishes this information.)

[33] Ibid., p. 31. Young provoked Burghley's remarks by first accusing Burghley of covetousness towards him. In defending himself, Young pointed out "that no man can well uphold his estate, if he spend above the third part of his yearly income in meat and drink" (whereas he was forced to spend three fourths).

Frankfurt Church declared itself a self-governing body: the domination of the minister was repudiated and the congregation was declared the source of law.[34] In the Convocation of February, 1563, Nowell and Watts supported the more radical group which tried (but failed by one vote) to eliminate certain Catholic ceremonies and apparel.[35] Young's views, then, would probably be closer to those of Mullins, who precipitated the publication of the *Troubles at Frankfort* by his criticism of Puritan views in a sermon at Paul's Cross in October, 1573.[36] But the very fact that Young's best friends were Calvinistic in their general religious attitudes would lead me to think that his reputed Catholic sympathies were not too pronounced, if indeed they existed at all. Like Spenser, Young attacked papal supremacy; and like Spenser, Young was fearful of Catholicism as a political force and of its possible danger to Protestantism and to the Protestant group in power in England. But what he thought about the Eucharist, for instance, we do not know.

Young, however, had no apparent Puritan sympathies, and here too he was like Spenser. He apparently did not believe in the prophesyings, for Grindal does not list his name among the supporters of the forbidden exercises. In an evaluation written to Burghley in November, 1581, Aylmer, bishop of London, recommended Young as a bishop most competent to deal with the Puritans of Norwich: Young, "for his quickness in government, and his readiness in learning, is the fittest man for that country

[34] Garrett, p. 22, and alphabetical census of these men.
[35] Judson, *Watts*, p. 9. Mullins, however, along with Watts and Nowell was one of the thirty-three signers of an earlier request that embodied substantially the same points (eliminating copes and surplices, the cross in baptism, organ music, etc.), so he was only slightly less Calvinistic in his religious sentiments than the other two.
[36] Garrett, p. 234.

that I know; and especially to bridle the innovators, not by authority only, but also by weight of argument. . . ."[37]

Since Grindal was one of the regular examiners at Merchant Taylor's School, Spenser may have become acquainted with Young as early as 1564, when the latter served as Grindal's chaplain. During Spenser's first six months at Cambridge, Young was in residence there as vice-chancellor of the University (he, of course, also served as master of Pembroke, Spenser's college, from 1567 to May, 1578). At this time, if not before, Spenser would certainly have become acquainted with him. Finally, as secretary to Bishop Young in 1578 and early 1579 Spenser would have had an opportunity to admire his character and to know him well. Hobbinol's eulogy of Young in the September eclogue attests to this knowledge and admiration. But again, as with Grindal, such admiration and acquaintance do not demand exact correspondence in religious views. But I do think that Spenser's religious ideas were influenced by Young, and that theologically Spenser was probably closer to him than to any other bishop.

[37] Strype, Aylmer, p. 58.

XI

Bishop Piers as Piers

PIERS, THE main critic of ecclesiastical abuses in the May eclogue, brands May games as harmless follies of the young but as inappropriate for "men of elder witt." He then uses them as a point of departure for his condemnation of the idle, ignorant, avaricious, and pleasure-loving clergy. To Palinode's provocative defense of a carpe-diem clerical philosophy, Piers asserts (quoting Algrind) that the clergy should not, like laymen, be concerned with laying up wealth for their children. In pastoral terms he then stresses the simplicity of life and trust in God's providence of an earlier era. "But tract of time and long prosperitie" have encouraged clerical ambition, greed, luxury, neglect of flocks, and consequent religious heresy. In a lighthearted fashion Palinode continues to defend a more worldly and tolerant way of life, but Piers absolutely refuses to compromise with evil. As an illustration of the folly and impossibility of such compromise he relates the fable of the Fox and the Kid.

If Algrind has long been recognized as a transparent disguise for Archbishop Grindal, it would seem that Piers would have been an equally recognizable and transparent representation of Dr. John Piers, bishop of Salisbury. But strangely enough, until the present century this identification was not considered. The late Percy W. Long, in objecting to Higginson's identification of Piers with Thomas Preston, first suggested Bishop Piers as Spenser's Piers.[1] In this chapter I will attempt to support Long's suggestion by documentary evidence—something which has not been done before—by connecting Bishop Piers to the Grindal-Young circle and by showing the appropriateness of Piers' sentiments in the May and October eclogues to the character of Bishop Piers.

Thomas Preston, Higginson's nominee for Piers, was a friend of Gabriel Harvey and fellow of King's College during Spenser's residence at Cambridge.[2] As Long indicates, Preston was not in orders; hence the statement of E. K. in the Argument of the May eclogue that Piers represents the Protestant pastor disposes of Preston's candidacy.

Since the name Piers had long been accepted as the stock denomination of the godly and unworldly spiritual shepherd, one may well ask, why look further for the prototype of the eclogues? But even with the Piers tradition in mind, Spenser could hardly have failed to associate a distinguished contemporary churchman of the same name with this stock character, especially if the churchman notably conformed to the type and won the admiration of the young poet. Furthermore, if in a fairly literal fashion or by readily penetrable disguises Spenser is representing Grindal, Young, Aylmer, and Richard Davies as Algrind, Roffyn, Morrell,

[1] In his review of Higginson's book on the allegory of the Calender. JEGP, XIII (1914), 350. While I was in graduate school, without knowing about Long's suggestion I wrote a paper arguing that Spenser's Piers was Bishop Piers. Professor Osgood read it and noted its conclusions in Var., p. 296.

[2] Higginson, pp. 185–87. Fleay (Var., p. 296) takes Piers to be William Percy, author of Sonnets to Coelia. Since Percy was only four years old when the Calender appeared, this suggestion can be dismissed.

and Diggon Davie, the presumption should be that Spenser is representing in the Piers of the eclogues—possibly in a highly direct and obvious manner—another bishop equally prominent and well known to him.

Born in South Hinksey, near Oxford, in 1523, John Piers was educated at Magdalen College, receiving his B.A. in 1545, and his M.A. in 1549.[3] He was ordained under the Catholic rite in 1558. Elizabeth's establishment of Protestantism was probably quite a strain on his religious convictions, for (while serving as rector of Quainton in Buckinghamshire from 1558 to 1566) he took to drink and became a drunkard.[4] Through the influence of an old priest he reformed and became a total abstainer. Apparently having solved his problems, he returned to Oxford, where he proceeded D.D. in 1566. Thenceforth, his course of promotion was steady and rapid. In 1567 he was appointed to the deanery of Chester, to which, in May, 1571, he added that of Salisbury. In the same year he received the deanery of Christ Church, Oxford, with permission to hold his other deaneries and livings *in commendam.* In 1575 Archbishop Parker recommended him (along with Whitgift and Gabriel Goodman) for the see of Norwich. On the elevation of Freake to Norwich, Piers was elected to the bishopric of Rochester and was consecrated on April 15, 1576. In November, 1577, he was translated to Salisbury. On the death of Sandys, he was translated to the archbishopric of York in 1589. He died in September, 1594.

This bare recital of biographical details gives us little relevant information about Bishop Piers except his steady and remarkable

---

[3] These facts about Bishop Piers are taken from the *DNB*, where the late Reverend Canon Venables gives an all too brief account of him.

[4] Anthony à Wood is inclined to blame the "companionship of rustics" for this phase of Piers' life; however, since it occurred immediately after Elizabeth's change of religion, I feel the religious explanation of Piers' taking to drink should be mentioned.

climb up the ladder of ecclesiastical preferment. Testimony as
to his character will be introduced later, but the fact remains that
we do not know very much about his precise religious views. His
progress in the church, however, should indicate that he became
a sound Protestant who probably accepted the Elizabethan Settlement in all its important aspects. His background would suggest that he was probably more conservative than Bishop Young
and that he would not desire further changes in religion in the
direction of continental Protestantism.

The possible significance of the May and October eclogues
aside, we have no direct evidence of Spenser's regard for Bishop
Piers. That the two men knew one another is, however, almost a
certainty. The knowledge that Spenser was secretary to Dr. John
Young, bishop of Rochester, in 1578, gives us this assurance.
Piers was Young's immediate predecessor at Rochester, having
been consecrated bishop of Rochester in April, 1576. Piers held
this bishopric for almost twenty months, and was translated to
Salisbury in November, 1577. On January 31, 1578, Young was
nominated by the Queen for the bishopric thus vacated. On February 18, he was elected by the chapter, on March 15, confirmed,
and on March 16, consecrated at Lambeth by Grindal. Assisting
were Bishops Piers and Aylmer.[5]

One cannot state with certainty how long or how intimately
Piers and Young had known one another, but before 1578 there
were many opportunities for one to become known to the other.
For instance, on May 9, 1572, Young, then a residentiary of St.
Paul's, gave the principal address before the convocation called
there by Archbishop Parker for ecclesiastical reform.[6] Another
opportunity was furnished when Archbishop Grindal summoned
all the clergy of the province of Canterbury to the Synod of

[5] Judson, Young, p. 14.
[6] Strype, Parker, II, 211.

March, 1576. Again, Piers attended the commission for ecclesiastical reform which met at St. Paul's on April 23, 1576.[7] During the year and a half that Piers was bishop of Rochester he resided at Bromley, in Kent, about ten miles from the heart of London. Since Young was then rector of St. Magnus the Martyr, London Bridge, and prebend of St. Paul's and of Westminster, he figured prominently in the ecclesiastical life of the city, and he and Piers must have been thrown together not infrequently.[8]

It seems extremely probable that, at the time of Young's elevation to Rochester, conferences took place between Young and Piers regarding the affairs of the bishopric. The fact that there is no evidence of any trouble over dilapidations and revenue is presumptive evidence that the two men respected one another and were on good terms.[9]

We do not know when Spenser entered the employment of the bishop of Rochester, or what he was doing between June 26, 1576, when he received his M.A. from Cambridge, and the period of his secretaryship to Young. It seems likely that Spenser was chosen secretary to Young shortly after the latter's election to Rochester and that he attended Young's consecration. And since Piers, Young's predecessor, assisted at the consecration, Spenser, as secretary to Young, would certainly be a party to the affairs of the bishopric, and to the information and arrangements necessary to the taking over. This would have provided opportunity for Spenser and Piers to become acquainted and to discover common interests. Furthermore, many of the clergy of the bishopric

[7] Strype, *Grindal*, pp. 289, 310.
[8] Judson, *Young*, pp. 5–14.
[9] As a contrasting example, the other assistant at Young's consecration, Bishop Aylmer, caused trouble over a period of seven years with his lawsuits over revenue and dilapidations against his predecessor Sandys. Strype, *Annals*, II. ii, 47, 245. (And Sandys, as we have seen, troubled Grindal over dilapidations.)

of Rochester served under Piers and Young, and may have been
a means of drawing them together after Piers' translation to the
neighboring diocese of Salisbury. For instance, Thomas Willoughby, who as a Marian exile lived in Frankfurt with important
members of the Grindal-Young circle,[10] was Dean of Rochester
under both Piers and Young.

The question then arises, was Bishop Piers the type of unworldly, devoted, and apostolic churchman that Spenser portrays
in the Piers of the May eclogue? All of the contemporary records
show him in a favorable light, suggesting a prelate who conforms
remarkably to the Piers of this eclogue. The asceticism of a shepherd who looked askance at the May games of Merry England is
found in Bishop Piers, who adopted such a strict rule of life that
"even in his last sickness his physician was unable to persuade
him to take a little wine."[11]

The fact that Bishop Piers did not marry, but devoted himself
entirely to his pastoral responsibilities, would attract Spenser to
him, for Spenser was antipathetic to clerical marriage. This fact,
too, would be significant in the light of Piers' long and vigorous
attack in the May eclogue on grasping pastors who pile up wealth
for their children, and his citing of the words of the unmarried
Grindal as his authority on the ideal clergyman—one who is set
apart, one who should not live like a layman.

Evidence suggests that Bishop Piers was characterized by generosity and meekness. Although prudence may have dictated
silence, in 1576 he did not object when Grindal, by importuning
the Queen and Walsingham, succeeded in taking away the archdeaconry of Canterbury (which hitherto had always been held
in commendam by the bishops of Rochester), and in giving it to

[10] That is, with Alexander Nowell, Thomas Watts, and John Mullins.
See Garrett, "census" of these men.
[11] Cited in *DNB*.

his chaplain, William Redmayn.[12] Again, in 1578 Piers manifested extreme fairness in his controversy with the Earl of Shrewsbury about deodands. Piers held that it belonged to him, as the
Queen's Almoner, to bestow these deodands at his discretion as
Her Majesty's alms. The matter was amicably settled.[13] In 1586
he showed his liberality by waiving a claim to a profitable lease
granted him by Elizabeth, in order to secure a provision for
Samuel Foxe, the son of the martyrologist.[14] As a large part of
the Piers portion of *May* is an attack on ecclesiastical avarice,
this trait of generosity might well have been in Spenser's mind
in the writing of this eclogue.

Bishop Piers opposed both Catholicism and Puritanism, and
in this opposition he corresponds with Piers of the *Calender*. In
1573, when dean of Salisbury, he began " 'the good work of
abolishing superstitions and popish statutes,' abrogating all observance there ordained 'repugnant to the Word of God and
statutes of the realm.' "[15] *The Calendar of State Papers* contains
several accounts of his activity against Catholics. For instance, in
October, 1577, he lists for the Council the Papists in the diocese
of Rochester who do not come to church or receive communion,
with a valuation of their lands and goods. A few days after this
first listing, he sends in another such list for Berkshire.[16] Again,
in July, 1582, he sends to Walsingham a certificate of the Recusants in his diocese of Salisbury, indicating those who have been
convicted, and those not convicted.[17] In January, 1581, Piers
aided the collection in behalf of Geneva, when the latter was

---

[12] Strype, *Grindal*, p. 312.
[13] Strype, *Annals*, II. ii, 183. Deodands were properties forfeited to the crown, which by law must be used for some pious purpose.
[14] Strype, *Whitgift*, I, 485.
[15] *DNB*. Canon Venables quotes from the *Report of Cathedral Commission* (1853), p. 377.
[16] *C.S.P., Domestic* I (1547–80), 559, 561.
[17] *Ibid.*, II (1581–90), 61.

threatened by "the Duke of Savoy, by the Pope, and other popish setters on."[18] In 1584 Piers was one of the preachers brought into Cheshire by Richard Hurleston, influential justice of the peace there, in order to lessen the "Romish power."[19]

Whereas Catholicism is attacked in the fable of the Fox and the Kid and in many of E. K.'s glosses, the only direct reflection on Puritanism occurs in a gloss in which those who would deny the "fatherly rule and godly governaunce" of the Church are explicitly condemned. Evidence, however, shows that Bishop Piers in his quest for conformity opposed Puritans as strongly as he did Catholics. For example, in December, 1583, he served on an ecclesiastical commission called to examine a group of rebellious ministers who refused to subscribe to the Book of Common Prayer. On the same commission were Whitgift, Young, Aylmer, and Gabriel Goodman.[20] Again, in 1583, Piers was one of the "relentless prelates" before whom Edward Gellibrand, fellow of Magdalen, was cited as being ringleader of the Presbyterian party in Oxford.[21]

Contemporary opinion of Bishop Piers would suggest that he was regarded as the ideal shepherd of this period of English Reformation history. Sir John Harrington summed his life up thus: "He lived and dyed a most reverent Prelate."[22] On December 10, 1594, the Lords of the Council sent a letter to Mathew Hutton, bishop of Durham, in which Piers is referred to as "a man of such learning and condition as her Majesty hath desired he should be imitated by you."[23] Canon Venables constructs this estimate of Piers from contemporary records:

[18] Grindal's Remains, pp. 429–30.
[19] Strype, Annals, III. i, 397.
[20] Strype, Whitgift, I, 256.
[21] DNB.
[22] As quoted by White, p. 201.
[23] HMC, Salisbury 5 (1594–96), IX (1894), 35.

At York, as in all his previous episcopates, Piers left behind him a high character as 'a primitive bishop,'[24] 'one of the most grave and reverent prelates of the age,' winning the love of all by his generosity, kindliness of disposition, and Christian meekness. His learning was deep and multifarious. He was called by Camden 'theologue magnus et modestus.'[25] On Piers' translation from Salisbury to York in 1589, Strype declares:

This was Dr. Piers' third remove: his first being from the deanery of Christ Church, Oxon, to the bishopric of Rochester. He obtained by his learning, good government, and Christian behavior, a great character from that college, when he went thence; in an epistle, anno 1575, they wrote to the Lord Treasurer for Dr. James to succeed him, viz. 'That his *benignitas in bonos, in praefractiores prudentia, in omnes moderatio*, were singular. That he was excellently furnished with the knowledge of all arts; and that he was the great instrument of the progress of good learning in that house.' They extol his learning, humanity, liberality, beneficence; and as he governed the college, so no question he behaved himself when he was advanced to the government of the church.[26]

Piers held the archbishopric of York until his death in September, 1594. His chaplain, Dr. King, eulogized him thus in the funeral sermon:

As he was not great by parentage, so it was his greater commendation that he became greater by virtues. The university tried his learning, the court his manners, the church his wisdom. He was translated from college to college: not by chance, but by advised choice. . . .
Even that malice which blotted and blemished the names

[24] See Piers' praise of primitive bishops in May, 103–116. Grindal, too (*Remains*, p. xii), was known as a "primitive bishop."
[25] DNB.
[26] Strype, *Whitgift*, I, 549.

of most of the lights of this land [viz., the bishops] never accused him.[27]

In every way, then, Bishop Piers fits the Piers of the May eclogue. He not only seems to have possessed every trait and virtue that Spenser admired, but in his actions too he would have won the poet's approval. For instance, his monument informs us that he resisted attacks on the possessions of his see.[28]

Does Bishop Piers also fit the Piers of the October eclogue? Piers' emphasis in *October* on the moral usefulness of poetry in its ability to restrain the "lust of laweless youth" and to spur them on to worthwhile action is what would be expected from a somewhat ascetic divine. But especially significant is Piers' advice to Cuddie to sing of Elizabeth and Leicester in epic fashion:

> Abandon then the base and viler clowne,
> Lyft up thy selfe out of the lowly dust:
> And sing of bloody Mars, of wars, of giusts,
> Turne thee to those, that weld the awful crowne.
> To doubted Knights, whose woundlesse armour rusts,
> And helmes unbruzed wexen dayly browne.
>
> There may thy Muse display her fluttrying wing,
> And stretch herselfe at large from East to West:
> Whither thou list in fayre Elisa rest,
> Or if thee please in bigger notes to sing,
> Advaunce the worthy whome shee loveth best,
> That first the white beare to the stake did bring. (37–48)

These lines are especially important and appropriate in view of the relation of Bishop Piers to both the Queen and Leicester.

[27] Strype, *Annals*, IV, 282. The brackets are Strype's.
[28] He was not, however, always successful, for a lease which he had been compelled by the Queen to grant, greatly troubled his conscience. White, p. 200 (refers to Hutton's *Correspondence*, p. 93).

Evidence indicates that he was one of Elizabeth's favorite bishops. In 1576 she appointed him Lord High Almoner, a position he held until his death. In January, 1583, he was chosen by the Queen to inform Grindal that he should resign his archbishopric because of failing health and increasing blindness. Grindal's death in July of the same year relieved Piers of the task.[29]

It might also be suggested that Bishop Piers was probably theologian and chaplain of the "War party," that group led by Leicester and Walsingham which advocated a militant policy against France and Spain, and open support of England's Protestant allies in the Low Countries. There is, I think, obvious satire directed against Burghley's policy of peace and non-intervention in those verses quoted above in which Piers advises Cuddie to celebrate those redoubtable knights "whose woundlesse armour rusts,/ And helmes unbruzed wexen dayly browne." To support this speculation I might mention that in 1585 Bishop Piers was consulted by Elizabeth as to whether she was morally justified in assisting the Low Countries in their struggle with Spain, and he gave a long affirmative reply.[30] On November 24, 1588, after the defeat of the Spanish Armada, he was appointed by the Queen to preach at the thanksgiving service at St. Paul's.[31]

There is also evidence indicating friendship between Bishop Piers and Leicester. (But this friendship we might almost take for granted, since Leicester was the chancellor of Oxford University, where Piers figured so prominently between 1566 and 1576.) For instance, on June 4, 1566, Piers wrote to Leicester from Oxford, complaining of the decay of readings and disputations at Corpus Christi College.[32] By May 5, 1569, he was appar-

---

[29] Grindal's *Remains*, p. 397.
[30] Strype, *Whitgift*, I, 437; and III, 165.
[31] Strype, *Annals*, III. ii, 28.
[32] *HMC, Pepys*, XVII (1911), 88.

ently in Leicester's entourage, for on that date Dr. Thomas Cooper, then vice-chancellor of Oxford, wrote to Leicester suggesting that Piers might well take a place in the disputations in divinity if he accompanied Leicester there.[33] In 1587 Leicester tried unsuccessfully to secure the bishopric of Durham for Piers.[34] Finally, in 1588 Piers wrote to Leicester seeking a favor for Thomas Jobson, an old servant.[35] Bishop Piers' relation to Leicester, then, would make dramatically appropriate Piers' narration of the fable of the Fox and the Kid in *May*, in which the French marriage (so opposed by Leicester and his group) was the hidden but main object of attack.

Finally, since Piers was Court bishop—the Queen's Almoner—it seems fitting that his counterpart in *October* should insist that the patronage of poetry is the proper business of the Court, and that he should encourage Cuddie, the disconsolate Court poet (Edward Dyer, as we shall see in a later chapter), who has received but slim rewards for his sprightly lyrics. It is also appropriate that he should encourage Cuddie to abandon lower kinds of verse for epic accounts of wars and princes, and should stress the glory and essential worth of poetry in contrast to its material rewards. And possibly as a tribute to Bishop Piers's reputation for "deep and multifarious" learning, Spenser makes Piers the spokesman of the famous stanza on the ennobling power of love. In context, Cuddie confesses his inability to make an epic flight; but Colin Clout (i.e., Spenser himself), were he not distraught with love, could easily do so. In reply, Piers emphasizes the Platonic nature of Love:

> Ah fon, for love does teach him climbe so hie,
> And lyftes him up out of the loathsome myre:

[33] *Ibid.*, XVII, 155.
[34] Strype, *Annals*, III. i, 682–84.
[35] *HMC, Montague*, Report 15 (1900), p. 2.

Such immortall mirrhor, as he doth admire,
Would rayse ones mynd above the starry skie.
And cause a caytive corage to aspire,
For lofty love doth loath a lowly eye. (91–96)

It may be a mere coincidence, but it can also be mentioned that Bishop Piers served on the ecclesiastical commission of April, 1583, which rejected Dr. John Dee's plan for calendar reform, a plan which would make England's calendar conform with that of the Continent. Other members of the commission were Grindal, Young, and Aylmer. Since this question of calendar reform was debated with sectarian bitterness in England between 1578 and 1583, it seems logical to connect Spenser's *Calender* with this controversy and the topical interest which this controversy begot.[36] It might well be that these four bishops had taken an early and prominent part in the controversy, and for this reason (as well as for many other more important reasons) were included in Spenser's poem and in the later ecclesiastical commission.

By way of summary, then, the prominence of Dr. John Piers, bishop of Salisbury, evidence of his relationship to the Young circle, the correspondence between the internal evidence of the May and October eclogues and the known facts of his life and character, and Spenser's practice in other generally accepted characters of the ecclesiastical eclogues—all create a strong probability that Spenser had him in mind in the Piers of the *Calender*.

[36] See, for instance, Parmenter, pp. 194–95. Spenser's starting his poetic calendar with January instead of March, and having E. K. defend this procedure in the "argument of the whole book," would make the *Shepheardes Calender* a part of this controversy, and would indicate that Spenser was more liberal in this matter than Grindal, Young, Aylmer, and Piers later proved to be.

XII

Bishop Aylmer as Morrell

In *July*, Morrell provocatively sets forth the superiority of the hill to the lowly plain—of ambition to humility. Although the Argument before this eclogue tells us that *July* is "made in the honour and commendation of good shepheardes, and to the shame and disprayse of proude and ambitious Pastours," it immediately adds that Morrell is, for the sake of a pastoral debate, "imagined to bee" a type of the latter. Furthermore, the tone of the eclogue is entirely that of good-natured banter. In fact, Morrell and his opponent, Thomalin, except for the necessity of carrying on an amiable debate (in terms of pastoral convention) over the respective advantages of highland and lowland, seem to be in remarkable agreement.

Thomalin readily accepts Morrell's contention that many hills are sacred to saints and carry saints' names, and that Christ Himself visited Mount Olivet. Morrell even cheerfully assents to the truth of Thomalin's statement that the higher clergy, in contrast to religious leaders of biblical times, are characterized by their pride, pomp, idleness, and devotion to wealth and pleasure. Mor-

188

rell and Thomalin are also in perfect agreement in their sympathy for the "long ypent" Algrind, and on this note they part in a friendly fashion at the end of the eclogue.

It has been generally assumed that in Morrell of the July eclogue of the *Shepheardes Calender* Spenser intended to satirize Dr. John Aylmer, bishop of London. Thomalin, Morrell's antagonist in this eclogue, has usually been considered a Puritan, but the Puritan so honored has been a matter of dispute among those scholars bold enough to hazard an identification. In this chapter, accepting Aylmer as Morrell, I intend, first, to study in detail the grounds for Spenser's presumed dislike of Aylmer; second, to question the satire and to suggest that Spenser's attitude towards Aylmer was rather that of friendly admiration.

Born in 1521, John Aylmer was sent to Cambridge by his patron, Lord Henry Grey, afterwards Duke of Suffolk.[1] There he diligently plied his studies and was reckoned among the best scholars and wits of his time. Proceeding B.A. in 1541, he became chaplain of his patron, tutor of Lady Jane Grey, and good friend of Ascham. Aylmer was early influenced by the Reformers: in the first convocation of Mary's regime (1553) he opposed the Catholic doctrine of Transubstantiation and was consequently deprived of his archdeaconry of Stow. Fleeing to the continent, he spent the years of Mary's reign largely in Strasbourg and Zurich, serving as a tutor and helping Foxe compile his *Acts and Monuments*. In April, 1559, he brought out his *Harborowe for Faithfull and Trewe Subjects . . .*, which he issued as a corrective to Knox's *First Blast of the Trumpet*. In it he applied Knox's generalizations about women rulers to Mary alone, and dissociated himself from the Marian exiles who were opponents of the Royal Supremacy.

[1] The following brief account of Aylmer is taken mainly from the *DNB*.

In 1562, through the influence of Thomas Dannet (a cousin of Cecil's whom he tutored on the Continent), Aylmer was promoted to the lucrative archdeaconry of Lincoln.[2] Although a Reformer, Aylmer was apparently satisfied with the Elizabethan Settlement: in the Convocation of 1563 he subscribed the Thirty-nine Articles, but absented himself on the voting to abolish certain Catholic ceremonies and practices. In 1573 he received by accumulation the degrees of B.D. and D.D. at Oxford. At Lincoln Aylmer was so effective in his preaching and in the execution of his official duties as archdeacon that "not one recusant was left in the country at his coming away."[3] On March 24, 1577, Aylmer was consecrated bishop of London, a position he held until his death in 1594. His rule of his diocese was characterized by his exceptional severity to both Puritans and Catholics.

The reasons advanced for the traditional acceptance of Aylmer as Morrell are: (1) the name itself: by analogy to the acceptance of Algrind as Grindal, *Aylmer*, with the variant spellings of *Elmer* and *Elmore*, is similarly formed and almost self-evident; (2) the use of the nickname "Morelme" for Aylmer in the Marprelate controversy of 1588 and 1589; (3) Aylmer's unpopularity in the diocese of London because of his repression of Puritans; (4) his general character, Aylmer being considered as possessing many of the faults which religious writers of the time attacked.[4]

It is almost certain that Spenser was at least slightly acquainted with Aylmer, who, with Bishop Piers, assisted Grindal at the consecration of Bishop Young, Spenser's employer, in 1578. And as Young, while bishop of Rochester, resided at Bromley in Kent,

[2] It was valued in the King's Books at 179 pounds, nineteen shillings (whereas the archdeaconry of Stow, which Aylmer left, was valued at twenty-four pounds). Strype, *Aylmer*, p. 12.
[3] *Ibid.*, p. 14.
[4] These reasons are not gathered in any one book or article. See, however, *DNB*, and Higginson, pp. 99–111.

about ten miles from the heart of London, Spenser, Young's secretary, would certainly be aware of Aylmer's doings and reputation. In fact, it is needless to labor this point, since Aylmer and
Young were present at practically all the convocations and ecclesiastical gatherings in London from 1563 to 1580. On other occasions, too, Aylmer and Young frequently met. For instance,
Young was one of Grindal's four assistants at the consecration of
Aylmer. Again, on August 2, 1579, at Croydon, Aylmer and
Young assisted Grindal at the consecration of John Wolton to
the bishopric of Exeter.[5]

After a thorough study of Aylmer's career, I am inclined to
think that it was not the constant and sturdy opposition of
Aylmer to the Puritans in the diocese of London that led Spenser
to portray him as the "defender" of proud and ambitious pastors
in the July eclogue. Spenser as secretary to a bishop who accepted
fully the Elizabethan Settlement would have no love for the
Puritans, a group that since 1570 had been the chief enemy of
the bishops and was trying to destroy diocesan Episcopacy and to
erect the Presbyterian system instead.

In the July eclogue, Thomalin (like Piers in *May* and Diggon
Davie in *September*) is not arguing against the rule of bishops,
but merely attacking those general abuses that all zealous and
right-minded churchmen censured. Thomalin is holding up the
ideal, praising those bishops who are meek, mild, humble, pure,
courageous, industrious and careful of their flocks, and characterized by a simplicity in clothes and in life. What Thomalin objects
to is the ambition, wealth and power of bishops, not to bishops
themselves. Furthermore, with marked caution, Thomalin re-
stricts his attack on episcopal splendor and tyranny to Catholic

---

[5] Strype, *Grindal*, p. 359. The fact that this consecration was at Croydon
indicates that Grindal's confinement to his palace at Lambeth was beginning to be relaxed.

bishops, though this procedure should fool no one.

First, let us consider why Aylmer has been regarded as a typical representative of ambitious pride in the ranks of the Elizabethan bishops. During Spenser's first three years at Cambridge, Aylmer, according to his critics, exhibited that contentious and grasping spirit that later often showed itself. In 1571 and 1572 Aylmer, then archdeacon of Lincoln, disturbed that diocese (which borders on Cambridge University) with his lawsuits against Thomas Cooper, the newly appointed bishop. The contests were over the exercise of spiritual and ecclesiastical jurisdiction and especially over the revenue coming from this jurisdiction. Finally in 1572 the matter was settled through the arbitration of Archbishop Parker and Bishop Horne of Winchester.[6]

When Aylmer was consecrated bishop of London in succession to Sandys in March, 1577, trouble immediately began. According to Sandys, Aylmer made outrageous demands, requiring "as his due, the whole incomes and benefits of the last half year, that is, from Michaelmas to Lady-day, though Sandys continued bishop of London the best part of that time, namely, till Candlemas, before his remove to York. Both of them appealed to the Lord Treasurer."[7] Sandys, answering sharply, charged Aylmer with "coloured covetousness and an envious heart covered with a coat of dissimulation," and reviewed at length Aylmer's ingratitude, Sandys having been instrumental in his advancement to the see of London, recommending him highly to the Queen, entertaining him at his house, assisting at his consecration, and leaving several things in the houses of the bishopric, when he departed for York, for his successor's use and benefit.

Also about the same time, Aylmer sought a commission for dilapidations against Sandys. The latter wrote to Secretary Wal-

[6] Strype, *Aylmer*, p. 15.
[7] *Ibid.*, pp. 17–18.

singham, through whom Aylmer was proceeding, recalling the promise that Aylmer had made him at his consecration never to trouble him in this regard. Aylmer, refusing to arbitrate the matter, as Sandys suggested and Walsingham was willing to do, held "that for the security of his posterity it must be decided by law." This suit dragged on, and Aylmer, when a new review was taken of the dilapidations in 1580, increased the amount sought from the 1,200 pounds of 1578 to 1,602 pounds. In 1584 Aylmer received a favorable verdict.[8]

Again, in 1578 and early 1579 Aylmer made a great fall of timber, and in May, 1579, was charged by the Council with wasting the revenues of the bishopric. Lord Burghley, Aylmer's chief patron and friend at Court, severely reprimanded him, relating how a bishop was once replaced for such a deed. About six months later, Aylmer was forbidden by the Queen to cut down any more timber. In regard to this matter, Strype asserts that "though this information was partly true, yet it had more of malice than truth in it."[9] Nevertheless, Bishop Bancroft later sued Aylmer's son for dilapidations, charging that "Bishop Aylmer made 6,000 pounds of his woods, and left scarce enough to find the present Bishop yearly fuel; and that he let out leases, some for an hundred years and above, and some for fifty."[10]

Furthermore, Aylmer might be judged to reflect that lordly living and love of ease that Spenser reprobates in the ecclesiastical

---

[8] *Ibid.*, pp. 48–50. In 1571 Parliament passed an act against frauds for dilapidations. It was directed against churchmen allowing buildings, mansions, etc., for want of proper repair, to fall into ruin; or selling timber, lead, or stones for their own benefit; or making deeds of gift, long or unreasonable leases, or alienating goods or chattels in such a way as to defraud their successors. The act empowered the latter to commence suit and seek remedy in ecclesiastical courts for the amendment and reparation of such dilapidations and decays. See Strype, *Annals*, II. i, 103.

[9] *Ibid.*, pp. 46–48.

[10] *Ibid.*, p. 128.

eclogues. Strype notes that "our Bishop kept a good house, having eighty servants with him in his family."[11] And despite the signal honor, Aylmer in 1574, when chosen by Archbishop Parker to answer *De Disciplina Ecclesiastica*, the famous Puritan attack on episcopal government, refused to comply. "Grindal, also, then Archbishop of York, reputed Aylmer the fittest for this work, but concluded he would not take the pains."[12]

Spenser's dislike of a married clergy, and of those prelates who pile up wealth for their heirs, or alienate the revenues of their bishoprics for the sake of wife and children, is reflected in the speeches of Piers in the May eclogue and of Diggon Davie in the September eclogue. On all of these counts, it has been suggested, Spenser would look on Aylmer with disfavor. Unlike Achbishop Grindal and Bishop Piers, ideal shepherds who were unmarried, Aylmer, as we have seen above, "for the security of his posterity" —seven sons and three daughters—insisted that his suit for dilapidations against Sandys "must be decided by law." As Strype remarks, Samuel, Aylmer's "son and heir, was left in good circumstances, as may be guessed from a purchase or purchases of land which cost the Bishop 16,000 pounds."[13]

But there are still other reasons offered why Spenser should satirize Bishop Aylmer in the *Calender*. In 1579 Spenser was a client of the Earl of Leicester, and the connections of Aylmer with Lord Burghley would make him a likely target of satire. Aylmer was also extraordinarily active in assisting Burghley and the Queen in keeping the London clergy from discussing the Alençon marriage in their sermons and private conversations.[14] Spenser, then, closely connected with Leicester and Philip Sid-

---

[11] *Ibid.*, p. 127.
[12] *Ibid.*, p. 15. Strype infers that Aylmer's refusal was due to his discontent in not getting a bishopric before this time.
[13] *Ibid.*, p. 115.
[14] See, for instance, Knappen, pp. 257–58.

ney, who were opposing the French marriage, would be naturally inclined to look askance at Bishop Aylmer.

For all these reasons, then, ecclesiastical and political, general and personal, it has been suggested that Spenser was satirically representing Aylmer as Morrell of the July eclogue, a shepherd who ambitiously strives for high places. But apart from the fact that very little satire, if any, is found in the eclogue itself directed against Morrell, I wish to suggest that Spenser would probably not interpret the above-given incidents and evidence as they have been interpreted by Aylmer's enemies.

It is a mistake to assume that Aylmer was always in the wrong. In his quarrel with Cooper at Lincoln, the arbitrating bishops awarded Aylmer half of the fees and other emoluments (from proving of wills, commissions, administration of estates of intestate persons deceased, etc.) that his archdeaconry provided.[15] And in the quarrel with Archbishop Sandys, Aylmer's claims were adjudged just in the ecclesiastical courts. Furthermore, we should consider the character of Sandys, who notoriously despoiled the diocese of Worcester (to which Grindal's friend Whitgift was elevated in 1577) and had scant sympathy for the sequestered Grindal in 1577. Sandys also troubled Grindal over dilapidations at both London and York, and it might well be that as one of Grindal's friends Aylmer was encouraged to make Sandys pay for his covetousness. Although neither bishop showed to advantage in the matter, Aylmer, in his over-all character, was certainly superior to Sandys.

Whether Spenser knew about the Council's investigation of Aylmer's sale of episcopal timber in May, 1579, is doubtful. But even if he did know, Spenser would be fully and sympathetically aware of the financial problems of bishops and the ways they attempted to meet their expenses. In his letter to Burghley about

[15] Strype, *Aylmer*, p .15.

the felling of the woods, Aylmer defends himself well, outlining his expenses and mentioning that he has threescore persons in his houses to provide for.[16] Aylmer had his limitations, but he certainly would not be ranked among the "bad bishops." Sale of episcopal timber was one of the least reprehensible schemes that bishops employed to make ends meet.

Likewise the number of servants should not indicate "lordly living." As bishop of London (and all that it implied) and as father of a family of ten children, Aylmer probably needed more servants than other bishops. And the mere fact that Aylmer did not wish to answer the Puritan *De Disciplina* should not indicate that he was indolent, for even the Puritans could regretfully testify to his diligence, conscientiousness, and zeal.[17]

And although Spenser preferred a celibate clergy, it does not mean he condemned clergymen who were married. If a cleric were learned, zealous, and honest, his marriage was a minor matter. Many of the bishops that Spenser undoubtedly admired were married. Likewise, the fact that Aylmer had Burghley for his main patron would not prejudice Spenser against him, for Aylmer was also friendly with Leicester. In 1569, Grindal, through Leicester, in vain tried to recommend Aylmer for the bishopric of London; finally in 1577, again through Leicester, Grindal was more successful.[18]

It has been overlooked that there is a good deal of humor in the representation of Aylmer as Morrell in *July*, a humor which I think Spenser was conscious of. In his *Harborowe for Faithfull and Trewe Subjects* Aylmer attacked fiercely the arrogance, splendor, avarice, wealth, luxury, and civil authority of bishops. He declared that bishops should be content with a lowly station in

[16] *Ibid.*, p. 48.
[17] *Ibid.*, pp. 182–84.
[18] See, Long, "Spenser and the Bishop of Rochester," p. 731.

life, and that a large part of their wealth should be appropriated by the Queen for the better ordering of the kingdom: "Come off, ye bishops. Away with your superfluities: yield up your thousands. Be content with hundreds."[19] Aylmer's friends sometimes twitted him about these radical sentiments, and the Puritans never allowed him to forget them, for they were many times hurled at him and at the other Elizabethan bishops. Although Aylmer had Catholic bishops and their "domineering tyranny" in mind, his generalizations against bishops were nearly as damaging to him as were Knox's against women rulers.

Thomalin in *July*, like Aylmer in his *Harborowe*, attacks the pride, ambition, wealth, and splendor of bishops but has the foresight to add a protective reference to Catholic prelates, a qualification which Aylmer unhappily forgot. When Morrell in *July* asserts that one shall receive small thanks for censuring bishop's wealth (11. 209–210), he is perhaps speaking with the wisdom of experience, for Aylmer was never allowed to forget his published sentiments of 1559. There is also a certain humor in making Aylmer reverse his position of twenty years earlier in a comic and brief defense of the wealth of bishops:

>   When folks bene fat, and riches rancke,
>   it is a signe of health. (211–12)

Aylmer undoubtedly possessed virtues and abilities which Spenser would respect and admire. The poet would probably be aware of Aylmer's record, which included his courageous stand

---

[19] Quoted by White, p. 204. This material on the *Harborowe* has been gathered from Strype, *Aylmer*, pp. 16, 147–49; and Knappen, pp. 174, 250. This attack on bishops was one of the reasons often cited for Aylmer's not being named to a bishopric before 1577, for his undoubted abilities and prominence made such a promotion long overdue. Strype, *Aylmer*, p. 16.

Aylmer was one of the wittiest of the Elizabethan bishops. On one occasion when the above-noted sentiments were recalled to him, he gave a scriptural reply: "When I was a child, I spake as a child." Quoted by White, p. 204.

in the Convocation of 1553 (the first of Mary's reign), when Aylmer

> bravely offered to dispute the controverted points of religion in that synod against all the learned Papists in England; and learnedly argued . . . with one Moreman there against the doctrine of Transubstantiation.[20]

Spenser would also probably be aware of the scholarly assistance furnished by Aylmer to Dr. Foxe, the martyrologist, while both were Marian exiles.[21] Aylmer was undeniably one of the most talented divines of the Elizabethan period, and Strype testifies to his antiquarian interests, his skill in Hebrew, Greek, and Latin, his knowledge of history, civil law, and theology[22]—all of which abilities Spenser would probably know and admire. Aylmer was also an able preacher,[23] and was invariably recommended as the one most able to answer any printed attack by either Puritan or Catholic on the Anglican Establishment.[24]

Most important of all, Aylmer was always careful to provide fit persons for the ministry. According to White, "His correspondence shows him to have been influenced by a sincere desire that the highest posts in the church should be filled by men best fitted for them, and for that with him piety and learning were the first considerations."[25] And his ideal was one which all teachers and scholars, as well as churchmen, can subscribe to: "To preach the

[20] Strype, *Aylmer*, p. 6. Aylmer's courage (or boldness) was noteworthy. Once in a sermon before the Queen, with a glance towards the royal wardrobe of six hundred gowns, Aylmer "inveighed against excess in female apparel." The Queen told her ladies afterwards: "If the bishop held more discourse on such matters she would fit him for heaven; but he should go there without a staff and leave his mantle behind him." Cited by White, p. 212 (from Harrington, *Nugae Antiquae*, I, 170, 217).

[21] Strype, *Aylmer*, p. 8.

[22] *Ibid.*, pp. 158–74.

[23] *Ibid.*, p. 168.

[24] Besides the Puritan *De Disciplina* mentioned above, Aylmer was the first cleric asked to answer Campion's *Ten Reasons*. *DNB*.

[25] White, p. 213.

truth fully was his first and great aim, but to preach it so as to be understood was his second."[26]

Now Spenser would be just as cognizant of Aylmer's admirable qualities as he would of his defects, and to get a fair picture of Spenser's probable attitude towards Aylmer one must realize this. In *July* Thomalin argues above all for meekness, mildness, humility, and plain living; on all these points Aylmer's character, especially as interpreted by his personal enemies, would make him a worthy spokesman for ecclesiasts who preferred to play a more ambitious and princely role in life. And although satire cannot be ruled out, I do not think that Aylmer would be offended at Spenser's portrayal of him as Morrell. Aylmer was learned enough to appreciate the literary side of the July eclogue, the imitation of Mantuan's seventh and eighth eclogues, as well as the *débat* form where both the valley and the heights have their advantages as set forth in the arguments of their respective representatives. He would also clearly realize how, in the eyes of the Puritans, Morrell's cap fitted. It is more probable, however, that Aylmer would smile at the genial pastoral banter of *July*. The eclogue was not the product of an enemy Puritan or Catholic, but from the pen of the talented secretary of a friendly fellow bishop. In fact, E. K. takes great pains to tell us in the Argument before *July* that it is merely for the sake of a good debate or contrast that Morrell is "imagined to bee" proud and ambitious. And Thomalin, we must remember, apart from the banter never makes any personal charges against Morrell. After relating Palinode's experiences with ecclesiastical abuses on his late trip to Rome, Thomalin concludes (though no doubt ironically) that

> Sike syrlye shepheards han we none,
>   they keepen all the path.[27]   (203–204)

---

[26] *Ibid.*, p. 212.
[27] E. K. glosses syrlye as "stately and proud."

Morrell, then, before relapsing into his opposition role, readily agrees that

> Here is a great deale of good matter,
>   lost for lacke of telling. (205–206)

And when in his concluding speech Thomalin relates through the fable of the Eagle and the Shell-fish how the sequestered Grindal still "lyes in lingring payne," Morrell expresses his sympathy. This sympathy accords with Aylmer's position, for Grindal, in his famous letter to the Queen, wrote that Aylmer was one of nine bishops who supported him and believed in the value of the suppressed prophesyings.

From the time of his elevation to the see of London, Aylmer worked manfully with the other bishops of the realm in behalf of Elizabeth's ecclesiastical settlement. Except for his concern for a full measure of justice for himself in his suits for dilapidations and revenues, and his desire to leave his ten children financially secure,[28] there is no evidence that—nor are there reasons why—the rest of the Anglican hierarchy looked, or should look, down upon him. The later bitter attacks of the Puritans on Aylmer have little bearing on the matter. Martin Marprelate in 1588 attacked Bishops Young, Cooper, and Whitgift, as well as Aylmer, and Bishop Cooper's famous reply, *An Admonition to the People of England* . . . ,was a defense of all bishops attacked by the saucy Martin,[29] as well as a wiping out of all those "foul and lying representations" with which Puritan spite and malice had besmirched Aylmer.[30]

---

[28] We must remember that Spenser in 1579 would not have the full information of modern scholars who tend to judge Aylmer in terms of his full record. When the *Calender* appeared, Aylmer had been a bishop less than three years, and his arbitrary and unconciliatory disposition had not been fully revealed. (Here, of course, I am not trying to defend Aylmer, but merely to indicate how Spenser probably regarded him.)

[29] Strype, *Annals,* III. ii, 155.

[30] Strype, *Aylmer,* p. 136.

All of the evidence given thus far would suggest that Bishop Aylmer and Bishop Young (and probably Spenser, too) were friends who would be in agreement on most ecclesiastical issues. Young assisted at Aylmer's consecration, and Aylmer at Young's, and both had a marked antipathy for Puritans. We have already quoted Aylmer's praise of Young as one "fit to bridle innovators, not by authority only but by weight of argument." This estimate of Young was written to Burghley in November, 1581, on the death of Gilbert Berkeley, bishop of Bath and Wells, when Aylmer wished to emphasize the importance of having fit bishops,

> advising therefore that Cooper, the bishop of Lincoln, a learned and active man, might be translated to Bath and Wells; Freke of Norwich, less fit for that place, to go to Lincoln, and Young, a good governor, . . . to be removed to Norwich.[31]

In his zeal for conformity, Aylmer worked hard to restrain or to reclaim both Catholics and Puritans, and the latter, exhibiting what Strype calls a "calumniating spirit," cast many slanders at his door. He was charged with detaining stolen goods, cheating his grocer, keeping an innocent man in prison, ordaining his porter, playing at bowls on Sunday, and being a great swearer—sometimes saying "By my faith."[32] But as Strype indicates, all these charges are so false, ludicrous, or distorted that they tell us more about the Puritans than about Aylmer.

Yet notwithstanding Aylmer's orthodoxy, and his diligence on behalf of the Established Church, his harshness of disposition and hot temper[33] were, for instance, a decided contrast to the habitual humility, mildness, and sweet reasonableness of Archbishop Grindal. In some ways, then, Aylmer would be a well-chosen

[31] *Ibid.*, p. 58. At this time Bath and Wells was troubled by Catholics, and Norwich by Puritans.
[32] *Ibid.*, pp. 134–42.
[33] *Ibid.*, p. 185.

model for a pastoral character like Morrell who is "imagined to bee" proud and ambitious, and I have no doubt that Spenser had him in mind. But satire directed specifically against Morrell is hard to find in the July eclogue. Furthermore, the total background of Spenser, Young, and Aylmer, as well as the tone of the eclogue, suggest that Spenser probably admired Bishop Aylmer as much as he did Bishop Young and Archbishop Grindal.

XIII

Bishop Cooper as Thomalin

As WE have already seen, Thomalin, Morrell's friendly antagonist in the July eclogue, indulges in a bantering attack on clerical ambition as symbolized by the hilly places, and then slips into a high praise of the shepherds of an earlier era who were satisfied with a lowly station in life and were characterized by their humility, meekness, devotion to duty, and purity and simplicity of life. But in the new order of things, the higher clergy are now noted for their luxury, splendor, and tyranny. Thomalin then softens his accusations somewhat by directing his criticism to Catholic bishops that the mysterious Palinode has studied on a late trip to Rome ("if such be Rome"), and ironically adds that the Established Church has no such examples of clerical ambition, pride, and addiction to wealth and lavish living. Furthermore, he has learned from the misfortune visited upon the shepherd of high rank, the "long ypent" Algrind, "to love the lowe degree."

In this chapter I wish to suggest that Spenser was representing Dr. Thomas Cooper, bishop of Lincoln, in Thomalin of the July

eclogue of the Shepheardes Calender. Spenser's acknowledged use
of real characters in the other eclogues, E. K.'s gloss to September
by which we are informed that by the names of shepherds Spenser "covereth the names of divers other his familiar freends and
best acquayntaunce," and the general acceptance of Morrell and
Algrind as Aylmer and Grindal in the July eclogue, should lead
us to suspect that Spenser had some living churchman in mind
as the spokesman for "the honour and commendation of good
shepheardes."

Up to the present time two identifications for Thomalin have
been offered. Higginson would identify this character with
Thomas Wilcox,[1] an extreme Puritan who was the co-author of
the famous Admonition to the Parliament, a pamphlet which appeared in the summer of 1572 attacking the Established Church
and advocating the abolition of episcopacy. Wilcox caused trouble
in the London area for the next ten years, frequently being
confined to prison for his religious nonconformity.

The Rev. A. F. Scott Pearson, while agreeing with Higginson
that Thomalin is a Puritan, suggests Thomas Cartwright as a
more likely identification.[2] Cartwright caused trouble at Cambridge in 1570 with his sermons against the Anglican discipline,
holding essentially the same views as Wilcox. But whereas the
latter came into conflict with Aylmer in 1577, Cartwright went
to the Continent after his deprivation at Cambridge (December
11, 1570). He was back in England again in April, 1572, a central
figure in the Admonition controversy, but in 1574 he returned
to the Continent, remaining abroad this time until 1586.

From what has been already written, it should be clear that

[1] Higginson, p. 199. With Higginson I agree that the Thomalin of
March is not the same character as the Thomalin of July. The March
Thomalin, like Spenser (i.e., Colin Clout) in September, is a "shepheard's
boy," not a shepherd.
[2] Thomas Cartwright and Elizabethan Puritanism, p. 188.

Spenser, a bishop's secretary and a strong critic of Puritanism, would have little regard for either Wilcox or Cartwright. Furthermore, there is strong internal evidence in *July* that Spenser would not have been honoring either Puritan in this eclogue. It is mainly given over to the celebration of Archbishop Grindal, an authority on the ideal shepherd and, since he was a cleric of courage and conscience, the praiseworthy but unfortunate victim of the Queen's anger because of his refusal to put down the prophesyings. As we have already seen, Grindal was by no means a Puritan. Elizabeth and her Council would not have elevated him to the archbishoprics of York and Canterbury if he had not devoted himself to the Establishment in a satisfactory manner. Such Puritans as Cartwright and Wilcox were anathema to Grindal—as they were to all bishops—and Grindal, then lately elected to the archbishopric of York, was instrumental in the deprivation of Cartwright at Cambridge and his consequent state of exile on the Continent.

Even the Rev. A. F. Scott Pearson, who would have Thomalin represent Cartwright, indicates how little Grindal and Cartwright agreed. He writes:

> In a pointed letter to Cecil, written from St. Paul's, London, on the 25th of June, 1570, he [Grindal] hurls the shafts of his ire at Cartwright as the chief ringleader of the University malcontents. He assures Cecil that the youth of Cambridge are thronging to Cartwright's daily lectures in which the external government of the Church is being attacked. The Vice-chancellor and the heads are not dealing as roundly as they should with the case. Grindal suggests that Cecil should instruct Dr. May and the heads to command Cartwright and his adherents to silence both in schools and pulpits, and that after examination the offenders should be reduced to conformity or duly punished by expulsion out of their colleges or out of the University as the cause should require. Meanwhile, the Vice-chancellor should not allow Cartwright

to proceed D.D. at the ensuing commencement, for he is not only guilty of the present singularity but is also not conformable in his apparel, and contemns many other laudable orders of the University.[3]

But the Archbishop of York did not let matters rest at this point.

A few days before his journey to the north, Grindal, in a letter to Cecil from Westminster, 27 July, 1570, urges the expulsion of the nonconformists from Cambridge if they do not renounce their factious assertions. He thinks, however, that even if Cartwright revokes his doctrines, he should never be permitted to lecture again in the University. He has conceived a definitely adverse opinion of the Puritan Professor, accusing him of having a busy head, stuffed full of singularities.[4]

It should be unnecessary to give here a further list of Grindal's many repressions of the Puritans both before and after 1570. With the appearance of the *Admonition* in 1572 and Cartwright's *Reply* to Whitgift's *Answer Against the Admonition* in April, 1573, there could be no doubt of the revolutionary nature of Puritanism, both pamphlets attacking not only the Prayer Book, ceremonies, and apparel of the Established Church, but especially making a frontal assault on espiscopacy itself. The bishops were now regarded as the "chief and implacable foes of Puritanism,"[5] and it would be unthinkable that extreme Puritans like Cartwright or Wilcox would be holding up Grindal as an authority on the ideal shepherd or sympathizing with his sequestration, as Thomalin does in the July eclogue. If a counterpart, then, is to be discovered for Thomalin, it would be more logical to look for him among the ranks of the bishops, especially since Algrind and Morrell of this eclogue are generally admitted to represent bishops.

[3] *Ibid.*, pp. 29–30.
[4] *Ibid.*, p. 34. (See also *Grindal's Remains*, pp. 304–305, 323–24.)
[5] *Ibid.*, p. 61.

And since Spenser is fairly literal or easily decipherable in the characters of Algrind, Roffyn, Piers, and Morrell, we might normally expect a certain amount of literalness in the character of Thomalin. Dr. Thomas Cooper, bishop of Lincoln, who often signed his name *Thom Lincoln* in his communications to Court and to other bishops, would immediately spring to mind.[6] If the Bishop of Rochester, Spenser's employer in 1578, signed his name officially as John Roffensis, and Spenser used Roffyn as a character in *September's* fable, by analogy why not see in Thomalin, Thom Lincoln or its further abbreviation, Thom Lin. Furthermore, the middle syllable of Thomalin often = of.[7] Since the official style was also sometimes Thomas of Lincoln, we could thereby get the full name, Thom-a-lin. And if Spenser in Grindal, Young, Piers, and Aylmer is using bishops whose sees border the city of London on the south, west, and east, it would at least be geographically fitting to use another bishop whose see directly touches the city of London on the north, taking in all of Hertfordshire. Then, if Bishop Cooper was well known to the Spenser-Young group in 1578 and 1579, and if he was a type of bishop who would win their admiration, and if his character fits the

[6] For example, see Strype, *Annals*, III. i, 254, for Cooper's use of this signature in a letter to Burghley. Lincoln was also sometimes abbreviated to Lin. in ecclesiastical documents.

[7] See *NED*, which offers such sixteenth-century examples of a = of as: men a war; cloth a gold; time a day; inns a court; John a Gaunt.

Elizabethan literature further confirms a = of. For instance, W. J. Thoms' edition of *Early English Prose Romances*, 3 vols. (London, 1858), II, furnishes two examples from romances of the 1590's: (1) "The History of George a Green" (p. 163), ". . . whence the name of George was given him, and surnam'd of Green, of the town which is called Wakefield, on a green"; (2) "The History of Tom a Lincoln, the Red Rose Knight" (p. 240), in which the child was "christned and called by the name of Tom a Lincoln (after the towne where it was found), a name most fitting for it, in that they knew not who were his true parents." Professor D. T. Starnes graciously furnished me the last two examples.

speeches of Thomalin in *July*, it is quite possible that Spenser had him in mind. All of these possibilities will be examined, but first I will give a brief account of Cooper.

Born in Oxford in 1517, the son of a poor tailor, Thomas Cooper was educated at Magdalen College, of which he later became a fellow and master.[8] Having early adopted Protestant views, Cooper was checked in his intention to take orders by the accession of Queen Mary. He therefore took a degree in medicine and practiced in Oxford. On the death of Mary, he returned to his original purpose and was ordained, quickly becoming known as a zealous preacher. After proceeding D.D. at Oxford in 1567, he remained dean of Christ Church, becoming at Leicester's insistence vice-chancellor of the University (1567–70), then dean of Gloucester in 1569, and bishop of Lincoln in 1570. In 1584 he was transferred to the bishopric of Winchester, which he held until his death in 1594. Cooper was popularly regarded as the most learned of the Elizabethan bishops, and was most active in the defense of the Establishment against both Catholic and Puritan. So much for the bare facts of his life.

Since Bishop Young and Bishop Cooper were neighboring prelates and had attended convocations together as early as 1567, it is practically certain that they knew one another. However, aside from this eclogue we have no evidence of Spenser's friendship with Cooper, who was elevated to the bishopric of Lincoln in 1570, but it is quite possible that the poet of the *Calender* had met him in his college days. Cambridge University was close to the boundary line separating the bishoprics of Lincoln and Ely, and Spenser in his last five years at Cambridge would certainly have heard of Cooper, ordinary visitor to King's College, who in 1577 was granted extraordinary authority by Burghley to put down

[8] The following biographical details are taken from the *DNB*, which gives a scanty account of Cooper.

disorders there and to settle the complaints of the fellows against Dr. Goad, the provost.[9] Cooper was also well known to the Earl of Leicester and to Philip Sidney, with whom Spenser was connected in 1579. He was Philip Sidney's second tutor at Oxford, and Sidney lived with him during his entire stay there.[10] In 1565 Cooper dedicated to Leicester his famous *Thesaurus*, and in 1567, Leicester, chancellor of Oxford, appointed Cooper his vice-chancellor. On May 5, 1569, Cooper wrote to Leicester, suggesting that Dr. John Piers, later bishop of Rochester and Salisbury, should take part in the disputations in divinity if he accompanied Leicester to Oxford.[11] In 1584 Leicester appointed Cooper Prelate of the Order of the Garter.[12]

Cooper was equally well regarded by Queen Elizabeth, to whom he had written congratulatory verses in Latin at her accession.[13] In 1573 he helped Archbishop Parker entertain the Queen at Croydon.[14] The *Thesaurus Linguae Romanae et Britannicae*, usually known as *Cooper's Dictionary*, "delighted Queen Elizabeth so much that she expressed her determination to promote the author as far as lay in her power."[15]

Cooper was very helpful to the other bishops in meeting the printed attacks of the Puritans. In a sermon on June 27, 1572, he answered Wilcox and Fields' *An Admonition to the Parliament*,

[9] Strype, *Annals*, II. ii, 36–38.
[10] Mona Wilson, *Sir Philip Sidney* (New York, 1932), p. 38.
[11] *HMC, Pepys*, XVII (1911), 155. Both Piers and Cooper attended Magdalen College, and proceeded D. D. a year apart, Piers in 1566, and Cooper in 1567. Piers and Cooper took important parts in the disputations held for Queen Elizabeth when she visited Oxford in 1566. Each gave an address in Latin to the distinguished visitors. John Nichols, *The Progresses and Public Processions of Queen Elizabeth*, I, 5, 9, 99 (under the year 1566).
[12] *C.S.P.*, Domestic (1547–80), p. 173.
[13] *HMC, Salisbury*, 13, Addenda I (1915), 39.
[14] Strype, *Annals*, II. ii, 50.
[15] *DNB*.

vindicating the Church of England and its liturgy.[16] A little later the same year he was consulted by Whitgift, and looked over the latter's *Reply* to the *Admonition* before it was published.[17] The year before he sat on a commission with Archbishop Parker and five bishops, examining Christopher Goodman, a noted Puritan.[18] However, as mentioned already, in 1589 he did his greatest service for the bishops in his book answering Martin Marprelate, *An Admonition to the People of England*.[19]

Cooper was also active against Catholics, being a member of a commission which visited Oxford in 1566 and expelled three Papists. In 1562 he answered a Catholic pamphlet entitled *An Apology of Private Mass* with his *Answer in Defence of the Truth Against the Apology of Private Mass*.[20] In 1580 he published a collection of twelve of his sermons entitled *Certain Sermons Wherein Is Contained the Defence of the Gospel Against Cavils and False Accusations by . . . the Friends and Favourers of the Church of Rome*.[21] Bishop Milner, the Roman Catholic historian of Winchester, charges Cooper with a cruel persecution of Catholics, but as the *Dictionary of National Biography* explains, the increase of persecution was due rather to the new acts of 1581 and 1585, and the beginning of the hostilities with Spain. But

[16] Strype, *Annals*, II. i, 286.
[17] Strype, *Parker*, II, 140.
[18] Strype, *Annals*, II. i, 141.
[19] For a brief analysis of this *Admonition*, see Knappen, p. 497: Cooper pointed out that Puritanism was equivalent to Anabaptism and indicated the various stages Puritanism had gone through. "Beginning as a private scruple about apparel, it soon became a conviction that the Anglican costume was not a thing indifferent but a matter for public protest and political opposition. Then church government was added to the grievances; a spirit of separatism developed, which was willing to divide the church; and finally a fierce war was being waged on education, class distinctions, and property rights, under the guise of an attack on the episcopal system."
[20] *DNB*.
[21] *Ibid.*

Cooper did have a "short way" with Catholics. As we have already seen, with archdeacon Aylmer as his able assistant, Cooper had been spectacularly successful in Protestantizing the shire of Lincoln between 1570 and 1577, before Aylmer's elevation to the bishopric of London.

In character and ability Cooper was outstanding in the ranks of the Elizabethan bishops. In 1584, on the death of Bishop Watson, he was translated to Winchester, where, according to Anthony à Wood,

> as in most parts of the nation, he became much noted for his learning and sanctity of life. . . . The course of his life in Oxon was very commendable, and, in some sort saint-like; if it be saint-like to live unreprovable, to bear a cross patiently, and to forgive great injuries freely, this man's example was without pattern.[22]

In historical, linguistic, and antiquarian scholarship Cooper was eminent. In 1549 he published a *Chronicle of the World*, a continuation of the *Chronicle* of Thomas Languet, who had brought it down from the creation to 17 A.D. Cooper carried it down to the reign of Edward VI, his portion being about three times as long as Languet's. Under the title of *Cooper's Chronicle*, a second edition appeared in 1560, and a third in 1565. At this same time Cooper was engaged in another work which was published in 1548, *Bibliotheca Eliotae. Sive Dictionarium Lat. et Angl. auctum et emend. per. Tho. Cooper.* A second edition appeared in 1552, a third in 1559, both entitled *Eliot's Dictionary* . . . "enriched and more perfectly corrected by Thos. Cooper, schoolmaster of Maudlen's in Oxford." His greatest literary work, *Thesaurus Linguae Romanae et Britannicae*, which he handsomely dedicated to Leicester, and which greatly delighted the Queen, appeared in 1565. To this work was added a dictionary of

---

[22] *Athenae Oxonienses*, ed. Bliss (London, 1813), II, 609.

history and poetry, and the whole was commonly known as *Cooper's Dictionary*. It was reprinted in 1573, 1578, and 1584.[23]

The *Thesaurus* was the "recognized authority in the schools and among scholars generally in the last quarter of the sixteenth century."[24] In the *Calender* both Spenser and E. K. show a considerable dependence on this standard reference work—and Spenser in the rest of his poetry as well.[25] The *Thesaurus* won for Cooper the reputation of being one of the most learned men of his age. With Spenser's well-known admiration for learning and wisdom—Sapientia—as the highest of the human and divine attributes,[26] Spenser could not have helped but admire Cooper.

In the Latin dedication to Leicester before the *Thesaurus*, Cooper undoubtedly reached a large number of readers with his plea for greater respect and material rewards for clergymen and scholars. Though he mainly deals with the general utility of learning, he also points out that the clerical and scholarly vocations bring to those who follow them only disgrace and ruin: hence "parents have prescribed other ways of life for their sons."[27]

As a teacher, a theological writer, and a preacher, Cooper had remarkable talents. Philip Sidney and William Camden were among his notable pupils at Oxford. Archbishop Parker thought so highly of Cooper's *Brief Exposition* of the Sunday Lessons, published in 1573, that he wrote the Lord Treasurer requesting him to recommend to the Council that orders be given to have a

[23] *DNB*.

[24] DeWitt T. Starnes and Ernest W. Talbert, *Classical Myth and Legend in Renaissance Dictionaries* (Chapel Hill, N. C., 1955), p. 4.

[25] *Ibid.*, pp. 44–61. DeWitt T. Starnes, *Renaissance Dictionaries* (Austin, Texas, 1954), pp. 85–110, analyzes the *Thesaurus*.

[26] See, for instance, Joseph B. Collins, *Christian Mysticism in the Elizabethan Age* (Baltimore, 1940), p. 223.

[27] Rosenberg, p. 124. (On pp. 124–28, Miss Rosenberg comments on this dedication.)

copy placed in every parish church.[28] And of all the bishops of
the realm, Cooper was chosen to give the funeral sermon for
Parker in 1575.[29] He also, as Strype relates, preached a powerful
sermon at St. Paul's Cross in Lent of 1577

> upon Luke XVI: *Reddite rationem dispensationis tuae*, i.e,
> Give an account of thy stewardship. A proper test for magis-
> trates, and all that were in public place and authority: and
> before such the bishop now preached. His sermon he man-
> aged with so great life, and application to his auditory, that
> Fleetwood, the recorder of London, who was among those
> that were present, was so affected with the discourse, that he
> resolved to forsake a speech that he had prepared to use be-
> fore the Queen the next week, when the lord mayor was, in
> some occasion, to be present, and to follow the matter that
> the bishop had taken in hand.[30]

The way, then, that Bishop Cooper towered as a scholar and
as a zealous and brilliant churchman above the great bulk of the
Elizabethan clergy would certainly call him to Spenser's attention
and regard. He was so outstanding that I imagine even his married state was overlooked by Spenser—especially since he gave
himself primarily to the responsibilities of his high spiritual calling and to scholarship. Furthermore, he was so unlucky in his
marriage, his wife possessing the worst traits of Xantippe and
Messalina, that he was a shining argument for the wisdom of
clerical celibacy.[31]

[28] *DNB.*

[29] Strype, *Parker*, II, 433.

[30] Strype, *Annals*, II. ii, 36.

[31] The married life of Bishop Cooper was notoriously unhappy. His
"wife was utterly profligate. He condoned her unfaithfulness again and
again, refusing to be divorced when the heads of the University offered to
arrange it for him, and declaring that he would not charge his conscience
with so great a scandal. On one occasion his wife, in a paroxysm of fury,
tore up half his *Thesaurus*, and threw it into the fire. He patiently set to
work and rewrote it." *DNB.*

The profligacy of Cooper's wife was reflected in contemporary doggerel

But there are perhaps other reasons, besides Cooper's general reputation, why Spenser should have him in mind in Thomalin. The main burden of *July*, Thomalin's quoting Grindal on the character of the ideal shepherd and Thomalin's sympathy for the sequestered Archbishop, should give us a cue. What was Cooper's stand on the prophesyings, and did he support Grindal in the latter's contention with the Queen over the exercises? In his letter to the Queen, Grindal declared that Cooper was one of the nine bishops who supported him. Cooper also seems to have been Grindal's predecessor and mentor in the prophesyings, for in 1574 he made arrangements to hold them in his diocese of Lincoln, appointed moderators, and laid down regulations for their taking place. The rules that he drew up were practically the same ones that Grindal would retain in obviating abuses to these discussion groups of the clergy.[32] And after Grindal's refusal to transmit the Queen's orders for the suppression of the exercises, the Queen expressed her will in a peremptory letter to every bishop. Cooper, who had also been commanded by word of mouth of the Queen herself to stop the prophesyings in his diocese, allowed them to continue in Hertfordshire. The Queen, now thoroughly angry, wrote Cooper a stern letter, commanding that they be put down, and "to avoid the contrary at your peril."[33]

Cooper and Grindal also stood together in brave opposition to the Crown and rapacious courtiers in the despoliation of church properties. As early as 1573 Grindal had protested to Burghley

---

verses and in the Marprelate tracts. (See Starnes, *Ren. Dict.*, p. 85.) Two of her better known paramours were Dr. Day, canon of Christ Church, and Cooper's brother. As Rowse puts it (p. 411), while Cooper "slept with his Dictionary," his brother "took his place at his wife's side."

[32] For Cooper's position, see Strype, *Annals*, II. i, 472–73. Grindal expressed similar views in his letter to the Queen that led to his confinement. Strype, *Grindal*, p. 327.

[33] Strype, *Annals*, II. ii, 114, 612.

about the oppression of the clergy by the Queen's gentlemen pensioners in the latter's fraudulent commissions for conceal-ment.[34] Cooper complained to Burghley in 1582 about these same commissions for concealment, which, he wrote, "created great perplexities and wrongs to the clergy."[35]

All in all, then, there are the many above-stated reasons why Spenser should know and admire Bishop Cooper, and why he should celebrate him in the *Shepheardes Calender*. In conclusion, I think that all the evidence marshalled in this chapter makes it strongly probable that Spenser intended to represent Dr. Thomas Cooper, bishop of Lincoln between 1570 and 1584, as Thomalin of the July eclogue.

[34] Strype, *Grindal*, p. 264.
[35] Strype, *Annals*, III. i, 162.

XIV

Bishop Richard Davies
as Diggon Davie

DIGGON DAVIE of the September eclogue gives the most detailed and pointed analysis of ecclesiastical evils in the *Shepheardes Calender;* consequently his identification has been of considerable interest to scholars. Although the dramatic action of *September* has been already reviewed in Chapter VIII, I will here briefly recall that Hobbinol is the friendly interlocutor who elicits Diggon's experiences with the clergy in a "farre countrye." The far country (or "forraine countryes") of Diggon's wanderings is a part of the convention taken from Spenser's sources—Virgil's first eclogue as developed in Mantuan's ninth—as is also the shepherd's reason for traveling, the desire to better himself. These far countries, then, need not be taken too literally, even though, as I will show later, they might also fit remote sections of Wales. So, too, we should not be puzzled by the conventional desire of the wandering shepherd to be enriched, even though this desire seems to conflict with Diggon's later condemnation of clerical avarice.

Before telling the fable of the Wolf in Sheep's Clothing, Diggon, in a series of answers to Hobbinol's promptings, emphasizes

216

the disgraceful traffic in church livings, and the pride, idleness, avarice, disobedience, and contentiousness of the clergy, presumably in the far country of his travels. His plainest speaking, however (after an initial blunt remark that the best of the clergy are a bad lot), is an elaboration of what people say about the bad behavior of the clergy in general. Of the various classes of critics, some assert that because of the ignorance and corruption of the clergy the world is much worse than in the past; others, that the clergy have only contempt for their calling and scorn for their charges; still others, that the clergy are so interested in adorning their wives and enriching their heirs that they neglect hospitality; the last group of critics, who shoot closest to the mark, declare that powerful courtiers plunder church properties and that the clergy are powerless to resist. Furthermore, the people under these pastors are equally corrupt and ignorant, and many have succumbed to false religious prophets.

As with Piers, there has been a certain reluctance among scholars to consider the plain and obvious in seeking the identity of Diggon Davie. Not until 1942 did Viola Blackburn Hulbert suggest that Spenser was representing Richard Davies, bishop of the Welsh diocese of St. David's, as Diggon Davie.[1] About a year before Mrs. Hulbert's suggestion had appeared in print, I had written a study also advocating Bishop Richard Davies as Diggon Davie.[2] In this chapter, then, the various candidates for Diggon Davie will be reviewed, and the arguments bolstering the identification of Bishop Davies with Diggon Davie will be presented.

First, it should be emphasized that Diggon Davie is not a literary creation. In a gloss to *September* E. K. informs us that

---

[1] "Diggon Davie," *JEGP*, XLI (1942), 349–67.
[2] Paper read in Professor Padelford's Spenser seminar in the Spring of 1941. Professor Osgood noted its conclusions in *Var.*, p. 354. Later, as a supplement to Mrs. Hulbert's article, it appeared as "Diggon Davie Again," *JEGP*, XLVI (1947), 144–49.

Diggon, Hobbinol's friend and the main exponent of the ecclesiastical satire of this eclogue, is the "very freend to the Author
hereof." If such is the case, it should be possible to discover the
identity of Diggon in the Young circle, that group of friends
which Dr. John Young, bishop of Rochester, possessed when
Spenser entered his employment in 1578.

In all, five identifications have been suggested for Diggon
Davie. A. B. Grosart proposed Jan van der Noot, the wealthy
citizen of Antwerp, who, because of his Calvinistic sympathies,
sought refuge in England in 1567, and shortly afterwards employed Spenser to make twenty-two verse translations in the English version of the *Theatre of Voluptuous Worldlings* (1569).
Grosart thought some of the dialectal expressions used by Diggon
might suggest van der Noot's presumed "broken or imperfect"
English.[3] F. G. Fleay suggested Thomas Churchyard, soldier of
fortune, and author, among other poems, of *Davy Dickar's
Dream*.[4] Higginson, the next scholar to advance an identification
for Diggon Davie, rejected the first two nominees because he felt
that a shepherd with a flock in an ecclesiastical eclogue must be
a clergyman,[5] an observation that I would agree with.[6]

Higginson, after dismissing every lead that E. K. gives as either
irrelevant or intentionally misleading, then suggests that Diggon
Davie "may have been intended for Richard Greenham, a promi-

[3] Edmund Spenser, *Works*, "Life of Spenser by Rev. Alex. B. Grosart"
(London, 1882–84), I, 25–28.
   [4] *Guide to Chaucer and Spenser* (London, 1877), p. 87.
   [5] Higginson, p. 188.
   [6] In all the eclogues, the characters are, of course, generally shepherds,
but Spenser distinguishes sufficiently to point his allegory. For instance in
September, Diggon Davie, like Roffyn, is a shepherd with a flock (and
hence presumably a bishop); Colin Clout is a shepherd's boy (in this case,
a bishop's secretary); and Hobbinol, specifically identified as Gabriel
Harvey in a gloss, is not a clergyman and apparently has no flock, not even
an academic one.

nent nonconformist divine, whom Spenser almost surely knew."[7]
In his summary account, Higginson tells us that Greenham was
a fellow at Pembroke for a year and a half after Spenser's matric-
ulation, sided with Cartwright in the religious controversy at
Cambridge in 1570, and in the same year was instituted to the
rectory of Dry Drayton (three miles from Cambridge), where he
remained for twenty years. In 1573 he was examined by Dr. Richard Cox, bishop of Ely, for refusing to subscribe to, or use, vestments and the communion book. In 1576 or 1577 Greenham was
deprived of his living for a time, but finally was returned to his
flock. Robert Browne, the founder of the Separatists, was a member of Greenham's household in 1578, because he thought Greenham was "most forwarde" in religious reform.[8] All of this, of
course, makes Greenham an extreme Puritan. Higginson then
offers the similarity of names: "Diggon or Dickon, which are
only slight variations of the same name, is colloquial or rustic for
Richard. . . . The Davie in Diggon's name is as close in sound to
Drayton, where Greenham lived, as many of Spenser's coined
names are to their originals."[9]

As we have already seen, Higginson, somehow missing the published fact that Spenser was a bishop's secretary, misinterpreted
the poet's religious position and the religious allegory of the *Calender*. Because W. L. Renwick could not accept an extreme
Puritan like Greenham as Diggon Davie, he suggested that William Harrison, vicar of Radwinter (about five miles from Saffron
Walden) and a friend of Gabriel Harvey, might be Diggon. It
it certainly true that Harrison's religious views were fairly close
to Spenser's, and that Harrison would be the type of clergyman

[7] P. 192.
[8] *Ibid.*, pp. 192–97. Knappen, p. 383, asserts that while Greenham was
troubled by Bishop Cox, he was never actually suspended; he then gives
(pp. 382–86) a most sympathetic account of Greenham.
[9] Higginson, p. 196.

that Spenser would admire, but Renwick did not press the identification.[10]

Finally in 1949, Ruth Mohl, rejecting the strong arguments in favor of Bishop Richard Davies, proposed Philip Sidney as a likely Diggon Davie. In an ingenious manner Miss Mohl argued that Philip Sidney, a good friend of both Spenser and Harvey, would make an acceptable Diggon.[11] All of her arguments and assertions will be, I think, satisfactorily answered in this chapter. Miss Mohl has incidentally touched on certain weaknesses wherein earlier commentators (myself included) have failed at times to isolate the conventional or imitative elements in *September*, and have tried to work these elements into the allegory in too literal a fashion. As Renwick and others before him have indicated, the first seventy-nine lines of *September* are a fairly close imitation of Mantuan. The wandering shepherd's motive for traveling—his desire to better himself—his unfortunate experiences with shepherds in distant regions, his (in the language of *September*) having "measured much grownd" and "wandred . . . about the world rounde," are all a part of the convention and straight from Spenser's sources. Furthermore, we must not confuse E. K. with Spenser, nor should we be led astray by E. K.'s remarks that do not fit *September*. For instance, E. K.'s statement about "Popish prelates" (in the Argument) is a figure of speech that accommodates the anti-Catholic propaganda of 1579 provoked by the Alençon marriage negotiations and the growing Catholic missionary activity. Significantly, Diggon mentions that one of the accusations against the clergy is that they are too interested in adorning their wives and enriching their heirs: hence the Catholic clergy cannot be the ones under attack.

[10] In his edition of the *Shepheardes Calender* (1930), p. 210.
[11] *Studies in Spenser, Milton, and the Theory of Monarchy* (New York, 1949), pp. 15–30.

Here let us cite a few basic facts about Bishop Richard Davies.[12] He was born, of an old Welsh family, at Plas Y Person (in North Wales) either about 1501, if it is true that he was eighty when he died, or about 1509, if he was (as episcopal records testify) fifty when he was consecrated bishop. He was educated at New Inn Hall, Oxford, a house popular with Welsh students. Proceeding B.D., he became rector of Maidsmorton; in 1550 Edward VI conferred on him the vicarage of Burnham in Buckinghamshire. When Mary came to the throne, he was already married and a staunch reformer. Deprived of his preferments he fled to Frankfurt, where he seems to have remained until Elizabeth's accession. In Frankfurt he was one of the conservative group who voted against the "new discipline" and supported Horne in the famous "troubles."[13]

On his return to England, Davies was placed on a commission to visit the four Welsh dioceses and the adjacent sees of Hereford and Worcester. In January, 1560, he was consecrated bishop of St. Asaph. In the spring of 1561 he was translated to the larger diocese of St. David's, where he remained until his death in November, 1581. In Wales he was an important person, a member of the Council of Wales, and the trusted adviser of Parker and Burghley on Welsh affairs. Active in the reformation of his diocese, he was interested in all schemes for the intellectual and religious enlightenment of his countrymen. He contributed to the Bishop's Bible of 1568, and with William Salesbury he translated the New Testament and the Prayer Book into Welsh (both published in 1567). Archbishop Parker thoroughly respected his scholarship and linguistic abilities, and often consulted him.

[12] These facts are taken from T. F. Tout's account of Davies in *DNB*.
[13] Garrett, p. 141, cites documentary evidence for Davies' residence in Frankfurt. On the authority of Sir John Wynne (who knew Davies' sons at Oxford), Tout had suggested that Davies fled to Geneva and there lived in extreme poverty.

In our consideration of Bishop Davies as Diggon Davie, let us first explore Davies' connections with the Grindal-Young circle. The first extended relationship of Davies with this group seems to have been during his four-year exile at Frankfurt. The English male community in Frankfurt numbered but sixty-two in 1557,[14] but included at times between 1554 and 1559, besides Davies, Alexander Nowell, John Mullins, Thomas Watts, and Edmund Grindal, all old and intimate friends of Bishop Young.[15] The Frankfurt exiles had a church of their own to worship in and started a university. It would, of course, be impossible for Davies not to know this group of men, isolated as they all were in a foreign land.

Davies, after his return to England and his consecration to the bishopric of St. Asaph in January, 1560, apparently spent most of his time in Wales, but he had occasional opportunities of renewing his friendship with the London group of the Frankfurt exiles. On March 27, 1560, Davies ordained two deacons and six priests "in the name and by the order of the reverend father, Bishop Grindal." A few days later, Davies ordained for Grindal two deacons and three priests. Both of these ordination ceremonies were performed in the Bishop of London's chapel.[16] Davies, now bishop of St. David's, was present at the synod of January, 1563, which drew up the Thirty-nine Articles. All the bishops of the realm were present, and Archbishop Parker made Alexander Nowell, dean of St. Paul's, his Prolocutor.[17] Davies also attended the convocation of bishops at London in April, 1571, and signed the canons of discipline.[18] On February 15, 1576, Davies was pres-

[14] *Ibid.*, p. 22.
[15] *Ibid.*, "Census" of these men. For Young's relationship with this group, see Judson, *Young*, pp. 16–18.
[16] Strype, *Grindal*, p. 58.
[17] Strype, *Parker*, I, 240.
[18] *Ibid.*, II, 60.

ent in London at the confirmation of Grindal to the archbishopric of Canterbury. Of the old Frankfurt group, Sandys, bishop
of London, Horne, bishop of Winchester, and Cox, bishop of
Ely, were also present. The oath of allegiance was taken for Grindal by Thomas Watts.[19] Davies stayed over for the convocation
of March, 1576, which was attended by all the bishops and clergy
of Canterbury.[20] Here, of course, he had an opportunity to meet
Dr. John Young, if he had not met him through mutual friends
before. Bishop Davies was in London again on April 23, 1576,
as a member of a commission called by Grindal to inquire into
ecclesiastical abuses. Thomas Watts and Alexander Nowell were
among those present.[21] As the commission was held at St. Paul's,
Young, the holder of the Cadington Major prebend, was also
probably among the "others." In fact, it would be indeed strange
if Dr. Young, prominent in the ecclesiastical life of London, did
not know Richard Davies, ranking Welsh bishop and one of the
most important prelates of England, before his (Young's) consecration to the bishopric of Rochester on March 16, 1578.

However, aside from the possible significance of the September
eclogue, I have discovered no direct evidence of any relationship
between Davies and Edmund Spenser, Young's secretary in 1578.
But Thomas Willoughby, canon of Canterbury and dean of
Rochester under Young, was a member of the Frankfurt community along with Davies, and may be suggested as another possible connecting link. Philip Sidney and his father are other
possible links. The former, who was in "some use of familarity"
with Spenser shortly before the publication of the *Calender*, was
instituted (as a "scholaris") by Davies to the prebend of Llan-
guulo in the collegiate church of Christ at Brecon on November

[19] Strype, *Grindal*, p. 286.
[20] *Ibid.*, p. 289.
[21] *Ibid.*, pp. 309–310.

2, 1564.[22] For over twenty years (1560 to 1581), Davies was a member of the Council of Wales under Sir Henry Sidney.[23] Daniel Rogers, friendly with Spenser in late 1579, was also a member of the Frankfurt community for a short while.

In the second place, by making Diggon Davie represent Richard Davies, Spenser would be following his normal procedure in using the outstanding prelates of his time in the ecclesiastical eclogues of the *Shepheardes Calender*. For a good many years now, Algrind, Roffyn, and Morrell have had a wide acceptance as Grindal, Young, and Aylmer. As I have pointed out, it also seems probable that Spenser, in an equally obvious manner, was representing Bishops Piers and Cooper as Piers and Thomalin. If Richard Davies was known to the Young circle (and I have above indicated the probability), and if the inner evidence of the September eclogue fits the known facts of his life and character—and I will shortly demonstrate this congruity—the normal assumption should be, from the similarity of names, that Spenser intended to represent Bishop Richard Davies as Diggon Davie.[24]

The arguments, many and cogent, for Bishop Davies as Diggon Davie, have convinced many scholars.[25] Before taking up the first

[22] HMC, Lord de L'Isle and Dudley, LXXVII, Part I (London, 1925), 271. Davies' letters of presentation, dated January 14, 1565, were endorsed by Sir Henry Sidney. Philip was ten years old at the time.

[23] Sir Henry Sidney, during the early part of 1580, was a frequent visitor at Wilton, the seat of Arthur Grey, who, having been nominated for the post of lord deputy of Ireland, was anxious to profit from Sidney's experiences. Later in the same year Spenser went to Ireland as Grey's secretary.

[24] Miss Mohl (p. 22), accepting Grindal and Aylmer for Algrind and Morrell, refuses to accept Davies as Diggon Davie because Hobbinol and Colin Clout do not sound like Harvey and Spenser. It might be answered that as a bishop, Davies should be grouped with the other bishops and considered accordingly. Also, perhaps because their names do not sound like their pastoral pseudonyms, Harvey and Spenser are specifically identified in the glosses.

[25] For instance, Whitaker, p. 15, writes: "Hulbert and McLane proved that Diggon Davie was beyond doubt Richard Davies, bishop of St. David's."

strong argument, it should be mentioned that Alexander Pope in 1713 pointed out the Welsh dialect in the first four lines of *September*.[26] In 1933 Mary Parmenter, without attempting to determine the identity of Diggon, on the basis of these four lines was certain that Diggon must have been a Welshman.[27] Then in 1942 Mrs. Hulbert demonstrated that the use of *her* for *I*, *he*, and *him* in the opening lines of *September*, and even the name *Diggon* itself, was characteristic of Welsh speech in Tudor times.[28] Although Miss Mohl later attempted to argue that *Diggon* (instead of the usual *Diccon*) was western English as well as Welsh, she entirely missed the point on the Welsh dialectal *her* by inquiring why Hobbinol (who had never been in Wales) also used *her* in his initial address to Diggon. The answer, of course, would be that Hobbinol was being humorous and was giving the readers a cue. Moreover, in his first gloss E. K. tells us that *her* characterizes only Diggon, the wandering shepherd. His "Dialecte and phrase of speache" differs somewhat "from the comen. The cause whereof is supposed to be, by occasion of the party herein meant, who being very freend of the Author hereof, had bene long in forraine countryes, and there seene many disorders, which he here recounteth to Hobbinoll." And if we consider the conditions and modes of travel in the sixteenth century and the different language used in Wales, Davies' remote, sea-girt diocese—even apart from the conventions that Spenser was borrowing from his sources—should amply fulfill the requirements of E. K.'s "farre countrye" or "forraine countryes." Davies, like Diggon, had traveled widely in his years as a Marian exile, in his visitations of his large and distant diocese, and in his periodic trips to London to

[26] In the *Guardian*, 40 (April 27, 1713). See Var., p. 355.
[27] In her excellent unpublished dissertation, *Colin Clout and Hobbinoll: A Reconsideration of the Relationship of Edmund Spenser and Gabriel Harvey* (Johns Hopkins University, 1933), p. 182.
[28] Hulbert, pp. 349–50.

attend ecclesiastical meetings or to visit old friends. Further, we should note that the first meaning of *country* in the *New English Dictionary* is a "district or region."

There is a wealth of evidence to show that the experiences of Bishop Davies and the condition of the clergy and the Church in St. David's (and in the other Welsh dioceses as well) fit the complaints of Diggon Davie. In 1570 Bishop Davies wrote an extended report on his diocese to Burghley. In it Davies pointed out that the clergy were both inadequate and incompetent. The once well-endowed livings "had been seized at the Reformation and made royal impropriations, their lands leased out to laymen, who, retaining the chief part of the revenues, put four or five benefices into the charge of some utterly incompetent clergyman to serve them, and that at a starvation salary."[29] He urged that the Council provide "competent stipends for vicars in the numerous churches impropriated to the crown, whose condition had become far worse than before the suppression of the monasteries."[30] He admitted the ignorance and immorality of his flock, and hoped some part of the fruits of the impropriated benefices could be sequestered to pay preachers to spread the Word of God.[31]

When Walter Devereux, the first Earl of Essex and Davies' great friend and patron, died in Dublin in September, 1576, Bishop Davies preached an eloquent funeral sermon in Carmarthen Church. In this sermon (which was printed in London in 1577), Davies again threw a clear light on the state of his diocese. He complained bitterly "of the careless and bad justices and sheriffs, the timid and superstitious churchwardens, who thwarted all

[29] As summarized by White, p. 125.
[30] DNB.
[31] White, p. 126. William Pierce, *John Penry* (London, 1923), p. 126, also gives a good account of this report.

his efforts for reform. But he had to deal also with great earls and courtiers, greedy for church spoils and contemptuously intolerant of the Church's rulers." [32] And although Davies suffered much from his enemies and from the ignorance, indifference, and vice of his flock, he was apparently not troubled by Catholics or Puritans. In a 1577 report to the Privy Council, he affirmed that there were no recusants in his diocese. [33] According to the celebrated Puritan, John Penry (from Davies' diocese), there was very little religion of any kind in all Wales.

This testimony is borne out from other sources. In 1582, Davies' successor, Marmaduke Middleton, on making his initial visitation, found the diocese in exceedingly bad shape: "small poperie" but much "Athisme," and the few clergy ignorant and incompetent. [34] Penry wrote that there were twenty parishes in Wales that had no sermons from one year's end to another as compared to the one parish that had a quarterly sermon. [35] From another point of view, Father Robert Persons, writing to Aquaviva in October, 1581, declares Wales "not so hostile to the Catholic religion as lapsed into a dense ignorance about it due to the lack of priests working there, and lapsed also into a kind of approbation of heresy through being accustomed to it." [36]

There are some interesting parallels between Davies' experiences and the speeches of Diggon Davie. In his summary of what

[32] DNB.
[33] C.S.P., *Domestic, 1547–80,* p. 564. There was a revival of Catholicism somewhat later. In the early seventeenth century, Catholics on the Continent thought Wales to be well inclined towards Catholicism. Hulbert, p. 358.
[34] White, p. 255. Middleton was deprived of his bishopric in 1592, the year before his death, for embezzling episcopal property and other crimes against the church.
[35] As cited by White, p. 125. See also Albert Peel, ed., *Notebook of John Penry 1593* (London, 1944), p. x. Penry's account of the Church in Wales corresponds closely with Davies' 1570 report to the Council.
[36] Quoted by Hughes, III, 315 n.

the people say about the clergy, one group, according to Diggon, say the "world is much war then it wont" (i.e., presumably much worse than before the suppression of the monasteries). Davies had said the same thing in his 1570 report to the Council. Again, the only charge that Diggon apparently reacts to is that of those who declare that there is no hospitality because the clergy are too interested in adorning their wives and enriching their heirs. This accusation so provokes Diggon that he would put a hot coal on the tongues of these critics. This is an interesting reaction, since Bishop Davies was noted for his bountiful hospitality. Lavish and somewhat improvident, he always kept an "exceeding great port," and he had in his service the younger sons of some of the best houses of North Wales, giving them good maintenance and education along with his own sons.[37] Whatever his failings, lack of hospitality was not one of them, and so it is not surprising that Diggon should react strongly to this accusation.

The main charge hurled by the ecclesiastical critics—and these, according to Diggon, shoot closest to the mark—is that powerful courtiers relentlessly plunder the clergy.

> For bigge Bulles of Basan brace hem about,
> That with theyr hornes butten the more stoute:
> But the leane soules treaden under foote.
> And to seeke redresse mought little boote:
> For liker bene they to pluck away more,
> Then ought of the gotten good to restore. (124–29)

This is a subject on which Bishop Davies should have been able to speak feelingly, for he had suffered much from Elizabeth's favorites. In early 1566 Davies was involved in a quarrel with the Earls of Leicester and Pembroke. In four peremptory letters they ordered Davies to accept a Mr. Bowen as their presentee to an

[37] DNB.

advowson to which there were already two pretenders with stronger claims. Bowen offered as evidence forged and counterfeit credentials. Davies was so alarmed at the pressure of the Earls that he tried to persuade Mr. Gwynne, the lawful holder, to resign. Meanwhile, another claimant, Samuel Ferrar, the son of Davies' martyred predecessor, had also appeared on the scene. A violent letter from the Earls, rebuking Davies for his delay, finally gave him courage to resist. In a letter to Parker, he complained of their bad usage and lamented how, in conjunction with "the insatiable cormorants in his own diocese," his powerful enemies defamed and oppressed him.[38]

Another Bull of Basan that Davies had trouble with was Sir John Perrot. In late 1578 Davies was appointed to a commission to investigate piracy off the coast of Wales. Davies was unlucky enough to discover that the powerful Sir John was profiting from the piracy. Rumor had it that Perrot worried Bishop Davies to death in revenge for his share of the investigation.[39]

But, besides these, Davies was the victim of one of the most brazen acts of despoliation in Elizabeth's reign. For over fifteen years (from 1566 to 1582), a Mr. Edward Carey, a groom of the Queen's chamber, aided by his solicitor, Dodington, by means of a commission of concealment plundered the diocese of St. David's and was successful in alienating almost half of the revenues of Davies' bishopric. Strype considers this one of the most flagrant and notorious examples of despoliation in Elizabethan church history. In a series of lawsuits, though usually defeated at first in the courts, Carey persevered until he received a verdict in his favor. He finally obtained the judgment of a jury that Llandde-

[38] *DNB.* This contentiousness (and litigiousness) over church livings was quite common in Wales. Hence it is not surprising that Diggon stresses it in *September*. See Hulbert, p. 361.

[39] Hulbert, p. 367, and *DNB.* Davies had other troubles with Perrot which are not too well defined.

wibrevi was a "college concealed," thereby robbing Davies of the patronage of that important living and of twelve other churches annexed to the prebends of the dissolved college as well. Carey afterwards obtained, in a series of new trials, the churches of Llanarth and Llanina as parcels of Llanddewibrevi.[40]

This long and merciless plundering by Carey might well be the "old griefe" of Diggon Davie that is the basis of the September eclogue, and might account for Diggon's misery and blasted hopes. Strype asserts that Carey reduced the revenues of St. David's from 457 pounds to the 263 pounds which remained at the time of Davies's death.[41] Professor Tout quotes Wynne that Davies "died·poor."[42] If so, the Carey despoliation would give point to Diggon's final plea to Hobbinol:

> What shall I doe? what way shall I wend,
> My piteous plight and losse to amend?

Diggon's emblem—*Inopem me copia fecit*—would also be pertinent to Carey's robbery of Davies. Plenty had made Davies poor because it had made him a target for avaricious courtiers who successfully stripped him of his rightful revenue. In another way, too, plenty had made Davies poor, for it encouraged him to indulge in bountiful hospitality that further stripped him of what little remained after the Bulls of Basan had butted him about.

Before giving the positive grounds for Spenser's probable admiration of Bishop Davies, it must be conceded that he was not a perfect shepherd. His successor, the disreputable Marmaduke Middleton, with some truth charged Davies with neglect of his

---

[40] Carey, in 1582, less than a year after Davies' death, continued his merciless plundering, suing the bishop's widow for arrears of rent due when the property involved was in her husband's unquestioned possession. Strype, *Annals*, III. ii, 226–28, and III. i, 175, gives a full account of these matters.

[41] *Annals*, III. i, 175.

[42] *DNB*.

diocese, sale of livings, lavishness, and improvidence. The sale of livings was, of course, the most serious charge. Middleton reported the testimony of Davies' brother-in-law that Davies "never gave any living within his own gift, nor admitted any to other men's gift without consideration: alleging he could not otherwise have lived."[43] But all of this information was revealed after Davies' death by his successor, Middleton, who was chagrined at not being able to lay his hands on church funds and was jealous of Davies' judicial powers which did not descend to him along with the ecclesiastical office.[44] Furthermore, if Davies was, as E. K. assures us Diggon Davie was, "the very freend to the author" of the *Calender*, Spenser would be inclined to overlook certain faults, especially when Davies was more sinned against than sinning. Spenser's general presentation reveals that Diggon, thoroughly fleeced by Elizabeth's greedy courtiers and tasked by his ignorant and corrupt clergy, has evoked all of Spenser's sympathy. We should not confuse, however, the conventional motives which Spenser borrows from his source, Mantuan, wherein Diggon "was bewitcht/ With vayne desire, and hope to be enricht," and try to argue from the borrowed convention that Spenser was aware of Davies' shortcomings and was satirizing him.

There are many reasons, other than the fact that Davies was an old friend to the chief members of the Grindal-Young circle, why Spenser should admire him. Davies was a writer of Welsh poetry and a dependable linguistic scholar. He was able to read Welsh, Old and Middle English, German, Greek, Latin, and Hebrew, and often aided Archbishop Parker in deciphering old manuscripts.[45] He was also devoted to education: for instance, in 1576, with the aid of the first Earl of Essex, he succeeded in founding

[43] As quoted by White, p. 127.
[44] *DNB*, and Strype, *Grindal*, pp. 401–402.
[45] See Strype, *Parker*, I, 418, and *DNB*.

the Carmarthen grammar school.[46] Next, he was an industrious Biblical scholar. He had a small part in the Bishop's Bible of 1568; the year before, with the assistance of William Salesbury, he brought out editions of the Prayer-Book and the New Testament in Welsh. In the preface to the latter, Davies pointed out that the Reformation grew from the new learning; as a patriot, he desires his countrymen, "glorious in their past history, to partake of the new intellectual and spiritual growth."[47] In the preface of the complete Welsh Bible of 1588, William Morgan highly praises the great work of Davies.[48] The Queen, too, highly regarded Davies, calling him "her second St. David."[49] After Davies' death, Sir John Wynne eulogized him as one of the glories of the Welsh nation: "O how my heart doth warm by recording the memory of so worthy a man."[50]

In two of the most critical ecclesiastical abuses of the time, Bishop Davies courageously supported the cause of the bishops against the Crown and the lay patrons. The first, the oppression of the clergy by the Queen's gentlemen pensioners in the latter's fraudulent commissions of concealment, is one of the main themes of September. As we have seen, Davies fought Carey from court to court and became a martyr to the cause of those who would protect the property of the Church. The second and perhaps greater evil, the ignorance and sloth of the clergy, is reflected in all the ecclesiastical eclogues. Davies was one of the nine bishops who supported the prophesyings, by means of which Grindal and other bishops hoped to obtain a zealous and educated ministry. He also labored hard to get competent clergy and bishops.

---

[46] DNB.
[47] Hulbert, p. 352, who cites Pierce, pp. 112–13.
[48] DNB.
[49] Encyl. Brit., 11th ed., "Wales: Religion."
[50] Cited by William Hughes, A History of the Church of the Cymry (London, 1916), p. 262.

For instance, in 1565 he wrote to Secretary Cecil, protesting that William Hughes, who was then seeking the bishopric of Landaff, was not fit to be a bishop, for he was deficient in learning and even ignorant.[51] And in his 1570 report to the Council, Davies tried to get the Crown to relinquish some of the royal impropriations to the Church, so that learned and competent preachers could be obtained for his diocese.

As one of the outstanding Elizabethan bishops, Davies would be a good spokesman for the Church in attacking ecclesiastical abuses. But it should not be thought that Spenser was limiting himself to a single Welsh diocese, or even to all the Welsh dioceses. The evils he was attacking were general in the English Church; they were almost as bad, in fact, in England as in Wales. In typical fashion, Spenser lets the prominent individual case stand for the general abuse: the despoliation of Davies for the universal plundering of the English Church, and the conditions in a single diocese for the conditions in all dioceses. In addition, it was safer to attack abuses in Wales, just as it was safer to reflect Scottish political affairs and to attack Aubigny rather than to reflect English political affairs and to attack Alençon in the fable of the Fox and the Kid. By indirections, Spenser's first readers could easily find directions out. Furthermore, Spenser has Diggon report what the people are saying about church affairs: some say this, and some say that, and all together they pretty well cover the ground. But don't blame Diggon or Spenser, who are merely rehearsing what the many-headed multitude are saying.

In conclusion, the identification of Bishop Richard Davies with Diggon Davie would emphasize the direct, literal way in which Spenser was reflecting contemporary affairs and ecclesiastical

[51] Strype, *Annals*, II. i, 463. In 1573, Hughes, in spite of Davies' warning, was appointed to St. Asaph, where he misbehaved in a scandalous fashion.

abuses in the *Shepheardes Calender*. And in the light of Spenser's extreme literalness in other portions of his poem, I doubt whether many in high political and ecclesiastical circles in 1579 could refrain from leaping to the identification which Dr. Hulbert originally made, and which I have attempted to strengthen in this chapter.[52]

---

[52] Since Miss Mohl argued at length for Philip Sidney as Diggon Davie (in the face of two articles making a strong case for Bishop Davies), some of her main arguments and assertions should be met. As I have intimated, the big weakness of her suggestion is that Sidney is neither a Welshman nor a clergyman. She never succeeds in explaining away the Welsh dialectal *her* in the opening lines of *September*. Her argument that Spenser is dealing with the world and not with England and Wales, while not too probable in terms of the whole *Calender*, depends on phrases where Spenser is following his source; these phrases, too, would fit Wales as well as the Continent. I have also explained some of her other difficulties: that Spenser was attacking continental Catholicism (based on E. K.'s references to Polish prelates); or that since Davies' record wasn't clear, he could not with propriety denounce others; or that since Bishop Davies desired to be enriched, he could not, as Diggon, complain of such ambitions in others.

Miss Mohl holds that Harvey, as Hobbinol, would not dare scold Davies, as he would Sidney. But there is no scolding—only banter and tongue-in-cheek advice to elicit further complaints from Diggon. In reality, too, Harvey would no more scold Sidney than he would Davies.

I would deny her assertions that criticism of Church affairs would be more appropriate for a layman like Sidney, or that Sidney could better denounce the rapacity of rulers and courtiers. A bishop would be in a better position to know the problems of the Church and be more interested in solving them. And Davies would know from bitter experience the rapacity of courtiers. On the other hand, Sidney was breaking Church law by holding three preferments. Moreover, Sidney's uncle, Leicester, could be considered a "Bull of Basan." Sidney was not only in league with Leicester but was preparing himself to step into Leicester's shoes, to be his heir and to assume his political mantle.

Personal Allegory -- Poets and Scholars

XV

Gabriel Harvey as Hobbinol

GABRIEL HARVEY plays a prominent, if not central, role in the *Shepheardes Calender*, being honored by both E. K. and Spenser. As G. C. Moore Smith writes, the *Calender* is "an eternal monument to the friendship of Edmund Spenser for Gabriel Harvey, of Colin Clout for Hobbinol"[1]—even though this friendship has been something that posterity has found difficult to explain. But the whirligig of time has taken its revenges, and today Harvey instead of being regarded as a learned blockhead or the pedant *par excellence*—an attitude fostered by the biased and unsympathetic treatment accorded him by his first editor, Dr. Grosart—stands as one of the most learned scholars of his age,

[1] In his introduction to Gabriel Harvey's *Marginalia* (Stratford-Upon-Avon, 1913), p. 24. This introduction is perhaps the fairest and most complete treatment of Harvey we have. Another excellent treatment of Harvey (centered around his quarrel with Nashe) can be found in Ronald B. McKerrow, *Works of Thomas Nashe*, V, 65–110.

a thoroughgoing humanist and Renaissance man,[2] and perhaps the Elizabethan Englishman whose mind we know best.[3]

In this chapter I shall attempt to determine the extent to which Hobbinol is a fictitious character in the pastoral world of the Calender, the extent to which he dramatically represents Spenser's friend Gabriel Harvey, and the extent to which Harvey and Spenser differ in their fundamental attitudes.

The identity of Hobbinol has never been a mystery, for Hobbinol is the only character in the Calender that E. K. definitely identifies in the glosses. There are probably two reasons for this frankness: (1) no political danger was involved in this particular admission; (2) Harvey was probably the only character in the Calender who went back to Spenser's Cambridge days, and needed to be identified: all the others were members of the London groups connected with Bishop Young and Leicester, and would be readily identifiable by these groups—and others "in the know"—for whom Spenser largely wrote this poem.

It was no doubt with the full approval of Spenser that E. K. addressed the introductory Epistle "To the most excellent and learned, both Orator and Poet, Mayster Gabriell Harvey," asking Harvey to defend the Calender against envious critics "with your mighty Rhetorick and other your rare gifts of learning." Such recognition was not unfitting, for in 1579, when the Calender appeared, Harvey could be regarded as one of the most promising scholars of his time. He had distinguished himself as Praelector or Professor of Rhetoric at Cambridge in 1575

[2] Professor Harold S. Wilson, in his introduction to his edition of Harvey's Ciceronianus (Lincoln, Nebraska, 1945), and in articles on "The Humanism of Gabriel Harvey," Joseph Quincy Adams Memorial Studies (Washington, D. C., 1948), pp. 707–21, and on "Harvey's Orations on Rhetoric," ELH, XII (1945), 167–82, has indicated the importance of Harvey and how he reflects the learning of his time.

[3] G. C. Moore Smith, Marginalia, p. 1.

and 1576, and had made an impact on the scholars of his age through the publication of *Ciceronianus* and *Rhetor* in 1577, Latin orations which are now regarded as "among the most interesting literary documents of the time";[4] he had been chosen to dispute before the Queen and her Court on her visit to Audley End in July, 1578, and to express the customary "Gratulations" of Cambridge; finally, he had been noticed by the Queen and allowed to kiss her hand at a dance given for Court ladies on this occasion.[5] Harvey celebrated in Latin verses the part he played at Audley End, bringing out his *Gratulationes Valdinenses* later in 1578, addressing the first three books of this work to the Queen, Leicester, and Burghley respectively, and the fourth to Lord Oxford, Philip Sidney, and Christopher Hatton.[6]

E. K. was evidently doing his best to increase Harvey's prestige and to prepare the ground for the publication of more of Harvey's works. In the postscript to the Epistle, Harvey is invited to publish his "gallant English verses" as he had already done with his Latin poems, which, says E. K., "both for invention and Elocution are very delicate, and superexcellent"; and the gloss to *September*, which identifies Harvey, gives the titles of five unpublished works of his worthy of print. This same gloss points to Harvey's reputation in poetry and rhetoric, as well as to his "choyce learning." A gloss to *January* had earlier indicated the high nature of the Hobbinol-Colin friendship, a

[4] H. S. Wilson, Gabriel Harvey's *Ciceronianus*, p. 1.
Moore Smith (p. 13) writes: "No scholar can read these discourses without surprise and admiration for Harvey's command of the Latin language, his eloquence, his scholarly openmindedness and readiness to learn, and his extraordinary width of reading."
[5] Moore Smith, pp. 17–18.
[6] Moore Smith, p. 20. In his indiscreet urging of the Queen's marriage to Leicester in his *Gratulationes*, and in his seeking the favor of the great, Moore Smith feels that Harvey showed "his lack of restraining good sense" and perhaps exposed himself to ridicule.

union of kindred souls; and Hobbinol is called Spenser's "very speciall and most familiar freend, whom he entirely and extraordinaryly beloved."

Harvey, as Hobbinol, appears in five eclogues of the *Calender*, playing a major role in *April*, *June*, and *September*. In the *January* eclogue Hobbinol is referred to in one stanza: Colin, absolving Hobbinol from all responsibility for his misery, tells how he rebuffs the latter's daily kindnesses in his obsession for Rosalind.[7] In *December*, Colin reviewing his life, cites Hobbinol's appraisal of his poetry:

> And if that *Hobbinol* right judgement bare,
> To *Pan* his owne selfe pype I neede not yield:
> For, if the flocking Nymphes did follow *Pan*
> The wiser Muses after *Colin* ranne. (45–48)

In saying farewell to life in the last lines of this eclogue Colin fondly remembers the loyalty of Hobbinol:

> 'Adieu, good *Hobbinol*, that was so true,
> Tell *Rosalind*, her *Colin* bids her adieu.'

In *April*, the first eclogue in which Hobbinol is presented as a dramatic character, he explains to Thenot, the other shepherd and speaker of the eclogue, his concern because Colin

> Now loves a lasse that all his love doth scorne,
and in his anguish has forborne
> His wonted songs, wherein he all outwent. (11, 16)

Hobbinol then identifies Rosalind as the cause of Colin's woe. In answer to Thenot's request for an example of Colin's poetic skill, Hobbinol recites the beautiful lyric that celebrates "Fayre Elisa, Queene of Shepheardes all." At the conclusion of this lyric, Hobbinol replies to Thenot's expressions of sympathy for the lovelorn Colin:

[7] Ll. 53–60.

Sicker I hold him, for a greater fon,
That loves the thing, he cannot purchase. (158–59)

Hobbinol's position in *April* is quite characteristic of Harvey in many ways. First of all, from the Spenser-Harvey letters we know that Spenser sought Harvey's critical reaction to his verses and valued his judgment. From these letters, as well as from his commendatory verses to Spenser, the "Learned Shepheard," on the publication of the first three books of the *Faerie Queene*, and from his own practice in his poems in his *Letter-Book*, we know that Harvey esteemed the pastoral vein and the homely, simple, vernacular style. From the passage already cited in *December*, and from another passage in *June* which will be noted later, Harvey appears in the *Calender* as the friendly critic who appreciates Colin's excellence as a poet and acknowledges this excellence in gracious terms. Now Harvey's values were not Spenser's—as this chapter will try to bring out—but Spenser, I feel sure, would not have made Harvey commend Colin's skill as a poet if this praise did not accord with the facts.[8]

Another point that can be made here is that Hobbinol would be an ideal reporter for Colin's eulogy of Queen Elizabeth, for of all the eclogues this would fit in best with Harvey's program of

[8] Too much has been made of Harvey's presumed insensitivity to certain aspects of Spenser's poetry. We have no means of knowing what part of the *Faerie Queene* Harvey was referring to in his "Gallant Familiar Letter" in his mention of "Hobgoblin runne away with the garland from Apollo." In his letters to Nashe, Harvey highly praised the *Faerie Queene*. For instance, in his *Letter of Notable Contents* (1593) he asks: "or is not the verse of M. Spencer, in his brave *Faery Queene*, the virginall of the divinest Muses, and gentlest graces?" Harvey, *Works*, Grosart, ed., 1884, I, 265. Sidney Thomas, "Hobgoblin Runne Away With the Garland From Apollo," *MLN*, LV (1940), 419–20, makes the sensible suggestion that Harvey was protesting only against Spenser's use of barbaric and irrational material in the *Faerie Queene*. McKerrow (Nashe, V, 71n) suggests that Harvey was reacting to Spenser's sham antiquarianism, which he thought unsuitable for epic poetry.

action: assiduously seeking the favor of those in power through adulatory verse—as he himself had done in his *Gratulationes Valdinenses*. Hobbinol's final words to Thenot on the folly of aspiring to the thing that cannot be realized are perfect Harvey on two counts: (1) Harvey was a great condemner of both romantic and Platonic love, as we know from his notations in his copy of Hoby's translation of *The Courtier*,[9] and from Spenser's jocular Latin verses to Harvey in his letter of October 5, 1579; (2) Harvey was the supreme realist of his period and he filled the margins of the books he read with assertions on the necessity of being practical, keeping one's feet on the ground, and avoiding all fantastic or unrealizable schemes.

In the June eclogue there is a dramatic contrast between Colin and Hobbinol. The eclogue and glosses suggest an actual episode is being recorded: Spenser has made a visit to Harvey at Cambridge, where Harvey advises that Spenser should

> . . . to the dales resort, where Shepheards ritch
> And fruictfull flocks bene everywhere to see. (21–22)

E. K. informs us that the dales are the "Southpartes, where he [Colin] nowe abydeth," and that this advice is "no poetical fiction, but unfeynedly spoken of the Poete selfe who, for . . . his more preferment removing out of the Northparts came into the South, as Hobbinoll indeede advised him privately."

> Lo *Colin*, here the place, whose pleasunt syte
> From other shades hath weand my wandering mynde.
> Tell me, what wants me here, to worke delyte?
> The simple ayre, the gentle warbling wynde,
> So calme, so coole, as no where else I fynde:
> The grassye ground with daintye Daysies dight,

---

[9] Caroline Ruutz-Rees, "Some Notes of Gabriel Harvey's in Hoby's Translation of Castiglione's *Courtier* (1561)," *PMLA*, XXV (1910), 637.

The Bramble bush, where Byrds of every kynde
To the waters fall their tunes attemper right. (1–8)
Colin replies:
O happy *Hobbinoll,* I blesse thy state,
That Paradise hast found, whych *Adam* lost. (9–10)
Hobbinol then suggests the seeking out of wealthy patrons in the
South where the Muses make sweet music, and Fairies and
Nymphs dance in the gloaming. But Colin feels that riper age,
with its experience of the anguish of love, now reproves his earlier
carefree life of song and poetry. Hobbinol then praises Colin's
poetic skill, which silences the birds and confounds with shame
Calliope and the Muses. Colin admits no such skill, is without
ambition, and is only concerned with pleasing himself and expressing his lovelorn state in rough rimes. Colin then pays his
respects to Chaucer, poet of love complaints and merry tales, and
relates how Menalcas has won Rosalind from him. Hobbinol
brings the eclogue to its conclusion by lamenting Colin's sad
situation.

The unqualified cheerfulness of Hobbinol's opening lines in
this eclogue expresses a fundamental point in Harvey's philosophy
of life. Perpetual cheerfulness was a motto that he always held up
before himself. To him the three greatest sins were sloth, sadness,
and coldness, and sadness was perhaps the greatest of these. For
instance, in his "Commonplace Book" he wrote:
It is on speciall poynt of mans foelicity to make the best of
everything; and to passe over a thousand busye impertinent
accidentes slighly and cunningly, without the least urging of
your mind, to or froe.[10]
His *Marginalia* is full of such items as these: "Hilaris animus et
hilaris frons, perpetuum convivium"; "fuge a moroso, et melan-
cholico: aut visus sit tui materia illius, tua foelicitas"; "Nunquam

---

[10] *Marginalia,* p. 88.

ullo memento Melancholicus aut abjectus: sed semper alacris, et iocundissimus."[11] Harvey was also fond of making lists of things bad for one's health, and anger and heaviness of mind always had a prominent place among these.[12]

Colin's reply to Hobbinol has elements of irony. The academic security of Cambridge was a point on which Spenser and Harvey were at variance. To Spenser now in the world of affairs, Cambridge with its opportunities for leisure, scholarship, and poetry no doubt had its appeal as that Paradise which Adam lost. Spenser, too, well aware of Harvey's defects of character that would—and did—hamper his ambition to become another Sir Thomas Smith or Lord Burghley, would be interested in emphasizing the conventional, attractive aspect of the academic life. In his splendid account of Harvey's life, G. C. Moore Smith quotes the sonnet which Spenser wrote to Harvey (dated Dublin, July 18, 1586), in which Spenser congratulates Harvey on his position of independence and detachment with no need of fawning "for the favor of the great," accounting him the "happy above happiest men" because he is "sitting like a looker-on of this worldes stage." Smith suggests that Spenser did not know Harvey as well as we do today, else he would not have so written about him.[13] But Spenser could not have been so mistaken, because Harvey's letters to Spenser are filled with his ambitions, and even Harvey's enemies, as Thomas Nashe later demonstrated, knew perfectly well

[11] *Ibid.*, pp. 187, 176, 143, respectively.
[12] *Ibid.*, p. 177.
[13] *Ibid.*, p. 57. Harvey knew that this sonnet's stress on his happy detachment, as well as on his supreme critical ability, was overly complimentary, for in his *Foure Letters* volume he apparently referred to this sonnet as "a token of his [Spenser's] affection, not a testimony of his judgement." *Works*, I, 212. Warren B. Austin, "Spenser's Sonnet to Harvey," *MLN*, LXII (1947), 20–23, offers strong reasons for thinking that Spenser wrote this sonnet as an introductory poem to an intended edition of poetic satires (never published) by Harvey.

the driving force of Harvey's life. As Professor Judson wrote in his *Variorum* life of Spenser, this sonnet was perhaps written "to console Harvey for his disappointments, since the preceding six years had contained little but frustration of his ambitious schemes, or it may have been merely the expression of a mood —composed at a moment when Spenser coveted his friend's leisure for literary work and freedom from the uncertainty and tyrannous demands of Irish life."[14]

Harvey best expresses his contempt for the romantic view of university life in the draft of a letter in his *Letter-Book* which was presumably sent to Spenser in 1579. This letter, in answer to a letter, "or rather bill of complaynte," was to represent the re-action of Harvey and of three of his drinking companions to whom he read Spenser's letter. Harvey wrote:

> You suppose us students happye, and thinke the aire prae-ferrid that breathithe on these same greate lernid philoso-phers and profonde clarkes. Would to God you were on of there men but a sennighte. I doubte not but you would sweare ere Sundaye nexte, that there were not the like wofull and miserable creaturs to be fownde within the cumpass of the whole worlde agayne. None so injurious to themselves, so tyranous to there servantes, so niggardlye to ther kinsfolkes, soe rigorrous to ther acquayntance, soe unprofitable to all, so untowarde for the common welthe, and so unfit for the worlde, meere bookeworms and verye idolls, the most intol-erable creatures to cum in any good sociable cumpanye that ever God creatid. Looke them in the face: you will strayte-wayes affirme they are the dryest, leanist, ill-favoriddist, abjectist, base-minddist carrions and wretcheckes that ever you sett your eie on.[15]

Hobbinol's advice to Colin to seek preferment is well illustrated

[14] P. 119.

[15] *Letter-Book of Gabriel Harvey, 1573–1580*, E. J. L. Scott, ed. (Cam-den Society, 1884), pp. 86–87.

in Harvey's own life and works. Harvey firmly believed that "the Prynces Court" was "the only mart of praeferment and honour— a goulfe of gain";[16] he further thought an obscure life was no life at all.[17] His futile attempts to make the life of scholarship a steppingstone to greatness in public affairs evoke a sense of pity in a sympathetic reader. Oratory and eloquence, he thought, were only a prelude to the life of action. He was sure that "early rising, spare diet, and perpetual cheerfulness" would lead to "the gaining of tyme, and winning of honour";[18] but, alas, for him this prudential regimen brought no material rewards.

Colin's disavowal of personal ambition—"With shepheard sittes not, followe flying fame"—was not only a pastoral convention but an idea that Spenser often entertained in his poetry; such moods, however, were more often produced by his disillusioning experiences with the frivolity, corruption, and uncertainties of Court life than by a temperamental inclination to a life of pastoral retirement. Harvey was undoubtedly influential on Spenser, and he, as well as the spirit of the age, made Spenser eager for preferment and a career of worldly achievement. As Hallett Smith has brought out in his recent book on Elizabethan poetry, pastoralism to the Elizabethans symbolized the good life of content and contemplative self-sufficiency free from ambition, greed, and the vicissitudes of fortune.[19] Spenser at times could, and did, respond to this positive ideal, whereas Harvey, for all his love of learning, found it alien to his nature to do so.

In the September eclogue Hobbinol is the friendly interlocutor who elicits Diggon Davie's sad experiences with ecclesiastical

[16] *Marginalia*, p. 142.
[17] *Ibid.*, p. 152.
[18] *Ibid.*, p. 199.
[19] *Elizabethan Poetry*, pp. 2–8. Professor Smith here gives an excellent account of Spenser's use of pastoral conventions.

abuses in the "farre countrye" of Wales. Diggon curses his bad luck, being so foolish as

> To leave the good, that I had in honde
> In hope of better, that was uncouth.[20]

These conventional sentiments provoke from Hobbinol the pastoral doctrine of content:

> Ah fon, now by thy losse art taught,
> That seeldome chaunge the better brought.
> Content who lives with tryed state,
> Neede feare no chaunge of frowning fate;
> But who will seeke for unknowne gayne,
> Oft lives by losse, and leaves with payne. (68–73)

Diggon then gives a more complete account of ecclesiastical evils, with the greatest emphasis falling on the plundering of diocesan properties by the Queen's favorites, powerful courtiers who are termed "Bulles of Basan." Hobbinol then replies:

> Nowe Diggon, I see thou speakest to plaine:
> Better it were, a little to feyne,
> And cleanly cover, that cannot be cured.
> Such il, as is forced, mought nedes be endured. (135–39

Diggon next relates the fable of the Wolf in Sheep's Clothing, which gives Hobbinol a chance to praise Bishop Young, Colin's master, as an ideal shepherd, one who is meek, wise and merciful, devoted to his flock, and given to practicing what he preaches. Then in reply to Hobbinol's question, Diggon asserts that wolves can only be coped with through a continual, night-and-day watchfulness. Hobbinol protests against such extremes:

> Ah Diggon, thilke same rule were too straight,
> All the cold season to wach and waite.
> We bene of fleshe, men as other bee.

[20] Ll. 59–60.

Why should we be bound to such miseree?
What ever thing lacketh chaungeable rest,
Mought needes decay, when it is at best. (236–41)

Then to Diggon's plea for aid and counsel his "piteous plight and losse to amende," Hobbinol laments his hapless situation but points out that he too has been a victim of "froward fortune," and he offers the comfort of his lowly cottage.

Of the more important speeches of Hobbinol—the only ones, in fact, that I have reported—the first on "content with the tryed state" is, of course, banter or irony. As we have already seen, Harvey's whole life was a vain attempt to escape from the "tryed state," and it is rich irony that the ambitious Harvey should utter these sentiments. But the irony is not at all inappropriate, for Harvey was a great student of irony, very often encouraging himself to be "a continual ironist, like Socrates, Sannazarious, and our Sir Thomas More."[21] On one occasion he briefly noted the ironic practice of Sannazaro: "Semper laudabat homines, reprehendo: reprehendebat, laudando."[22]

Hobbinol's next significant speech is his mild protest against speaking too plainly, with his prudent advice "a little to feyne,/ And cleanly cover that cannot be cured:/ Such ill, as is forced, mought nedes be endured." This again, though perhaps spoken with tongue in cheek, is pure Harvey. Harvey thought that to be successful one must mask all feelings that would not be politic to express.[23] As pointed out earlier, he stressed the necessity of making the best of everything: his *Commonplace Book* has many such items as "Chi la dura, la vince"; and "He bearith his misery best, that hydith it most."[24] Harvey also did not believe in attack-

---

[21] *Marginalia*, p. 155.
[22] *Ibid.*, p. 143.
[23] *Ibid.*, p. 56.
[24] *Ibid.*, pp. 91, 95.

ing or fighting back against those in power. Under the year 1579 he writes in his *Marginalia*:

"Frowardness towards any is one of the basist, vilest, rudest, and grosest qualities in the world; but toward the prince or any princely peere, a most absurd, senceles, and pernitious property." He then cynically adds that such frowardness doesn't do any good anyway.[25] Among his Latin maxims occur such gems as the following: "Learn from a dog how skillfully to treat a Lord or a King. Endure anything in the way of wrongs and fawn none the less."[26]

Hobbinol's praise of Bishop Young would be most appropriate, for Young was Harvey's firm friend, and had supported him in an earlier crisis at Cambridge (in 1573), when some of the fellows at Pembroke, irked by Harvey's arrogance, unsociability, intellectual independence[27] and tolerance for widely divergent shades of religious thought and opinion, tried to prevent Harvey from getting his M.A. degree. Young, then master of Pembroke, after vainly writing letters in Harvey's behalf, made a trip to Cambridge from London and smashed the opposition to Harvey.[28] In his quarrel with Nashe, Harvey in his *Pierces Supererogation* lists "milord the bishop of Rochester" among the illustrious who have supported and commended him.[29]

[25] P. 150.
[26] *Marginalia*, p. 56.
[27] Harvey was sometimes considered arrogant because he did not bow to ancient prejudices. He thought that a man should receive that consideration which his abilities and achievements deserved, and the fact that his father was a ropemaker should not have any bearing on the matter. According to McKerrow (*Nashe*, V, 68), in the struggle between servility and independence Nashe stood for the past, the Harveys for the future: "This indeed is the very head and front of their offending, that they did not realize their proper station, and could never by any slights or ill usage be made to learn it."
[28] *Marginalia*, p. 12. Five of Harvey's letters in the *Letter-Book* are addressed to Bishop Young in relation to this quarrel.
[29] *Works*, II, 83.

The next speech of Hobbinol's that squares with Harvey's character is his statement that night-and-day watchfulness is too much for flesh and blood. This extreme interference with play and sleep—even though for a good reason—went against Harvey's philosophy of moderation, which was one of the main rules of his life. Twice in eight pages in his collected *Marginalia* he writes: "Labor, cibus, potus, somnus, Venus: omnia Mediocria."[30] To Harvey all extremes were bad; moreover, he seems to have regarded moderation not so much as a philosophic or ethical principle as a ladder to success. In his quest of fame, however, Harvey was most immoderate. Spenser was well aware of this contradiction between Harvey's theory and his inordinate ambition, and poked good-natured fun at this contradiction. In Latin verses addressed to Harvey in his letter of October 5, 1579, Spenser makes Harvey the philosopher of the golden mean. He writes:

> But a safe road still divides the abyss through the middle,
> For you would describe as a wise man only one who wished
>   to appear
> Neither too much of a fool nor a mentor shrewd beyond
>   measure.

Spenser then goes on to say that Harvey, in his pursuit of fame and glory, should not spurn love, marriage, and money, but should also follow the mean here.[31]

Hobbinol bows out in this eclogue with emphasis on his own lowly financial position: but if God favored him, Diggon would in turn "find favour and ease" through Hobbinol's generosity. Nevertheless Hobbinol offers the comfort of his modest cottage, "Till fayrer Fortune shewe forth her head." Poverty was indeed Harvey's constant attendant during his life, and even a friendly

[30] Pp. 175, 183.

[31] *Variorum Spenser, The Prose Works*, Rudolf Gottfried, ed. (Baltimore, 1949), p. 257, lines 188–95 (as translated by Gottfried).

interpreter like Smith suggests that the ascetic life adopted by
Harvey, with its emphasis on moderation, was probably forced
on him by his impecuniosity as well as by his principles.[32] But at
least in 1579 he could hope for "fayrer Fortune." After 1580,
however, he was thwarted in almost everything he undertook, and
one can only admire his resiliency and fortitude, meeting, as he
did, defeat after defeat in practically every academic and worldly
ambition.

After this examination of Hobbinol as a dramatic presentation
of Gabriel Harvey, we might ask some pertinent questions. Is
Hobbinol-Harvey, as H. S. V. Jones declares, "the philosopher of
the *Calender*," and do we find in the principles of Harvey, especially that of moderation, a principle of unity for the *Shepheardes
Calender* as a whole? And do the sentiments of Palinode in *May*,
as Jones declares, also somewhat represent Harvey?[33] And how far
does Hobbinol also express Spenser's views?

All of the characters of the *Calender* are in a sense philosophers,
and many of them utter sentiments that Spenser would be in
accord with, but, in my judgment at least, Spenser would be poles
apart from practically every philosophic attitude expressed by
Hobbinol. I do think Jones is right when he singles out two lines
of Palinode in *May*,

> Let none mislike of that may not be mended
> So conteck soone by concord mought be ended;[34]

and declares that these lines represent a point of view of Harvey's.
This is a shrewd observation, for they certainly do. And in other
ways, too, Palinode expresses points of view characteristic of Harvey, such as his suggesting that the clergy should not criticize each
other in public and thereby furnish ammunition for their ene-

[32] *Marginalia*, p. 56.
[33] *A Spenser Handbook* (New York, 1930), pp. 44–53.
[34] Ll. 162–63.

mies, and that we should make a sensible compromise with certain existing evils. Of course, if Spenser wished specifically to represent Harvey in *May*, Hobbinol and not Palinode would be the interlocutor who elicits Piers' account of the shortcomings of the clergy. Like Hobbinol, Palinode is in part an opposition character in the dramatic framework of the *Calender*, whose purpose is to provoke Piers to elicit criticism of ecclesiastical evils.

Perhaps the best statement of the fundamental difference in outlook between Spenser and Harvey can be found in the draft of the letter already referred to, which Harvey wrote (probably in 1579) in answer to a letter, "or rather bill of complaynte," of Spenser's. This letter was widely quoted and analyzed in the journals over twenty-five years ago in relation to the dating of the *Cantos of Mutability*. Scholarly acceptance of Evelyn May Albright's contention that this letter refers to these Cantos (and hence she would date them as early as 1579) has been scant.[35] I intend to use this letter only as a statement of Harvey's views; however, it might well be suggested that there is a strong correspondence between the ideas that Harvey takes objection to in Spenser's "bill of complaint" and material in the *Calender*. As I have already quoted Harvey's rebuke to Spenser over his exalted notion of the envied lot of Cambridge scholars—the Paradise that Adam lost—I won't develop this point any further.

Another fundamental difference in outlook between Spenser and Harvey is that on the golden age. Harvey was not only a follower of the philosophy of Bodin, but was also temperamentally disinclined to look back to earlier ages of golden virtue. Such notions exasperated him. They were only folk tales based on an

[35] Evelyn May Albright, "Spenser's Reason For Rejecting the *Cantos of Mutability*," *SP*, XXV (1928), 93–127. Scholarly reaction to Albright's article is well summarized in the Variorum, *Faerie Queene, Books Six and Seven* (Baltimore, 1938), pp. 441–449.

ignorance of history and on a turning away from the central doctrine of Christianity—the fall of man which brought sin into the
world as well as man's never-ending conflict with the world, the
flesh, and the devil. And so he chides Spenser:

> Sir, yower newe complaynte of the newe worlde is nye as
> owlde as Adam and Eve, and full as stale as the stalest fashion
> that hath bene in fasshion since Noes fludd. You crie oute of
> a false and trecherous worlde, and therein ar passing elo-
> quent and patheticall in a degree above the highest. Nowe I
> beseeche you, Syr, did not Abel live in a false and trecherous
> worlde, that was so villanouslye and cruelly murtherid of his
> owne very brother? Na, did not ould Grandsier himself live
> in a false and trecherous worlde, that was so suttellye and
> fraudulentlye putt beside so incomparablely riche and good-
> lye possession as Paraside [sic] was?
>
> The storyes to this effecte—Tower of Babel, Sodome—are
> notoriouslye knowne; there be infinite thousands of examples
> to proove that the first men in the worlde were as well ower
> masters in villanye as either predecessours in tyme or fathers
> in consanguinitye. Lett us not be so injurious to remaender
> antiquitye as to deprive the fardest of, of his due commenda-
> tion, nether must we be so parcially affectionate towards any
> as, against ower owne consciences, to conceale these notori-
> ous and infamous trecheryes. Undowtidlye the verye worlde
> itselfe millions of yeares before the creation was predestinate
> to be a schoolehouse and shopp of all villanyes, and even
> then I suppose the ilfavoritid sprites and divells that nowe
> so truble and infecte the world were a devissinge and pre-
> meditatinge those infinite severall kindes and varietyes of
> wickednes, that immediately after the creation and ever since
> they have so basely blowne abroade and so cuninglye plantid
> in everye quarter and corner of the worlde.[36]

A little later in this letter he declares:

> You suppose the first age was the goulde age. It is nothinge

[36] *Letter-Book*, pp. 82–83.

soe. Bodin defendith the goulde age to flourishe nowe, and
owr first grandfathers to have rubbid thorowghe in the iron
and brasen age at the beginninge when all things were rude
and unperfitt in comparison of the exquisite finesse and
delicaye, that we are growen unto at these days.[37]

In the various eclogues all these points of view opposed by
Harvey have their spokesmen. For instance, in *February*, Thenot
adverts to the cyclic degeneration of the world.

Must not the world wend in his commun course,
From good to badd, and from badde to worse,
From worse unto that is worst of all
And then returne to his former fall? (11–14)

Piers in *May* gives a long exposition of the primitive purity of the
church when pastors lived simply and worked zealously for the
spiritual welfare of their flock. But times have changed, and now
there is a mad scramble for power, wealth, and luxury. Piers too
believes that this beautiful past can be recovered:

The time was once, and may againe retorne
(For ought may happen, that hath bene beforne). (103–104)

Thomalin in *July* goes over much the same ground as Piers.
That Abel who in Harvey's letter lived in "a false and trecherous
worlde" is pointed to by Thomalin (who has often heard Algrind
speak on this matter) as the ideal shepherd in an ideal society:

As meeke he was, as meeke mought be,
     simple, as simple sheep,
Humble, and like in eche degree
     the flocke, which he did keep. (129–32)

Thomalin cites other examples from primitive times such as the
twelve sons of Jacob, Moses and his brother Aaron, all of whom
are the very antithesis of the proud, ambitious, and avaricious
shepherds of the new age. But let us take the whole picture of

[37] *Ibid.*, p. 86.

antiquity, says Harvey: let us also consider the stories of the Tower of Babel and Sodom and Gomorrah.

To Harvey, the golden age was hoary nonsense. As a man of action, a would-be leader in the world of affairs, he scoffed at dream worlds, ideal republics, or theoretical societies. In his *Marginalia* he wrote: "Vivimus in Smithi Rep: non in Mori Utopia; aut Platonis Politeia; aut regno Xenophontis."[38] He thought that "ranging and transcending generalityes in abstracto et contemplativo, and in the clowdes [to be], nothing but idle and vain speculations. Idle heddes ar in their transcenditibus, et in nubibus: politique Witts, evermore in concreto activo."[39]

Another marked difference between Spenser and Harvey was their attitude towards romantic love. To Harvey romantic love was ridiculous on a number of counts: (1) it made man miserable —and we have already explored Harvey's attitude towards melancholy; (2) it was not agreeable to his philosophy of moderation in all things; (3) it was unrealistic in terms of his practical understanding of man's human nature; and (4) it interfered with the really important thing in life: the attainment of fame through public service. In the Latin verses to Harvey contained in the letter of October 5, 1579, Spenser develops, in a bantering fashion, this last point:

A Magnanimous spirit, I know, spurs you up to the summits
Of honor and inspires your poems with emotions more
    solemn
Than light-hearted love (yet not all love is light-hearted).
Therefore you prize nothing so much as perennial fame
Or more than the radiant vision of glory divine.
Other things which the giddy mob rabble adores as its gods—

[38] P. 197.
[39] *Marginalia*, p. 199.

Fat farmlands, gold, city freeholds, alliance of friends;
What gladdens the eye, pleasing forms, pageantry, paramours
comely—
These you trample like muck and call a mocking of reason.[40]

The neo-Platonic concept of love, which is so beautifully de-scribed by Piers in *October*—the "immortall mirrhor" that lifts one "up out of the loathsome myre" and raises "ones mynd above the starry skie"—was, of course, something that Harvey could never respond to. I have already mentioned his unsympathetic notations in his copy of *The Courtier*. He believed in the domi-nance of man's reason, but thought it reasonable and realistic to give the emotions and passions a moderate scope and satisfaction. In this same letter, he writes:

> You suppose it a foolish madd worlde, wherein all thinges are overruled by fansye. What greater error? All things else ar but troble of minde and vexation of spiritt. Untill a mans fansye be satisfied, he wantith his most soveraigne contente-ment, and cannot never be at quiet in himselfe. You suppose most of these bodily and sensual pleasures ar to be aban-dondid as unlawfull and the inwarde contemplative delightes of the mind more zelously to be imbracid as most commen-dable. Good Lord, you a gentleman, a courtier, a yuthe, and go aboute to revive so owlde and stale a bookishe opinion, dead and buried many hundred yeares before you or I knewe whether there were any worlde or noe![41]

Earlier in this paragraph Harvey had reproved Spenser for being bookishly naive about the facts of life:

> You make a wonderful great matter of it, that reason, con-trarye to all reason and the custom of former ages is forcibly constraynid to yeelde her obedience, to be in a manner vassal unto appetite. See, I beseech you, how you overshoote your-

[40] *Variorum, Prose Works*, p. 256. Translated by Gottfried.
[41] *Letter-Book*, p. 86.

selfe and mistake the matter, in beinge over credulous to beleeve whotsoever is unadvisedly committid to writinge. Towards the end of this letter Harvey writes that Spenser's "greatist and most erronious suppose is that Reason should be mistrisse and Appetite attend on her ladiships person as a pore servante and handmayden of hers."[42] Harvey has, of course, been so provoked that he is taking an extreme view here, and we can't take him too seriously. And he even begins to contradict himself on the golden age, as he seems to contradict himself on his usual philosophy of making reason the rule of one's life, when he states that the belief in the dominance of reason could be more plausibly held a thousand years ago, but all things change, both in nature and the opinions and judgments of men.

> On fortye yeares the knowledge in the tunges and eloquence karrieth the creddite and flauntith it owte in her sattin dobletts and velvet hoses. Then exspireth the date of her bravery, and everye man havinge enoughe of her, philosophy and knowledge in divers naturall morall matters, must give her the Camisade and beare the swaye an other while.[43]

In reference to the *Calender*, this speech might relate to Cuddie's sorrow in *October* over the contempt of true poetry and his feeling that the palmy days of Maecenas will never return.[44] Fashions change, Harvey says, so let's not get too discouraged over the present state of affairs.

Most of the eclogues of the *Calender* are complaints of one sort or another—on figurative unrequited love or the prophetic death of some "mayden of greate bloude," on the contempt of poetry, or on the many ecclesiastical ills of the time. With his philosophy of accepting the world as it is, cheerfully and realistically, Harvey believed that complaining was futile, and hence

[42] P. 87.
[43] P. 87.
[44] Ll. 55–78.

he would probably not be enthusiastic over the contents of the *Calender*, except for the opposition views of such characters as Hobbinol, Palinode, or Thenot in *February*.

Harvey's philosophy also led him to take an attitude towards satire much different from Spenser's. As an idealist and a perfectionist Spenser could be sharp and personal in his satire, as he often is in the *Calender*. Harvey, however, at least before 1580, was more of a philosophic critic of the world's evils; and on principle he thought it impolitic and futile to attack the great and the powerful or get unduly concerned about the sins of humanity. But Harvey was also writing satirical verses in 1579, for Spenser mentions in the Harvey-Spenser letters how well Dyer liked Harvey's satirical verses. Perhaps his *Speculum Tuscanismi*, which Harvey offered as an example of a "bolde Satyricall Libell," would not be characteristic of Harvey. Lord Oxford, incited by John Lyly, apparently took offense at it as an attack on himself (thereby admitting the cap fitted). However, Harvey, in his quarrel with Nashe, denied that any personal reference was intended, as he also denied that he had to hide out for two weeks in Leicester's house before being apprehended and sent to the Fleet.[45]

On this matter, I would not be inclined to believe Harvey, for Harvey would necessarily have to protect himself in a satire of Oxford. However, it is also true that his *Speculum Tuscanismi* is a portrait of an Italianate fop in most general terms. Harvey was genially amused at the typical court dandy, "a passing singular odde man," and his characteristic condemnation is that the fop is

Not the like resolute man, for great and serious affayres,

Not the like Lynx, to spie out secretes, and privites of states.

In other words, if the Italianate courtier became too interested in dress and in frivolous activities, he would never become another Burghley or Walsingham. More characteristic of Harvey is his

[45] Smith, pp. 31–32.

elegy to Gascoigne in his *Letter-Book*, written about this period, in which he envisions Gascoigne as protesting against the introduction of foreign manners and dress into English life, and as writing a "New Steele Glass,/A second girdinge Satyre." Harvey reproves Gascoigne and says that we must accept the world as it is and not be concerned about these things:

> What George? I pray thee spare the world
> And give men leave to temporize
> Our tyme is short, weele lawghe with the
> If once to heaven we take our rise.[46]

Temporizing, in fact, is almost too euphemistic a term for the extent to which Harvey would often go in placating the powerful in self-abasement and flattery and in philosophically accepting downright abuses. He writes in his *Marginalia*:

> It is an honest service to serve the Tyme
> When vice doith well, lett vertu go.[47]

Spenser, we hardly need remind ourselves, could never accept this point of view. Spenser thought that whenever evil is encountered it should be attacked immediately and resolutely.

At times, however, Spenser praises Harvey's pragmatic approach to life, his hard-bitten sense of the value of the practical. In his Latin verses to Harvey, Spenser confesses that he wins

> Every vote of approval who mingles use with delight.
> Long ago the gods made me the gift of delight, but not of the useful:
> O would they have given the useful, even now, along with delight.[48]

Spenser then goes on to say that Harvey has the combination of both, but it is fairly clear that Spenser is paying his respects to

---

[46] *Letter-Book*, pp. 68–70.
[47] P. 104.
[48] *Variorum, Prose*, p. 257. Translated by Gottfried.

Harvey's addiction to the practical, but that he himself has no real intention of changing.

We might well ask whether Spenser and Harvey had anything in common. A genuine friendship undoubtedly existed between the two men, but it is one of those perhaps not uncommon friendships where there is an opposition in temperament and fundamental philosophy. Both admired men of action, and, on the positive side, both believed that literature should exemplify ideals of valor and virtue. Harvey, of course, did not have the interest in pure literature that he had in the practical sciences of law and government, and he thought that authorship was a poor substitute for a life of action, but his conception of the proper function of the writer was similar to Spenser's. It was, in the words of Professor H. S. Wilson, "to praise and immortalize heroic deeds; to honor virtue and valor; to enhance the excellence of the English tongue and to excel the greatest writers in Europe."[49]

In religious attitudes Spenser and Harvey were fairly close together.[50] Both were thoroughgoing Anglicans, but Harvey unlike Spenser, had no tendencies toward mysticism; rather he was somewhat of a rationalist in his approach to religion. Harvey was

[49] Adams Memorial Studies, p. 717.

[50] The best treatment of Spenser's and Harvey's religious ideas can be found in Virgil K. Whitaker, Religious Basis of Spenser's Thought, Harvey's on pp. 63–68. Whitaker has, I think, made it clear that Spenser's sympathies were entirely with the conservative party in the Established Church, and that his few deviations from Anglican doctrine were Catholic rather than Calvinistic in origin.

Whitaker has also made it clear that Harvey had no sympathy for Calvinism as a theology or as a form of Church government. Harvey was repelled by the intolerance of certain Puritans, their daily "freshe span newe opinions," their subjectivism in condemning the "ancient fathers and Doctors of the Church" in their reliance on the "inner light," and their constant invective against the Pope: "the Divell not so hated as the Pope."

very interested in Lutheran and Catholic theological thought, and his extreme tolerance sometimes led to ridiculous interpretations of his position. He was sometimes called a Puritan, but, as Smith writes, he was "as little a Puritan as any man could be."[51] Smith calls Harvey's analysis of the Marprelate controversy in his letter to Lyly (dated November 5, 1589) as wise and far-sighted as anything written in the whole of the sixteenth century. Here, Harvey

> shows that a perfect system of church government is not to be had in a day, that the Primitive church adapted itself to temporal circumstances, and that the creation of a theocracy represented by ministerial rule in every parish would be intolerable. The better scholar, he says, the colder schismatic. We must have mutual charity or Church and State will be overthrown.[52]

In conclusion, then, it may be said that except for one or two cases of obvious irony, Hobbinol in the *Shepheardes Calender* is a dramatic presentation of Gabriel Harvey, a portrayal which, with fair accuracy, adjusts Hobbinol's speeches to the known character and philosophy of Harvey—a character and philosophy which stand in remarkable contrast to many of those values and attitudes which we consider Spenserian. And it is perhaps one of the great ironies of the Elizabethan age that Spenser, the dreamer and uncompromising idealist, succeeded, whereas Harvey, the practical man and compromising realist, failed.[53]

[51] *Marginalia*, p. 54.
[52] *Ibid.*, pp. 58–59.
[53] An excellent account of Harvey is given by Mary Parmenter in her unpublished dissertation, "Colin Clout and Hobbinol: A Reconsideration of the Spenser-Harvey Relationship."

XVI

Edward Dyer as Cuddie

CUDDIE, who appears in three eclogues, is one of the most interesting characters in the *Shepheardes Calender*. Both as malcontent and poet, he has attracted a variety of readers. If, as E. K. writes, the characters in the twelve eclogues represent Spenser's "familiar freendes and best acquayntaunce," it would be most reasonable to seek Cuddie's identification in the two circles of friends in which Spenser moved and worked in 1578 and 1579: (1) that of Bishop Young of Rochester (and the other Court and London-area bishops with whom Young was closely associated); (2) that of the Earl of Leicester and the group at Leicester House, where in late 1579 Spenser was employed in some capacity, resided at times, and enjoyed the friendship of Philip Sidney and Edward Dyer (as the Spenser-Harvey letters tell us). Here stressing Spenser's association with the Leicester group, I wish to present evidence in this chapter that Spenser intended to portray Edward Dyer in Cuddie of the *Shepheardes Calender*—a suggestion which, as far as I know, has never been made.

Scholars have not been able to agree on the identity of Cuddie.

262

Herford thinks Cuddie of the February eclogue is not the same character as Cuddie of the August and October eclogues, but the rest ignore this problem and concentrate on Cuddie of *October*. R. W. Church and Higginson suggest that *October's* Cuddie may be Edward Kirke; Fleay hesitantly suggests Fulke Greville. The others disagree over the extent to which Cuddie stands for Colin Clout or Spenser. Warton and Collier thought that Colin and Cuddie were different persons. On the other hand, Craik, Lowell, Grosart, and Jusserand identify them. Herford and Renwick believe that they are distinct persons, but that Cuddie in certain ways represents Spenser's position and attitude.[1]

The Spenser-Harvey letters amply attest Spenser's friendly association with Edward Dyer. Dyer is mentioned together with Sidney in eight places, and once separately.[2] In his letter of October 15 and 16, 1579, Spenser remarks that Sidney and Dyer have him "in some use of familiarity" and asks Harvey to imagine what things were said by the three of them to Harvey's "credite and estimation." Later in the letter Spenser promises to show Harvey's verses to Sidney and Dyer.

Spenser evidently felt a little freer with Dyer than with Sidney, for in the same letter he wrote that he intended to dedicate *My Slomber* and "other Pamphlets" to Dyer rather than to Sidney. Spenser had prefaced this remark by mentioning how the author of the *School of Abuse*, which was dedicated to Sidney, was for his labor scorned. "Suche follie is it not to regarde aforehande the inclination and qualities of him to whome wee dedicate oure Bookes." In his next letter (of April, 1580) Spenser wrote Harvey: "Truste me, you will hardly beleeve what great good liking and estimation Maister Dyer had of your Satyricalle verses. . . ." Harvey also intended to dedicate his virelays to Dyer, in his *Letter-*

---

[1] See Var., pp. 334, 374–76.
[2] See *Variorum, The Prose Works,* p. 250.

Book terming him "In a manner oure onlye Inglish Poett."[3] It would, then, indeed be strange if Spenser, in the many personal allusions in the Calender, should not celebrate his friendship for Dyer, influential courtier and the most important Court poet of the time.

That the mysterious Cuddie is a friend of Spenser's cannot be doubted, for he is twice referred to by Harvey in his "Gallant Familiar Letter" dealing with English Reformed Versifying. Harvey writes Spenser that he will henceforth give over trifling (i.e., his verses) and concentrate on studies and pursuits that will carry with them a certain material reward. "For, I pray you, what saith M. Cuddie, alias you know who, in the tenth Aeglogue of the foresaid famous new Calender?" He then quotes the two stanzas from October in which Cuddie bemoans the fact that from his poetry he "Little good has got, and much lesse gayne." Harvey then goes on to say that it might be different in Spenser's case ("Master Colin Clout is not everybody"); and even though Cuddie and Harvey ("old companions" of Spenser) have not profited from their verses, Spenser, by means of special favor of "Mistresse Poetrie," and "some personall priviledge, may happely live by Dying Pellicanes, and purchase great lands, and Lordshippes, with the money which his Calender and Dreames have, and will affourde him."

As I have pointed out in earlier chapters, many of the names in the eclogues are fairly literal or easily decipherable.[4] In itself the name Cuddie is not as obvious as many others, but it could represent Edward Dyer or Cosn (Cousine)[5] Dyer, one of the

[3] P. 89.
[4] I concede that what is literal and obvious to me might not be so to another scholar.
[5] See Ralph M. Sargent, At the Court of Queen Elizabeth: The Life and Lyrics of Sir Edward Dyer (London and New York, 1935), p. 66, for the use of Cosn, a term which was employed as a friendly or familiar term

foremost members of the group at Leicester House. But the literal closeness of the name, or absence of such closeness, has little to do with the strength of my arguments for this identification.

Cuddie first appears in the February eclogue. Although in the Argument we are told that *February* is "rather morall and generall then bent to any secrete or particular purpose," a gloss informs us that Cuddie, "whose person is secrete," is a real person in love with Phyllis, "the name of some mayde unknowen." Compared with the later ecclesiastical eclogues, *February* is indeed "morall and generall," but Spenser gives us a few clues to Cuddie's identity. In the Argument Cuddie is called an "unhappy Heardmans boye," a term whose significance has been hitherto overlooked. Although Spenser is not entirely consistent, a gloss either gives us direct information (Hobbinol is Harvey), or terms are used that reveal his intentions. In the ecclesiastical eclogues, for instance, a shepherd is a bishop, and a shepherd's boy (like Colin in *September*) is someone serving a bishop in some capacity or other. A "Heardmans boye" would suggest someone closely associated with Leicester, who in 1565 was given permission to establish a quasi-royal retinue of a hundred personal fol-

---

of address or designation in court circles. Sargent's excellent life of Dyer proved to be most useful to me in writing this chapter.

In the back of John Dee's *Pety Navy Royal* (which was printed in 1577 through Dyer's help) are verses addressed to Christopher Hatton. One cryptic stanza reads:

M' Instructor's freend did warrant me,
You would do so, as he did his:
*E.D.   That *Redy freend, can witness be
Esq.   For higher States, what written is:

In these lines M (or Mechanician) stands for Dee; the instructor is Hatton; and the friend is Dyer. Cited by Parmenter, *Harvey*, p. 210 (Library of Congress copy used by Parmenter).

Redy, identified by the intials on the margin, is a pun based on the sound of Dyer's initials—E. D. Perhaps *Cuddie* is another name for Dyer constructed in a similar fashion.

lowers—his herd.[6] Leicester was in fact the only Herdman,[7] i.e., powerful member of the nobility, with whom Spenser was closely connected in 1579. Dyer and Sidney were the most important "Herdman's boys" with whom Spenser was on friendly terms at this time, but the internal evidence of this eclogue, as well as of the later eclogues in which Cuddie appears, points to Dyer as the "unhappy Heardman's boye." In fact, most probably *February* good-naturedly satirizes the dominant note of Dyer's lyrics and mirrors his situation at the time of the composition of the *Calender*. To clarify my subsequent arguments, at this point I will give a brief sketch of the pertinent facts in Dyer's career.

Edward Dyer, one of the earliest and finest of Elizabethan lyric poets, attended Oxford between 1558 and 1561; there, according to Anthony à Wood, Dyer first revealed "his natural inclination to poetry" and also his "excellency in bewailing and bemoaning the perplexities of love."[8] Coming to Court (probably in 1565 after the death of his father), Dyer, the possessor of at least a dozen manorial estates of moderate size,[9] secured the patronage

[6] Sargent, p. 18. Dyer probably entered Leicester's service at this time. As an important member of Leicester's group, Dyer had dependents and followers (usually suppliants for royal favor). It should be noted that in Cuddie's misfortune the latter also suffer: His "ragged rontes all shiver and shake." *February*, 1. 5. In late 1579 Spenser could no doubt be included among the "ragged rontes."

[7] The main meaning of *herdman* is a keeper of a flock or herd of domestic animals. The term also means a keeper or guardian. See *NED*. The term is carefully used in the *Calender*. Cuddie is *never* a shepherd or shepherd's boy. This "cattle" metaphor is curiously used in the September eclogue, 1. 124, where powerful courtiers who alienate diocesan properties or make other exactions on churchmen are called *Bulls of Basan*. The engraver of the woodcut before *February* also carefully distinguishes between Cuddie's cattle and Thenot's sheep. This distinction is significant and must be intelligibly explained.

[8] Sargent, p. 9.

[9] According to one account, Sir Thomas Dyer left his heir Edward an income of four thousand pounds, besides fourscore thousand pounds in money (Sargent, p. 12).

of Leicester. Although nominally attached to the latter and serving him at first as a confidential agent or gentleman secretary, Dyer won a place for himself at Court and the friendship of Burghley, Hatton, Walsingham, and Henry Sidney. In 1570 the Queen, for "good and faithful service," granted Dyer the stewardship of the manor and woods of Woodstock, Oxford, for life. In 1571 Dyer experienced the capriciousness of royal favor, languishing for four years under the Queen's displeasure—and writing gloomy lyrics about his situation. In September, 1575, on the Queen's visit to the royal domain of Woodstock, and amid the pageantry prepared for Elizabeth, Dyer, as the mournful minstrel of the Oak, made a dramatic and personal appeal to her in his *Song in the Oak*. This performance returned Dyer to prominence and royal favor, winning for him as well the grant of the tanning monopoly. The latter did not prove too profitable, for in 1578 Dyer, burdened by the expenses of living at Court, importuned a loan from the Queen. On March 27, 1579, his petition was granted: three thousand pounds payable in three years, a sum which was far inadequate for his immediate needs and which he was never able to repay. With most of the Leicestrian faction who opposed the French marriage, Dyer was probably in retirement from Court—and in the Queen's displeasure—in late 1579 (when the *Calender* appeared).[10] It is generally accepted that most of Dyer's lyrics were written in the 1570's.[11]

The main purpose of *February* is, of course, the political allegory embodied in the fable of the Oak and the Briar. Cuddie and his elderly antagonist Thenot furnish the setting for the narration of this fable by their preliminary sharp-edged masculine banter. The subject of their pastoral debate is one's adjustment to misfortune, misfortune symbolized by "ranke Winter's rage,"

[10] Sargent, pp. 9–70.
[11] Sargent, p. 166.

whose "bitter blasts" Cuddie complains of in his first speech.
Thenot reproaches Cuddie for complaining of Winter's violence:
the cyclic degeneration of the world and the philosophic acceptance of adversity—based on his own experience—are the staples
of Thenot's argument. Cuddie banteringly replies that it is no
wonder that Thenot can cheerfully bear "Winter's wrathfull
cheere,"

> For Age and Winter accord full nie,
> This chill, that cold, this crooked, that wrye . . .
> But my flowring youth is foe to frost,
> My shippe unwont in stormes to be tost. (27–32)

Thenot, in pastoral fashion, then characterizes the presumption
and folly of Cuddie and other "heardgroomes": When the sun
once shines, they think spring has entirely arrived, scorn the cold,
and think they are "Lords of the yeare."

> But eft, when ye count you freed from feare,
> Comes the breme winter with chamfred browes,
> Full of wrinckles and frostie furrowes:
> Drerily shooting his stormy darte,
> Which cruddles the blood, and pricks the harte.
> Then is your carelesse corage accoied,
> Your carefull heards with cold bene annoied.
> Then paye you the price of your surquedrie,
> With weeping, and wayling, and misery. (42–50)

In reply, Cuddie chaffingly gives the argument a new turn when
he, scorning Thenot's wisdom as unsuitable for youth, declares:

> But were thy yeares greene, as now bene myne,
> To other delights they would encline.
> Tho wouldest thou learne to caroll of Love,
> And hery with hymnes thy lasses glove. (59–62)

Thenot philosophically answers that "All that is lent to love, will
be lost." Cuddie retorts that love is the vitalizing force of life.

As a final rebuke to the pride and folly of ambitious youth in scorning age, Thenot tells the fable of the Oak and Briar.

Both the bitterness of Cuddie's complaint against fortune and his general situation match Dyer's position in 1578–1579 and the tone of his characteristic lyrics. In such poems as *A Fancy, I Would It Were Not As It Is,* and *Divide My Times,* Dyer expresses his utter wretchedness in terms that echo Cuddie's complaint. For instance, in *Divide My Times* Dyer laments:

> For Carefull thought, and sorow sundry waies
> Consumes my youth before my aged daies.

His ambition has been thwarted:

> Kept from the reach wherto it would desire.[12]

In *I Would It Were Not As It Is* Dyer stresses the agonies of disappointed ambition. To his sorrow he has learned

> That he that lyfts his heart to hye
> Must be contente to pine and dye.[13]

In *February* Cuddie, of course, on one level represents ambitious youth fretfully and unhappily encountering disappointments and misfortunes; and Thenot (here the eclogue is perhaps "morall and generall") represents philosophic old age counseling patience and fortitude. In his thrice thirty years Thenot has faced life without complaint, never opposed fortune,

> But gently tooke, that ungently came.[14]

In his lyrics Dyer so often speaks the very sentiments of Cuddie that it is possible to believe that in *February* Spenser is indulging in some lighthearted banter and in a friendly fashion is mocking his friend Dyer's mournful lyrical note.

If we provisionally accept Cuddie as a portrait of Dyer, we can

[12] Sargent, pp. 177–79.
[13] Sargent, pp. 180–81, 11. 47–48.
[14] *February,* 1. 22.

detect some hidden meanings in *February*. For instance, when
Thenot advises Cuddie,

> The soveraigne of seas he blames in vaine,
> That once seabeate, will to sea againe,[15]

perhaps Elizabeth is referred to (in spite of the gloss on Nep-
tune), and Dyer is being told that since he knows from experience
the uncertainty of courtly favor, he has only himself to blame for
subjecting himself to such hazards. The further assertion against
Cuddie and other "Loytring" herdgrooms,

> And when the shining sunne laugheth once
> You deemen, the Spring is come attonce,

would likewise fit Dyer. In common Elizabethan symbolism, the
sun would represent the Sovereign. Dyer is being told in effect
that just because the Queen smiles with favor upon him once, it
is no sign that the game has been won and that thenceforth he
will bask uninterruptedly in the warm rays of the royal regard.
The reference to Phyllis in this eclogue and in the gloss would
also be significant, for Dyer, as Coridon, had been singing his
hopeless love for the nymph Phyllis in lyrics whose sprightliness
belied his broken heart. In *Alas, My Heart* Dyer concludes:

> Die, Coridon, the spoile of Phyllis eye:
> She cannot love, and therefore thou must die.[16]

The important thing to remember here is that Spenser was closely

---

[15] Ll. 33–34. Between 1576 and 1579 Dyer was closely associated with
Dr. John Dee, who (with the whole Leicester group) was a prime mover of
the idea of Elizabeth as Sovereign (or Queen) of the seas. In 1577 Dyer
made possible the printing of Dee's *Pety Navy Royal*, which stressed the
necessity of having in permanent commission an adequate fleet of vessels
to be used in commerce as well as war. Parmenter, *Harvey*, pp. 208–11.

[16] Sargent, p. 189, ll. 29–30. In Sidney's *Arcadia* Coridon represents
Dyer (Sargent, p. 66). Philisides (Sidney) declares in the song in the
third eclogue in *Arcadia* that (on his return from his three year continental
tour in 1575) Languet relinquished his mentorship and
> To worthy Coridon he gave me ore.

associated with Dyer in 1579, through him and Sidney and Leicester Spenser hoped to win preferment at Court, and Phyllis would have meaning principally in terms of Spenser's immediate circle of friends at this time.[17]

Cuddie does not play a very important role in the August eclogue as the judge in the singing match between Perigot and Willy, two shepherd boys. But note the consistency with *February* in the designation of Cuddie: the Argument before *August* carefully calls Cuddie a "neatheards boye," and three times in the eclogue proper Cuddie is called a "heardgroom." In the gloss it is intimated that Perigot is a real person, and in the eclogue we are told that he earlier had lost a spotted lamb in a song contest with Colin Clout. If Cuddie is Dyer, no better arbiter could be chosen, for Dyer at that time was the recognized and outstanding Court poet. *August* concludes with Cuddie's reciting a "dooleful verse of Rosalind that Colin made," a tribute to the poet of the *Calender*, but also a possible tribute to Dyer, who was Spenser's predecessor and possible model in "dooleful" love lyrics. In fact, the whole Rosalind portion of the *Calender*, its allegory aside, by way of imitation could well be a tribute to Dyer, for in such "bewailing and bemoaning" Dyer was justly famous.

The whole of the October eclogue fits Dyer perfectly. At times Spenser has, of course, himself in mind in the character of Cuddie, and a gloss intimates as much. Spenser's problem was also Dyer's, but it is easy to detect when Cuddie is speaking for poets in general at the Court of the Queen and when for himself. At one time in this eclogue Cuddie confesses his inability to write on heroic and epic subjects (as far as we know Dyer never wrote anything other than short lyrics), and that Colin Clout is better

[17] I recognize, of course, that *Phyllis*, besides occurring in Virgil and Horace, was widely employed in pastoral poetry.

able to attempt such flights—and would, too, were he not in love.[18]

Here it might be well to stress that the *Calender* is primarily a dramatic poem. The characters of the *Calender*—Spenser's "familiar freendes and best acquayntaunce"—express their own experiences and points of view, and at times these experiences and points of view are clearly not Spenser's. Cuddie of the October eclogue would exemplify the dramatic nature of the *Calender*: he is a recognized Court poet who has never been properly rewarded for his graceful lyrics; he has consequently become thoroughly disillusioned and has ceased to write poetry. Also he has apparently never written in the epic vein. This situation would certainly not fit Spenser, who was making his confident poetic debut in the *Calender* and was working on the first draft of his epic, the *Faerie Queene* (as the Spenser-Harvey letters tell us).

Dyer is, I think, the only poet of the time who in 1579 could be called "the perfecte patterne of a Poet"—as Cuddie is called in the Argument before *October*. For almost twenty years he had been recognized as the model courtly poet.[19] Philip Sidney, of course, was beginning to be known as a poet among the small group of kindred spirits at Leicester House; and Spenser, in his meetings with, or unpublished letters to, Harvey, must have spoken about Sidney's poetic abilities in glowing terms, for Harvey in the published letters praises Dyer and Sidney in extravagant fashion. For instance, in his "Gallant Familiar Letter" (probably written in late April, 1580) Harvey calls Dyer and Sidney "the two very Diamondes of hir Majesties Courte." Later in the letter he mentions that a "worshipfull Hartefordshyre Gentleman" of his acquaintance lacked a good poetic pattern for his verses such as Sidney or Dyer would have been able to furnish. In the same letter Harvey calls Dyer and Sidney the "incompa-

[18] *October*, 11. 85–90.
[19] See Sargent, pp. 166–73.

rable and myraculous *Gemini*," whom, as poets, he would chalk up in the "Catalogue of our very principall Englishe *Aristarchi*." But as we might gather from Gosson's dedication of the *School of Abuse* to Sidney, the latter was not generally known as a poet in 1579.[20]

Spenser is, of course, thinking of himself and his future as well as of Dyer, when Cuddie, "finding no maintenaunce of his state and studies, complayneth of the contempte of Poetrie and the causes thereof: Specially having bene in all ages, and even amongst the most barbarous, alwayes of singular accounpt and honor. . . ."[21] But if we can judge from Dyer's financial troubles in 1578 and 1579, as well as from his earlier experiences, there were real grounds for dissatisfaction on Dyer's part.

Let us examine *October* in part, noticing how the speeches fit Dyer, who had begun to give up verse-writing about 1579.[22] In the first six lines Piers tells Cuddie to hold up his "heavie head."

> Whilome thou wont the shepheardes laddes to leade,
> In rymes, in ridles, and in bydding base:
> Now they in thee, and thou in sleepe are dead.

In his reply, Cuddie complains that from his poetry he

> Little good hath got, and much lesse gayne.

Piers then points out the glory and moral usefulness of Poetry in its ability to kindle and restrain, but Cuddie reiterates the lack of material reward for poetry: something more substantial than praise is required. Piers then encourages Cuddie to abandon his "dapper ditties" and sing of heroic subjects—of Elizabeth and Leicester. Cuddie replies that Virgil through the encouragement

[20] See *Variorum Spenser, The Prose Works*, p. 251 (commentary on 11. 50–52).
[21] Argument before *October*.
[22] Sargent, p. 166. We have no certainty about the dating of most of Dyer's extant lyrics, but Sargent believes that Dyer's poetic activities "flourished in the 1570's."

of Maecenas did leave the pastoral for the epic vein, but such patrons, and heroic subjects for the poet's verse as well, have disappeared, and poetry has come into contempt or withered in the degeneracy of later ages.

> But ah *Mecoenas* is yclad in claye,
> And great *Augustus* long ygoe is dead:
> And all the worthies liggen wrapt in leade,
> That matter made for Poets on to play:
> For ever, who in derring doe were dreade,
> The loftie verse of hem was loved aye.
>
> But after vertue gan for age to stoupe,
> And mighty manhode brought a bedde of ease:
> The vaunting Poets found nought worth a pease,
> To put in preace emong the learned troupe.
> Tho gan the streames of flowing wittes to cease,
> And sonnebright honour pend in shamefull coupe. (61–72)

In the last part of *October* Cuddie stresses the tyrannical power of love: the poet cannot love or be oppressed by economic problems and be a poet at the same time. Wine is the only true friend of poetry. With the help of Bacchus, Cuddie could write of heroic subjects. But his ambition cools: true content is in the humble life.

Dyer certainly never profited from his verses, or from his services to Queen and country. In the latter he had by 1578 dissipated a modest competence, and had gone hopelessly in debt.[23] In the

---

[23] Not only from Dyer's poems, but from contemporary anecdotes we get the impression that Dyer was treated in somewhat shabby fashion by the Queen and given promises which were never fulfilled. William Oldys relates one encounter between the two. "Sir Edward," once said Elizabeth to the pensive Dyer, "what does a man think when he thinks of nothing?" "A woman's promise," Dyer answered with a smile. The Queen was nettled by his reply. Sargent, p. 131.

speeches of Cuddie and Piers and in the glosses of E. K. there is a direct plea for a return to an earlier doctrine of patronage which decreed that Princes should support poets "for the sake of the present fame and future remembrance."[24] At least by implication there is a strong criticism of Elizabeth and her chief minister Burghley for failing to sustain poetry. In the Argument before *October* E. K. bluntly writes that Poetry has "bene in all ages, and even amongst the most barbarous always of singular accompt and honor"; and his following glosses are full of examples of ancient princes rewarding and honoring poets.

Cuddie's complaints and E. K.'s glosses corroborate the fact that the Queen and her chief nobles neglected belles-lettres in the first thirty years of her reign. (Their record, however, was somewhat better in utilitarian writing, for they apparently encouraged histories, handbooks of information, and works of piety and religious controversy.) The Elizabethan chiefs of State, in default of direct royal generosity to writers, assumed the burden of patronage. Their support, however, was sometimes selfish, for they were often more interested in directing and controlling public opinion through propaganda for their own political and religious objectives.[25] Leicester and his sponsorship of Puritan writers in late 1579 would be a good example of this procedure. Although Leicester had earlier helped Gascoigne, and in 1579 was employing Spenser in some capacity, his munificence to poets was not extraordinary.

The position of Dyer was, of course, somewhat different from that of Spenser. Dyer, who was a servant of the Crown and held a recognized place at Court, had written distinguished lyrics for fifteen years but was hemmed in by the current conception that poetry was the avocation of a gentleman, who neither should look

---

[24] Rosenberg, p. 3.
[25] See Rosenberg, pp. 3–9, for a full discussion of this point of view.

for reward nor hazard the stigma of print. In lieu of adequate compensation for his services to Queen and country, Dyer was perfectly willing, in his dire need, to be rewarded in the ancient manner for his poetry. Spenser, too, as a friend and fellow poet, would be interested in seeing the old order of poetic remuneration restored so that his own future would be more secure.

In his life and lyrics Dyer well illustrates the truth of Cuddie's statement that a poet cannot properly function when he is suffering from the dual tyranny of love and economic problems. The latter tyranny has already been sufficiently dwelt upon, but apart from the fact that he never married we must depend on Dyer's lyrics for the elucidation of the former. In his songs of unrequited love Dyer employs the common Petrarchan conventions, and hence it is difficult to determine the reality behind his self-conscious melancholy. In such lyrics as *The Song of the Oak, A Fancy,* and *Amidst the Fairest Mountain Tops,* Dyer is apparently mirroring his sorrow at his undeserved capricious rejection by the Queen. In the last-mentioned lyric, his platonic relationship with her collapses. He states that he

Causles be scorn'd, despis'd,

and concludes

Oh, Cynthia, thou hast angels eyes,

But yet a woman's heart.[26]

In *Alas, My Heart* and *Amarillis* Dyer sings his unrequited love for Phyllis and Amarillis, respectively. In the latter poem Dyer (as Coridon) recounts his misfortune in falling in love with one of Diana's (i.e., Elizabeth's) maids. When Diana finally turns him into an owl, he flees to the wilderness and leads a solitary life. Sometimes Amarillis goes to the wood "to heare the lay and tune of his dispare." Lest we think that all is convention and

[26] Sargent, p. 183.

feigning, Dyer pointedly reminds us in the final lines of the poem,

> Well I wott what here is ment, and though a talle it seme,
> Shadowes have ther bodies by, and so of this esteme.[27]

In the speech of Cuddie in praise of wine in the last verses of *October* it is possible that Spenser (or Dyer) is twitting Bishop Piers (the Piers of *October* as I have indicated in an earlier chapter), a close friend of both the Young and Leicester circles and a recognized teetotaler.[28] The final four lines of Cuddie on content seem to echo Dyer's most famous lyric, *My Mind To Me A Kingdom Is* (a poem, by the way, which doesn't agree in its philosophy with most of Dyer's other poems, or with his life). We do not know when Dyer wrote this poem, but it was probably written before 1580—most probably between 1571 and 1575 when he had fallen from the Queen's favor and spent much time in semi-retirement at Woodstock Park—as an expression of one side of his character, the result of a temporary philosophic acceptance of the bitter disappointments and injustices of Court life. These four lines, then, could well be a complimentary reference by Spenser to Dyer's most famous poem.

Cuddie in *Colin Clouts Come Home Againe* probably represents the same person as the Cuddie of the *Calender*. As Professor Percy W. Long has explained, Spenser is here employing a literary device: the poem, addressed primarily to the Court, is ostensibly related to his Irish friends on his return from England.[29] But these friends are of England as well as of Ireland. Hobbinol stands for Harvey (as in the *Calender*), and Cuddie probably represents Dyer. Cuddie, one of the main interlocutors of the poem, helps to elicit from Colin Clout his experiences at Court. Of the six in-

---

[27] Sargent, pp. 193–95.
[28] *DNB*, "John Piers." Bishop Piers adopted such a strict rule of abstinence that even in his last sickness his physician was unable to persuade him to take a little wine.
[29] Var., p. 451.

terruptions of Cuddie,[30] the most important occurs after Colin's
relation of the passage of Raleigh and himself to Cynthia's land.
Cuddie feigns ignorance:

> What land is that thou meanest (then Cuddy sayd)
> And is there other, than whereon we stand?[31]

Colin then rebukes Cuddie for his ignorance, and proceeds to
contrast the happy side of English life with the dangers and mis-
eries of existence in Ireland. This is information which is, of
course, well known to Dyer, but is directed to those of the Court
circle who have no proper appreciation of conditions, or Spenser's
trials, in the Savage Island. Cuddie's next two interruptions are
likewise ironical. Cuddie feigns ignorance, seeking to know how
Cynthia's land is different and what heavenly graces exist there.
Cuddie then questions Colin's extravagant praise of Cynthia,
giving Colin an opportunity to be even more extravagant in his
eulogy of the Queen.

As far as I know, Dyer's influence on Spenser has never been
investigated. Scholars no doubt feel that most of Dyer's poems,
because of his aversion to printing them, are lost beyond recall,[32]
and that the thirteen or so poems to which Dyer's authorship can
be reasonably established, furnish scanty evidence for any study

[30] Ll. 80–87; 96–99; 290–91; 304–307; 616–19; 823–34.

[31] Ll. 290–91. The irony would be further pointed by the fact that Dyer
was one of the most traveled of Elizabeth's roving ambassadors and had
become internationally famous through his imprisonment at Prague by
Emperor Rudolph in early 1591 in an incident connected with the frauds
of Edward Kelley, the celebrated alchemist. Dyer, released through the
intercession of Elizabeth and Burghley, was back in England by August,
1591. Sargent, pp. 97–122, gives an interesting account of Dyer's experiences in Bohemia. Colin Clout was probably written in late 1591. Var.,
p. 451.

[32] Sargent, pp. 165–66. Sargent writes: "Dyer's songs were not intended
to pass beyond the circle of friends to whom they were read or sung. If a
friend made a copy of one of them he was expected to preserve the
anonymity of the author" (p. 57).

of this kind. Dyer, however, in his manuscript poems and through his personal influence may well have been an important factor in Spenser's poetic development. For instance, the employment of native English words, as well as the defense of their use in the poetry of the *Calender* in the *Epistle to Harvey*, may have been due in part to Dyer. At any rate, this concern corresponds with Dyer's practice. According to Sargent, "His contemporaries recognized the native quality of Dyer's verse. Dyer's direct poetic sources are all English." [33]

In conclusion, then, a great deal of evidence indicates that Spenser was probably representing Edward Dyer as Cuddie of the *Shepheardes Calender*. This identification helps us realize Spenser's mastery of irony, gay banter, and graceful parody as well as his easy familiarity with one of the most interesting personalities and Court poets of Elizabeth's reign.

[33] Sargent, p. 165.

XVII

Fulke Greville as E. K.

THE IDENTITY of E. K., the annotator of the *Shepheardes Calender*, is one of the darkest and most controversial mysteries in Spenser scholarship. When I began my study of E. K. for this book, I believed that E. K. was probably a mask for Spenser himself. In my investigation of this problem, I was forced, however, to reverse my position: I am now firmly convinced that E. K. was someone other than the poet of the *Calender*.

The scholarship on E. K. is so voluminous and complicated that I first intended to reserve my extended analysis of it for an appendix. Editorial economy, however, forced me to drop this plan; hence I refer my readers to the summaries of the various schools of thought on E. K. in the *Variorum*. In this chapter, then, I cannot fully discuss the strong reasons and evidence that led me to conclude that E. K. was not Edward Kirke or Spenser. I will, however, here try to isolate those specific points of view that characterize E. K. and distinguish him from Spenser; second, I will suggest that E. K. probably represents Fulke Greville, who, I think, possesses most of the qualifications, and fulfills most of the conditions, that the role of commentator on the *Shepheardes Calender* demands.

I have no real quarrel with those scholars who hold that Spenser may have at times worked with E. K. and contributed a few glosses, or may have made a few additions or revisions for reasons of greater clarity or obscurity. Professor Osgood in the *Variorum* inclines to this notion, and he lists Palgrave, Fletcher, Greenlaw, Draper, and Renwick as holding substantially the same view. I believe that Spenser selected E. K. as glosser (or accepted him as a volunteer or assignee), and that E.K.—certainly a member of the Sidney circle at Leicester House—was fully aware of Spenser's intentions in the *Calender*, for he was involved in the same political events that the allegory of the poem deals with and had, as he confesses, talked things over with Spenser. I further believe that the someone else designated as E. K. largely (if not completely) wrote the Epistle to Harvey, the arguments before the eclogues, and the following glosses, and that he was of sufficient stature as a critic of poetry and as an educated man so that Spenser would not radically tamper with his views, even if Spenser had a chance to do so in seeing the *Calender* through the press. In certain glosses, like others before me, I sense in E. K. a distinct personality who differed from Spenser in certain definite ways.

Perhaps the most impressive difference between Spenser and E. K. is their attitude on the Fairy world. In a gloss to *April* E. K. writes:

> Ladyes of the lake be Nymphes. For it was an olde opinion amongste the Auncient Heathen that of every spring and fountaine was a goddesse the Soveraigne. Whiche opinion stucke in the myndes of men not manye yeares sithence by meanes of certain fine fablers and lowd lyers, such as were the Authors of King Arthure the great and such like, who tell many an unlawfull leasing of the Ladyes of the Lake, that is, the Nymphes.

Similarly E. K. glosses *Frendly faeries* in his notes to *June*:

The opinion of Faeries and elfes is very old, and yet sticketh very religiously in the myndes of some. But to roote that rancke opinion of Elfes oute of mens hearts, the truth is, that there be no such thinges, nor yet the shadowes of the things, but onely by a sort of bald Friers and knavish shavelings so feigned; which as in all other things, so in that, soughte to nousell the comen people in ignoraunce, least being once acquainted with the truth of things, they woulde in tyme smell out the untruth of theyr packed pelfe and Massepenie religion.

As C. S. Lewis (who thinks E. K. to be a very ridiculous figure) recently wrote, these two glosses express E. K.'s "humanistic and Protestant detestation of that medieval or 'Gothic' mythology which was Spenser's lifelong delight," and show how far E. K. was from Spenser's way of thought.[1] In regard to these same two glosses Professor Judson recently wrote me: "If Spenser and E. K. are consistently one, how, for example, shall we explain, on the part of one already contemplating a poem like the *Faerie Queene*, the condemnation of those who invented the Arthurian legends and of those who encouraged a belief in fairies and elves?"

C. L. Wrenn, who detected in E. K.'s commentary a mind inferior to Spenser's and a lesser knowledge of earlier English, writes that E. K. "seems more of a stiff Protestant controversialist than Spenser, as several of his comments far outgo the text in emphasis, or imply more anti-Catholic feeling than the text seems to warrant."[2] Although E. K.'s knowledge of earlier English always seemed to me to be adequate, I would accept Wrenn's judgment in this matter. From a poetic point of view, I would also agree that E. K.'s mind was probably inferior to Spenser's. I myself

[1] *English Literature in the Sixteenth Century* (Oxford, 1954), pp. 354–60.

[2] "On Re-Reading Spenser's *Shepheardes Calender*," *Essays and Studies*, by Members of the English Association, vol. 29 (1943), 42–43.

have long felt that E. K. was more of a Protestant than Spenser, but some of the anti-Catholicism of the arguments and glosses I would be inclined to explain by the passions of the moment. When E. K. wrote most of his glosses (probably in November of 1579), the hysteria against the Alençon marriage was reaching its peak. E. K. surely knew the allegory but sharpened certain glosses in appealing to the popular resentment against the French and Catholics that the allegory lent itself to. As in the arguments to *May* and *September*, E. K. even injected into certain eclogues an animus against Catholics that the text does not bear out. He made Palinode of *May* (in large part just a pastoral opposition character) a Catholic, and applied Diggon's remarks (in *September*) about the clergy of the Established Church in England and Wales to the "loose living of Popish prelates."

The fable of the Fox and the Kid in *May*, reflecting Aubigny's success in Scotland, and secretly an attack on Alençon, gave E. K. his big opportunity. The Fox also represented "false and faithlesse Papistes, to whom is no credit to be given, nor felowshippe to be used." The text's mention of "bells, babes, and glasses" in the Fox's pack suggests to E. K. the "reliques and ragges of popish superstition which put no small religion in Belles: and Babies.s Idols: and glasses.s. Paxes, and such lyke trumperies." The Fox's hind leg is wrapped in a cloth, "For with great cold he had gotte the gout." The phrase *great cold* provokes E. K. to attack Catholics thus: "For they boast much of their outward patience, and voluntarye sufferaunce as a worke of merite and holy humblenesse." The Fox used the term *sweet Saint Charitee.* E. K. explains: "The Catholiques comen othe, and onely speache, to have charitye alwayes in their mouth, and sometime in their outward Actions, but never inwardly in fayth and godly zeale." In a gloss on Pier's emblem, E. K. asks: "For if fayth be the ground of religion, which fayth they [Catholics] dayly false, what hold then is of theyr religion?"

The above-listed quotations from May's glosses with their emphasis on faith rather than on good works, even with due allowance for passions aroused by the Alençon affair would suggest that E. K. was somewhat Calvinistic in his leanings. However, in his careful study of Spenser's religious position, Virgil K. Whitaker has made clear that Spenser was a thoroughgoing Anglican without the slightest tinge of Calvinism.[3]

Wrenn thinks that E. K. is at times "pompous and prosy." He also thinks E. K. makes a clumsy guess at *glen* as a "country Hamlet or borough," and indulges in such needless glosses as that of "*neighbor towne* as the next towne."[4] C. S. Lewis also comments that E. K.'s "positive contribution to our understanding of the text is pretty fairly represented by glosses like 'neighbor towne, the next towne: expressing the Latin *vicina*.' "[5] But all these glosses relate to the allegory: E. K. wishes to emphasize that *neighbor towne* is the next town, Greenwich, where Rosalind lives. And E. K., if we rightly understand, has his tongue in cheek when he mentions the "Latin *Vicina*." Knowledge of the allegory permits us to appreciate his sly touches of humor and the significance of certain emphases. "Pompous" and "prosy," I concede, are adjectives that at times may be applied to E. K. But the pompous pose and pedantry are, I submit, very often a way of underlining the allegory.[6]

Other impressions I have of E. K. will be briefly noted. E. K. is probably a young man, for in the gloss on the emblem of *February* he takes sides finally with youth, though in a bantering

[3] *The Religious Basis of Spenser's Thought.*
[4] Pp. 42, 47.
[5] P. 355.
[6] Edwin Greenlaw long ago noticed this. "*The Shepheards Calender*," *PMLA*, XXVI (1911), 423.

fashion, in the controversy between youth and age. Next, unlike Spenser—for in the allegory, in relation to Rosalind, Colin Clout represents in the main the English people, not Spenser—E. K. is cynical and disillusioned in regard to love, for in his gloss to the emblem of *March* he zestfully amplifies, and agrees with, the theme that love is "but follye mixt with bitternesse and sorow sawced with repentaunce." Further, E. K. has probably, as Nan Carpenter brought out, a greater knowledge of music than Spenser, as *October's* glosses might indicate.[7] He has also a greater and more technical knowledge of painting, as his analogy between poetry and painting in explaining archaic diction in the Epistle might suggest. When E. K. is not on dangerous ground, I also detect a certain characteristic straightforwardness and a sly humor.

In regard to the poet himself E. K. often attempts to distinguish beween fact and convention. For instance, in the gloss to *June* on *Forsake the soil* E. K. writes: "This is no poetical fiction, but unfeynedly spoken of the Poete selfe, who for speciall occasion of private affayres (as I have bene partly of himselfe informed) and for his more preferment removing out of the Northparts came into the South, as Hobbinoll indeede advised him privately." In a gloss to *December*, E. K. comments thus on *The flagraunt flowres*: they are the "sundry studies and laudable partes of learning, wherein how our Poete is seene, be they witnesse which are privie to his study." E. K. slyly emphasizes ab-

---

[7] Miss Carpenter's analysis fits very well my suggestion of Fulke Greville as E. K.: "The musical annotations, furthermore, weight the evidence considerably, it seems to me, for the actual existence of E. K., the poet's philosophical friend. Spenser's own references to the powers of music are highly poetical: although he refers frequently to Orpheus, occasionally mentions Amphion, and devotes an entire sonnet to Arion, nowhere in his poetry does he speak of Timotheus or call any of the modes by name. E. K.'s explanations, on the other hand, are painstaking, meticulous, and filled with specific detail—just what one would expect of a scholar and philosopher . . . rather than a poet." *PMLA*, LXXI (1956), 1150.

surdities, errors, or omissions by attributing them to the principle of pastoral decorum: rustics do not know any better. For instance, in *July* Morrell refers to the hill of Paradise where shepherds fed their flocks at will until Adam's fall deprived them of this place of delight. E. K. notes that this unbiblical peopling of Paradise is an "errour of shepheards understanding." Later in the eclogue Thomalin is unable to recall the name of Aaron. E. K. comments thus: "he meaneth Aaron: whose name for more Decorum the shephearde sayeth he hath forgot, lest his remembraunce and skill in antiquities of holy writ should seeme to exceede the meanenesse of the Person."

As a final point, the Epistle to Harvey, as Atkins has brought out, is a notable critical introduction that in a sensitive and intelligent fashion discusses aspects of literature in the concrete and endeavors to help readers to understand and appreciate by explaining the poem's classical coloring, rhetorical devices, and archaic and dialectal diction.[8]

First of all, in suggesting Fulke Greville as E. K. it should be emphasized that Greville was Philip Sidney's and Edward Dyer's closest and most intimate friend. Because of this fact biographers of these men have always wondered why Greville was never mentioned in the Spenser-Harvey letters along with Dyer and Sidney.[9] During the period of late 1579, as we know from these letters, Spenser, in his employment at Leicester House, was accepted as a member of a literary group by Sidney and Dyer. All read each other's poems, discussed literary problems, and even sometimes experimented with classical meters in English in an attempt to test the aptitude of the English language for more varied kinds of

[8] *English Literary Criticism of the Renascence* (London, 1947), pp. 147–51. I would add E. K.'s clues for the understanding of the allegory as a further contribution of the Epistle.

[9] For instance, see Geoffrey Bullough in his introduction to Fulke Greville, *Poems and Dramas*, 2 vols. (London, 1938), I, 5.

poetry and to accommodate verse to music.[10] Harvey even sent his poems to Spenser, who in turn showed them to Sidney and Dyer. At this same time, Dyer, Greville, and Sidney, that "happy, blessed Trinity," were writing verses in friendly competition, as we know from Sidney's songs in his *Arcadia* ("Striving with my mates in song"), as well as from the many affinities between the early sonnets of *Astrophel and Stella* and Greville's *Caelica* and such a poem as Dyer's *A Fancy*.[11] Hence it would be almost inconceivable that Spenser should not meet or know Greville, who apparently had written some of the *Caelica* poems as early as 1577. In this rivalry on set themes and conventions, Spenser, evidence suggests, was probably an occasional member of this group, for the first three lines of Spenser's *Amoretti*, VIII, are practically identical with those in *Caelica*, III. And since this is the only sonnet of the *Amoretti* not in the Spenserian sonnet rhyme scheme, it suggests early work done at the time of Spenser's association with Sidney and his circle.[12] Greville, like Spenser and Sidney, was also interested in classical meters: *Caelica*, VI, for instance, is one of the most successful poems of the period in classical meters.

But even before this close association with the group at Leicester House, Greville would have had an opportunity to know Spen-

[10] See John Buxton, *Sir Philip Sidney and the English Renaissance* (New York, 1954), p. 116.

[11] See Elizabeth Carrick, "The Life and Works of Fulke Greville." Unpublished M. A. thesis, University of London, 1936, pp. 81 f. Also Bullough, I, 44–48.

[12] Carrick, p. 83; Bullough, I, 232. Professor William Ringler has informed me that *Amoretti* VIII, exists in four mss. completed in the 1580's, and was probably written in 1579 or early 1580. His "Chronology of Spenser's Sonnets," which contains this information, was read at the Spenser section of MLA in December, 1956. Professor de Selincourt in his Oxford edition of Spenser (p. xxxv, n.5) thinks the Surreyan form of *Amoretti* VIII suggests very early composition. Bullough (I, 38) dates *Caelica* III roughly between 1578 and 1586.

ser and Harvey. Greville preceded Spenser at Cambridge by exactly one year; during his first two or three years at Cambridge Spenser may have become acquainted with Greville. To judge from the terms of the dedication ("long most dear to me") of one of the books of Harvey's *Gratulationes Valdinenses* (1578) to Philip Sidney, it is apparent that Harvey—also at Cambridge in these years—knew Sidney before the Court's visit to Cambridge in the summer of 1578. And since Harvey was in Leicester's service for a time in 1576 and 1578, it would be strange if he did not know Greville, who during these years was closely associated with Sidney and the Leicester circle. So with Greville as E. K., the friendly Epistle to Harvey preceding the *Calender* could be easily accounted for.

There is, of course, the problem of the initials. The allegorical attack on the Alençon marriage in the *Calender*, as well as the barbed nature of the glosses, would almost preclude the use of initials by which the commentator could be readily identified. Such a guess as that of Edward Kirke as E. K. was almost entirely predicated on an ignorance of the real meaning of the *Calender*: an attack on the French marriage decidedly less direct than Sidney's famous letter to the Queen and Stubbs' *Gaping Gulf*, the latter costing the author and the dispenser of the book their right hands. All three were written or printed in late 1579 within a few months of one another, all grew out of the concern of the group at Leicester House over the danger to England, the Queen, and the Established Church that the match threatened. Indeed, it would seem that Walsingham intervened in the punishment of Singleton, the printer of the *Gaping Gulf*, so that Singleton could go ahead with the *Calender*.

My theory is that Spenser took the last letters of Greville's first and last names, and reversed them, just as he reversed the syllables of *Grindal* and *Aylmer* (with its variant spellings of *Elmer*, or

Elmore) to get *Algrind* and *Morrell*. I also wish to emphasize that a common Elizabethan spelling of Greville's first name was *Fulk*, or *Foulk*, without the final *e* of the modern spelling. For instance, the spelling used in the signature on the letter to the Scottish Ambassador, telling of Greville's sorrow at Sidney's death, was *Foulk Greville*. Most of the spellings in the Essex letters are *Foulk*, or *Fulk*. A contemporary letter accusing Greville of being a deceiver of women spells the name as *Fulk Greville*. Even the writer of an article on Greville in *Biographia Brittanica* (1757) uses the latter spelling.[13] The use of the final letters of one's names as initials was not too common, but it sometimes occurred. For instance, Spenser's friend William Camden, who had Greville for a patron, brought out his *Remains* in 1605 signed only with the letters *M. N.*, the last letters of his name.[14]

The customarily cautious Greville, perhaps influenced by the state of unnatural tension and excitement at Leicester House that the Alençon marriage negotiations had created, presumably agreed to serve as annotator of the *Calender* and give, among other things, veiled clues to its allegory. But he also no doubt demanded that his part in the work be kept an absolute secret. If any more hands were to fly—and his position was just as perilous as Spenser's—he would wish to be suitably protected. In a tentative reconstruction of events, I would say that Spenser began to write the political eclogues of the *Calender* in August of 1579, with the full knowledge and encouragement of the group at Leicester House. Greville had agreed to serve as glosser shortly thereafter; Harvey was in on the secret and would know the identity of E. K. when Spenser was sending the latter's regards in the letter of

[13] For the *Foulk* or *Fulk* spelling, see Buxton, p. 172; Carrick, pp. 30–31; Bullough, I, 7; and Morris W. Croll, *The Works of Fulke Greville* (Philadelphia, 1903), p. 6.

[14] *DNB.* "Camden." Camden at first intended to dedicate the *Remains* to Fulke Greville.

October, 1579. And since E. K. was also doing glosses on Spenser's *Dreams*, I would suggest that this poem was of a political nature also, perhaps even dealing with some of the same events. Spenser would perhaps have finished most of the *Calender* by the time of his presumed marriage on October 27, 1579; he may or may not have been away on a confidential mission just after this marriage. Greville, then, acting on instruction, and with full permission of Spenser, wrote the Epistle to Harvey and the glosses during November. After a hurried reading and passing by a friendly licensor on December 5, the *Calender* was rushed to the printer and appeared before the end of the same month.[15]

It is significant that E. K. is referred to as a separate person in Spenser's letters to Harvey—letters (printed in the summer of 1580) in which Sidney and Dyer are mentioned in a way indicating that E. K. was a member of the same group. This fact might also suggest that Sidney, Dyer, and Harvey, except for giving their advice and moral support, had very little to do with the *Calender*. But Greville, still at Court while Spenser was on his way to Ireland, must yet be protected and remain anonymous. Greville's association with the group at Leicester House would also account for E. K.'s full knowledge of Spenser's other poems and of Harvey's Latin poems and English verses. If Greville were E. K., the praise of Spenser and Harvey, E. K.'s feigning of ignorance on certain aspects of the allegory, and his intentionally misleading arguments slanted to contemporary affairs (and hence not really

---

[15] I can not give evidence here for these suggestions, but my study has turned up ample evidence to support all of them. Spenser, Harvey, Sidney, and even Singleton changed the date of the new year on January 1 rather than on March 25 (as in English legal and political documents). Hence, apart from E. K.'s argument that the year begins with January, all available evidence in relation to the 1579 date of the *Calender* would suggest that it was printed before December 31, rather than between that date and March 25 of the following year.

misleading at all) would all be easily explainable. As a member of the Sidney-Dyer group Greville would also have the necessary full knowledge of the allegory, be sympathetic with Spenser's intentions, and be vitally concerned over the ill-will ("Envie") that the *Calender* would provoke in certain quarters at Court.

Greville, too, was sufficiently independent and of sufficient stature as an educated man to differ with the poet. For instance, Greville used alliteration sparingly in his poetry, and never to the extent of the verse in *October* which E. K. criticizes as a fault. In his prose (*Life of Sidney* and letters) Greville, like E. K. in the *Calender*, uses alliteration in a normally effective fashion. With his education at Shrewsbury and Cambridge, and subsequent period of travel on the Continent, Greville would also have the wide learning that the Epistle and glosses reveal: a knowledge of Plato, Castiglione, of the classics, and of Italian, French, and native poets and authors. Greville would also possess the "poetic mind," the "different, less flexible" mind, and the at times "prosy" mind that certain scholars see in E. K.'s contributions to the *Calender*. Both Spenser and Greville held many ideas in common. For instance, both, unlike Harvey, believed in a golden age of the past, and both in many of their poems are Platonistic in regard to love and poetry. Greville, even though his poetic practice was sicklied o'er with the pale cast of thought, like E. K. in the Epistle was an advocate of simple, colloquial diction in poetry. From what we know of him, Greville, too, would agree with E. K.'s praise of the author of the *Calender* for his "pithinesse in uttering," his "seemely simplycitie in handeling his matter and framing his words," the closely-knit style, and the plainness and directness of language. Unlike Sidney, Greville did not have the respect for poetic precedent and classical conventions that would lead him, as it did Sidney, to criticize Spenser's use of archaic and dialectal words. Like E. K. again, Greville would attack inferior

poets who overdo alliteration and other poetic adornment but
lack poetic substance. Greville, also, like E. K., would attack the
disparagement of native English by the unnecessary and excessive
importation of Latin, French, and Italian terms. Like E. K. again,
Greville had a prose style that was marked by clarity and force-
fulness.[16] Finally, like E. K., Greville was a sound judge of poetry.
In his *Polyhymnia*, Peele called Greville "Lover of Learning and
of chivalry,/ Sage in his saws, sound judge of poesy."

The stern Protestantism of many of E. K.'s glosses, with their
Calvinistic stress on faith rather than on good works, would fit
Greville.[17] Greville, too, with his growing realism that ruthlessly
tossed aside medieval fancies and romantic flights, would be likely
to write such un-Spenserian glosses as those which attack the authors of Arthurian legends as "lowd lyers . . . who tell many an
unlawfull leasing of the Ladyes of the Lake"; he, too, would like
"to roote that rancke opinion of Elfes oute of mens hearts."
Greville distrusted that "inchanted confusion imaged by the
Poets,"[18] and rejected romantic fictions "in which the affections
or imagination may perchance find exercise or entertainment, but
the memory and judgment no enriching at all."[19]

The other qualifications suggested by E. K.'s glosses Greville
closely meets: he is a young man (two years younger than Spenser), is extremely cynical about love, has an extensive knowledge
of painting and music, and has a tendency towards didacticism.
For instance, in the Epistle E. K. explains how through the principle of contrast Spenser's archaisms "enlumine and make more
clearly to appeare the brightnesse of brave and glorious words."
Similarly, in painting, exquisite beauty is often set off by a back-

---

[16] To support the judgments of this paragraph, see Bullough I, 19–47.
[17] On Greville's Calvinism, see Carrick, pp. 207 f.
[18] Buxton, p. 211.
[19] See Greville's *Life of Sidney*, Nowell Smith, ed. (Oxford, 1907), p.
233.

ground of "rude thickets and craggy clifts." In *Caelica*, XXIV, Greville also contrasts poetry and painting, and in his *Treatie of Human Learning* (st. 109), Greville explains that as those words are best which properly express the thought, so in painting that is best which eschews adornment and most closely captures reality.

Greville's startling and un-Spenserian cynicism about love in many of the *Caelica* poems is reflected in the last gloss to *March*:

> For besides that the very affection of Love it selfe torment-eth the mynde and vexeth the body many wayes, with un-restfulnesse all night, and wearines all day, seeking for that we can not have, and fynding that we would not have: even the selfe things which best before us lyked, in course of time and chaung of ryper yeares, whiche also therewithall chaungeth our wonted lyking and former fantasies, will then seeme lothsome and breede us annoyaunce, when yougthes flowre is withered, and we fynde our bodyes and wits aun-swere not to suche vayne jollitie and lustful pleasaunce.

Greville's tendency towards didacticism and his taste for gen-eral moral allegory (such as occur in his chapter summaries of the 1590 edition of *Arcadia*) are reflected in the "Generall Argument of the whole booke" when E. K. "safely" interprets the moral eclogues thus: "the second of reverence dewe to old age, the fift of coloured deceipt, the seventh and ninth of dissolute shepheards and pastours, the tenth of contempt of Poetrie and pleasaunt wits."

Perhaps the strongest reason that may be advanced for not ac-cepting Fulke Greville as E. K. is the tremendous difference between Greville and Spenser as poets. In his tendency towards realism and didacticism, his avoiding of poetic adornment and all the images of wit, his apostleship of the plain style in poetry (which is perhaps best exemplified in his disciple Daniel), the mature Greville, after the first imitative portion of *Caelica*, seems the very antithesis of Spenser, with his diffuseness and sensuousness and the rich decoration and elevated language of the *Faerie Queene*. But we forget that this Spenser is a radical change from the earlier Spenser.[20] In the *Calender* Greville could heartily approve of Spenser: the plain, even rustic diction; the seriousness of the subject matter; the emphasis on the moral allegory; and the basic political propaganda of the poem. Sidney and the Alençon marriage controversy probably brought two poets together between whom, in terms of their later development, there was little essential kinship. After Spenser's removal to Ireland and the death of Sidney, they probably would have had very little in common. The memory of the stirring days of late 1579 would no doubt later make Greville tremble at his uncharacteristic rashness. After Sidney's death, through his policy of wary walking Greville found favor with the Queen and began to amass a fortune. When he thought of the *Calender* and the impact it made on its age through its boldness in attacking the policy of Burghley and Elizabeth, he no doubt resolved to play it safe in the future. In his *Life of Sidney* Greville refers to his poems as pamphlets which "having slept out my own time, if they happen to be seene hereafter, shall at their own perill rise upon the stage when I am not."[21] Bullough suggests that "probably the fear which made him burn one play made him reserve publication of the rest of his work. There was ambiguous stuff in it, which could easily be distorted to a particular application."[22]

When Spenser returned from Ireland in late 1589 with the first three books of the *Faerie Queene*, I would suggest that Greville undoubtedly greeted him in a friendly fashion, even though po-

[20] Spenser, of course, had many styles: *Mother Hubberd's Tale* and *Colin Clouts Come Home Againe* are good examples of poems with styles far different from the style of the *Faerie Queene*.

[21] P. 220.

[22] Bullough, I, 24.

etically they were now far apart. And in *Colin Clouts Come Home Againe*, where Spenser celebrated his reception at Court on this visit, I have the feeling that Greville is perhaps among those honored in the poem, but not as E. K. Greville would undoubtedly prefer that his earlier political indiscretion of annotating the *Calender* still remain unpublicized, and Spenser would respect this wish.

In conclusion, it should be emphasized that my suggestion that E. K. of the *Shepheardes Calender* is Fulke Greville is pure speculation: however, it is speculation which is based on the known background of the poem, the circumstances of its publication, and the implications of its allegory. This chapter has also, I hope, advanced new arguments to indicate that E. K. was not Spenser, and in attempting to find a more likely E. K. has assembled evidence to support my conjecture that E. K. is probably Fulke Greville.

Problems Relating to the Allegory

XVIII

Spenser's Concept of Allegory

IT HAS long been recognized that Spenserian allegory has different levels of meaning. The single poem can operate on a literal or romantic level, on a religious or moral level, on a national level, or on a personal level—and often on all levels at the same time. At other times, the poem or a major part of it stresses a single level of meaning, and one would be rash indeed to try to work out in a coherent fashion for the whole narrative a particular level of meaning present in the single episode.

Spenserian allegory, however, for all its multiplicity of effects, rich allusiveness, flexibility, and episodic nature, is not as chaotic as, at first glance, it might seem. A knowledge of the contemporary scene and a close study of the poem in terms of this context and of literary tradition almost always make Spenser's intentions clear.

First, let us see how the single character in the poem can represent many characters. In the *Faerie Queene*, for instance, Duessa is a witch in league with the Devil, Archimago, but she is also Deception, the Catholic Church, the daughter of the Pope, and

Mary Queen of Scots. Of course, Duessa is not all of these characters in every scene that she appears; perhaps only in Book V, when she is tried and executed for treason against Mercilla, is she Mary Stuart. But in all these transformations it should be noted that there is a common denominator to the Protestant mind of the period, a denominator which the poet can add to at will. Again, the Red Cross Knight represents the Christian man in quest of holiness and salvation; on another level, as St. George, he is England or the English people. And Una represents the true Christian faith, the Church of England, and Elizabeth, the supreme governor of this Church.[1]

At other times, the single historical character is represented in the poem by a number of different characters. For instance, in the *Faerie Queene* Queen Elizabeth is certainly represented in "mirrors more than one." In her public and private character as Queen and virtuous and beautiful lady she is at times Gloriana, Belphoebe, Britomart, Una, and Mercilla.

Spenser's employment of allegory in the *Shepheardes Calender*, it seems to me, is exactly the same as in the later *Faerie Queene*. The single character of the poem either represents different characters at various times, or the single historical person is represented by many characters. Furthermore, the allegory can be both general and specific, and in its details it can point to different characters at different times. For example, in the *Calender* Pan represents Christ, the Pope, Henry VIII, and the shepherd deity— and all, apparently, without any confusion, for the context or E. K.'s helpful glosses explain everything. Again, Colin Clout stands for the English people, in love with and mystically wedded

---

[1] Leicester Bradner, *Edmund Spenser and the Faerie Queene* (Chicago, 1948), pp. 124–26, gives an excellent account of the multiple levels of allegory in the *Faerie Queene*.

to Elizabeth; Colin is also Spenser himself, the author of the poem.[2]

Queen Elizabeth has as many incarnations in the *Calender* as in the *Faerie Queene*. As Elisa she is beautiful lady, goddess, and "Queene of Shepheardes all." As Rosalind she is betrothed to the people of England, but in feminine fashion has allowed her affections to wander to that "faithlesse fere," Menalcas (or Alençon). As Dido she symbolizes the prophetic death that the Alençon marriage forbodes for England. As the Eagle of the fable she represents royal authority dropping a severe penalty on the hapless Archbishop Grindal. As the Husbandman of another fable she is the master woodsman of that forest, England; but in the supervision of her trees of state she has allowed the spite and malice of the Briar and her own anger to influence her royal justice and wisdom. Hence she cuts down the "King of the field," the tall and mighty Oak that represents the Earl of Leicester.

Sometimes the pastoral or fabular action has a single allegorical meaning. At other times general meanings also appear. For instance, the fable of the Eagle and the Shell-fish represents the suspension and sequestration of Archbishop Grindal. Although this fable may, in general, also bring out the capriciousness of fortune, it is difficult to discover further specific meanings in its personal allegory. The fable of the Oak and the Briar, in its specific details, represents Leicester and Oxford. In a more general sense, however, the Oak represents other English statesmen of the time whose faithful years of service and proven loyalty to Queen and country have been forgotten in the turmoil of party politics. In late 1579 Sir Henry Sidney and Walsingham would particu-

---

[2] In a later chapter on the unity of the *Shepheardes Calender* I suggest a third level of meaning for Colin Clout: in the equation of his life to the four seasons of the year he represents the Christian man, or Everyman.

larly spring to mind as other Oaks that were felled by the Queen's wrath or the malice of their enemies.

Sometimes the action of the allegory is flexible enough to cover a number of specific actions or even general conditions. For instance, in the September eclogue the ignorant and corrupt clergy in Bishop Davies' diocese stand for the ignorant and corrupt clergy in all dioceses in England and Wales; and the plundering of Davies' diocese by powerful courtiers stands for the universal robbery of the English Church by an unholy combination of gentlemen pensioners of the Queen and unscrupulous lay patrons. And the symbol of the Wolf in September's fable is flexible enough to cover both Bishop Young's unmasking of the heretical H. N. as a "secret" Catholic and the routing of those who had designs on the revenues supporting Chatham Hospital. In the October eclogue Cuddie represents a single poet, Edward Dyer, who was never properly rewarded for his graceful lyrics, but Spenser is also concerned with the contempt of poetry and learning in Elizabethan England by those in authority, who should foster both.

Perhaps the best example of multiple meanings in the Calender is the fable of the Fox and the Kid in the May eclogue. Here Spenser gives us in full measure—though perhaps not too consciously—the four levels of medieval allegory. First, on a literal level the fable is a story of a clever Fox and a credulous Kid. Second, tropologically, it teaches us to beware of flatterers and deceivers. Third, anagogically, as E. K. tells us, the Goat is Christ, the Kid the "simple sort of the faythfull and true Christians," and the Fox is the Devil—even though E. K., letting the political allegory for a moment intrude, defines the Fox as the "false and faithlesse Papistes, to whom no credit is to be given, nor felowshippe to be used." Fourth, allegorically, in terms of the specific details of the fable, the Goat is George Buchanan, the Kid is the youthful King James of Scotland, and the Fox is Duc d'Aubigny. But behind the figure of Aubigny we see the shadow of Alençon, Elizabeth's French-Catholic suitor. It was this shadow that Spenser was mainly interested in, and to it he was pointing, using every protection that the fabular art affords.

In conclusion, it can be said that common sense, a little imagination, and a knowledge of the historical and personal background of the poet and of the conventions of the particular literary form he employs, are the only requisites for the solution of a poetic allegory. And even when scholars possess all three, we should not expect perfect agreement on details or on the various levels of a multiple allegory, for the allegorist sometimes proceeds in a highly subjective fashion in his use of symbols and their reference to contemporary events. At other times, as in the case of the *Calender*, the poet is forced by circumstances to compromise between clarity and protective obscurity. A false step in one direction and he is in trouble with the authorities; a false step in another direction and all his fine intentions will be frustrated, for he will not be understood. But with the assistance of E. K., Spenser kept to the narrow path of safe comprehensibility.

XIX

Shepheardes Calender as a Dramatic Poem

IT HAS not been sufficiently stressed that the Shepheardes Calender is a dramatic poem as well as an allegory. As a dramatic poem
it can be discussed, of course, on a non-allegorical level: its characters may be regarded as independent and created (i.e., fictional)
with a dramatic relationship to each other in the context of a
dramatic poem. From this point of view, Colin is the central
character or hero of a poetic drama—not Spenser or anyone else.
The other characters are likewise fictional. When they discuss
themes of universal interest like love, friendship, poetry or
religion, the eclogues serve as the acts and scenes of the drama.

Now the Calender can certainly be read on this non-allegorical
level and often has been. The meanings such a reading reveals,
if based on the text and governed by common sense, are—to the
extent that the allegory may be safely ignored in an allegorical
poem—valid and acceptable. But from this point of view we
cannot discuss Colin as Spenser or Hobbinol as Harvey, for both
Colin and Hobbinol exist only as literary characters in the world
of the poem and have no existence outside it.

In many ways the *Shepheardes Calender* as an allegory is similar to a history play. For instance, Shakespeare's *Richard II* can be viewed as a literary document, a tragedy whose story and characters are in a sense all fictional. But it can also be viewed as a historical drama with a strong relation to historic fact. As such, Shakespeare's sources, his use and modification of his sources, would have a bearing on Shakepeare's meaning. The *Calender* can be approached in the same two ways: as a poetic drama which has no relation to history, or as a poetic drama which, because it is an allegory, depends on history in order to be fully understood.

My primary purpose in this chapter is to indicate how the allegory affects the *Calender* as a dramatic poem. But first let us consider literary influences on its dramatic character. E. K. never lets us forget that the *Calender* has been influenced by Spenser's pastoral predecessors. Virgil, Petrarch, Mantuan, and Marot are Spenser's main models; everywhere, according to E. K. in the Epistle, is Spenser following their footsteps. Particularly in its language has the *Calender* been influenced by the pastoral tradition.

Since the *Calender* is a pastoral, its characters are all shepherds. According to the principle of dramatic decorum, shepherds are rude and ignorant; hence not only their language but also their knowledge and manners are faulty. With the sanction of pastoral tradition, Spenser used dialect and colloquial terms. In the Epistle E. K. stresses Spenser's "dewe observing of Decorum everye where, in personages, in seasons, in matter, in speech, and generally in al seemely simplycitie of handeling his matter, and framing his words." In the glosses also, E. K. many times points out the influence of pastoral decorum. In regard to Colin's lay to Elisa in *April*, E. K. points out that the song is not

> what the worthinesse of her Majestie deserveth, nor what to the highnes of a Prince is agreeable, but what is moste comely

for the meanesse of a shepheards witte, or to conceive or to utter. And therefore he calleth her Elysa, as through rude-nesse tripping in her name: and a shepheards daughter, it being very unfit that a shepheards boy brought up in the shepefold, should know, or ever seme to have heard of a Queenes roialty.

Later in the glosses to *April* E. K. tells us that Colin's injunction to the shepherds' daughters to dress discreetly when they come into the presence of their Queen is "spoken rudely, and according to shepheardes simplicitye."

Again, in the glosses to *July* E. K. makes two references to de-corum. In explanation of Morrell's statement that shepherds used to feed their flocks at will on the slopes of Paradise until Adam's fall ruined this idyllic state, E. K. tells us that this is an "errour of shepheards understanding." Later Thomalin is unable to recall Aaron's name. According to E. K. this forgetfulness is "more de-corum . . . lest his remembraunce and skill in antiquities of holy writ should seeme to exceede the meanenesse of the Person."

In *October's* glosses E. K. makes two more references to de-corum. Piers had suggested that Cuddie sing of Elisa and the "worthy whome she loveth best." E. K. hints that this worthy is Leicester, declaring that it is not likely that "names of noble princes be knowne to country clowne." Later E. K. notes that Cuddie in certain majestic verses on the poetic effects of wine seems "to be ravished with a Poetical furie . . . and hath forgot the meanenesse of shepheards state and style."

Another somewhat ignored influence on the language of the *Calender* is the choice of Colin Clout, from Skelton's poem of the same name, as the main character. This choice is, of course, motivated by the allegory, for Colin, as in Skelton, at times repre-sents the people of England. Besides being a man of the people, Skelton's Colin is a rustic. Hence he uses a homely, colloquial speech and deliberately rough verses. His rimes are intentionally simple and dramatically appropriate. In the Latin Epilogue, Skelton acknowledges that Colin's lines are purposely unpolished and clumsy. Similarly, in the June eclogue Spenser's Colin confesses: "I wote my rymes bene rough, and rudely drest." Since Spenser's Colin is man of the people as well as shepherd, it is likewise fitting for him to speak as untutored rustic. But Skelton's Colin and the principle of pastoral decorum, however they affect the dramatic speech of the *Calender*, are largely literary influences.

But since the *Calender* is an allegory, we must expect to find its real subject and meaning in contemporary life, in Spenser's personal, political, and religious interests. The main character of the poem, Colin Clout, is at times Spenser himself, and the other characters represent Spenser's "familiar freendes and best acquayntaunce." Their subjects of dramatic discussion have reference to the life of the times and take on meaning in terms of this reference. Furthermore, the relationship of the characters of the poem to their counterparts in real life—as we have seen in earlier chapters—has an important bearing on the meaning of the poem, affecting both what the characters say and how they say it. The allegory, then, is exceedingly important, if not the actual heart of the poem, and we must expect the allegory to influence the poem in language, characters, action, and imagery.

The language of the *Calender* is not only influenced by the historical allegory but is also a clue to the allegory. E. K. was perhaps referring to this phenomenon in the Epistle when he warned against misinterpreting Spenser's use of "old and unwonted words." Before one judges the length of Spenser's cast, one should first mark "the compasse of hys bent." For instance, in the fable of the Fox and the Kid, which allegorically depicts Aubigny's dangerous influence on King James, Spenser used Scottish dialectal terms to indicate he was dealing with Scottish affairs. He used *gate*, the Scottish form for *goat*, to designate the Kid's dam (George Buchanan, James' tutor), as well as such Scottish terms as *sperre the yate* for "shut the door." E. K. assists us by noting that *gate* is "northernely spoken." And to help us realize that the Fox is the French-Catholic Aubigny, the French loan word *newell* is used for the toy with which the Fox enamors the Kid.

Spenser's use of dialectal terms in *September* is also much influenced by the allegory. In the first four lines, Hobbinol's bantering address and Diggon's reply, Spenser uses the Welsh dialectal *her* for *he* and *him* to indicate that Diggon is from Wales. E. K. comments that this term is meaningful in reference to Diggon Davie. Not much more is required for us to realize that Diggon represents Richard Davies, bishop of the Welsh diocese of St. David's. Up to the Roffyn episode (1. 170), Spenser does not need the words *he* or *him*, so that *her* in these senses is confined to the opening speeches.[1] But in the Roffyn episode, even though Diggon is the narrator, *he* and *him* are employed. The reason for Spenser's procedure is not difficult to fathom. A dramatic clue to Diggon's identity is given in the opening lines of the eclogue. But since the Roffyn episode deals with English affairs, with Bishop Young and his diocese, the normal English pronouns are used in relating it.

Let us now, for example, consider how the allegory affects the portrayal of character in Colin Clout. As we have seen, Colin is both the English people and the poet Spenser. A study of the allegory reveals, however, that Colin as lover is seldom if ever

---

[1] Hulbert, p. 350. She further writes: "*Her* does appear, however, in the first 170 lines in the sense of *their* (11. 39, 112, 115, 119, 141) and perhaps Spenser thought that in employing *her* he was consistently indicating the Welsh dialect in spite of the fact that *her* for the possessive plural is good Middle English and that he used it at least once in another eclogue in the Middle English sense (*May*, 1. 160)."

Spenser, for the eclogues in which Colin so appears do not square with Spenser's circumstances as we know them from other evidence. For instance, in *January* Colin neglects Hobbinol and his poetry because of his rejection by Rosalind. This neglect could well be symbolic of the expected consequences of the Alençon courtship on the English people: friendship and poetry, two of the most precious and enduring things in the world, are as naught in the light of the coming event. These consequences, however, do not affect Spenser as poet, for Spenser at this time certainly did not give up his friendship for Harvey or cease writing verses. Both friendship and poetry flowered all the stronger, as we realize from the Spenser-Harvey letters. And since his poetry mirrored the political turmoil of the times, the Alençon affair might be said to inspire Colin as Spenser, for under the pressure of disturbing events he created poetry which reflected these events. In un-Wordsworthian fashion, without benefit of tranquillity his emotion was immediately channeled into poetry. The excitement produced in Spenser by these events also required a confidant; hence Spenser was never closer to Harvey than he was in late 1579.

The death that Colin awaits in December could be symbolic for the people of England, for it does not seem to fit the poet Spenser. As we have seen, the Alençon marriage was popularly regarded (at least by the group around Leicester) as threatening fatal consequences to England, the English Church, and the Queen. In fact, most of the representations of winter and death in the *Calender* are symbolic, prophesying the misfortune that will come in relation to the French marriage: the death of Dido (who represents Elizabeth or England as identified with the Queen), and the approaching death of Colin in *December* (who represents England, on one level, as embodied in and symbolized by the English people.

E. K. places the eclogues dealing with Elizabeth as Rosalind and Dido in a separate category and calls them "plaintive." They express England's sorrow over the Alençon marriage, Colin here representing the English people. Colin's total devotion to Rosalind is a symbol of England's total devotion to the Queen. And Colin's lay to Elisa in *April* can be interpreted as an expression of the joyousness and serenity of the English people in an earlier day before Alençon cast his black shadow over England.

Other allegorical interpretations are likewise possible. For instance, the death of Colin, at hand in *December*, could symbolize the death of a callow and possessive form of love in the English people for their Queen, a love that would foolishly measure her constancy to them by the fiction of the mystic marriage of Queen and people. As lover of Rosalind, Colin (i.e., the English people) grows in experience and matures: the love-melancholy brought on by the Queen's projected foreign marriage is replaced in part by a spiritualized love that accepts rejection with no lessening of constancy or devotion. And even though this rejection forbodes disaster (winter and death) for the English people, Colin, as the embodiment of these people, in *December* testifies to his unswerving loyalty. And in *October* Piers declares that Colin's love, in neo-Platonic fashion, has raised his mind "above the starry skie." Now heavenly beauty, or this beauty as reflected in Rosalind, is enough for his constant devotion.

At times, of course, Colin clearly represents the poet Spenser. For instance, in *June* Hobbinol advises Colin to leave the hills
   And to the dales resort, where shepheards ritch,
   And fruictfull flocks bene every where to see. (21–22)
We perhaps do not need E. K.'s gloss to tell us that this suggestion is no poetical fiction, and that the author of the *Calender*, "for his more preferment," left the Northparts for the South, as indeed Hobbinol had here advised. Again, in *June*, Hobbinol's delight in hearing Colin's "rymes and roundelayes" would be a

reference to Colin as Spenser. Many other examples could be cited where Colin as poet represents Spenser. But as lover of Rosalind, Colin represents the people of England. E. K.'s statement that under Colin's name the author "secretly shadoweth himself" is in part a blind, a protective gesture, and not the whole truth. Only on one level of an allegorical poem that has multiple levels does Colin represent Spenser. A good rule of thumb to follow is that Colin as lover of Rosalind is the English people; Colin as poet is Spenser, even though some of his sad songs allegorically portray the relationship of the English people to their Queen.

Spenser's use of imagery, especially the imagery of the seasons, has marked reference to the allegory. Spring and summer seldom appear in the glory of their seasonal details, because both are symbolic of good fortune and concord. In his depiction of political and religious conditions and of the contempt of poetry in the England of 1579, Spenser was stressing the long winter of England's discontent. The whole year, from January to December, particularly in view of the contemplated French marriage, was unseasonably wintry and discordant. In fact, a good, if fanciful, case can be made that the sad year of the *Shepheardes Calender* is the sad year of 1579. In early January, Simier visited England and the Queen became seriously interested in Alençon; by December the marriage contract had been forced through the Council by the Queen, and the marriage seemed to be a foregone conclusion that nothing could change. It is small wonder, then, that Colin in *December* should prophecy that for him "after Winter commeth timely death," for that is how the English people regarded the French marriage.

As a single example of a specific image that Spenser develops in terms of the allegory, we might note the "water" image in *November*. Because Alençon is heir to the French throne, he is the Dolphin; hence the sun (the monarch symbol) is in the Fish's hask. As a consequence Dido (who represents Elizabeth) has prophetically drowned ("For deade is Dido, dead alas and drent") through associating with the Dolphin and succumbing to his dangerous and unnatural element.[2]

In earlier chapters we have seen how Spenser has dramatized his friends and their problems. For instance, Hobbinol is Spenser's best friend, Gabriel Harvey; in the *Calender* Hobbinol is the perfect friend to both Colin and Diggon Davie. Hobbinol also reflects Harvey's pragmatism, his tolerance of evils in Church and State that the individual is powerless to change, and his cynicism on all varieties of romantic and platonic love. Again, in Cuddie, Edward Dyer is represented. In *February* Dyer's pessimistic lyrical note is subjected to good-natured banter; in *October* the basis of his pessimism, his failure to receive proper rewards for his poetic skill, is dramatically brought home to us. As a further example, the troubles of Bishop Davies are dramatized in the speeches of Diggon Davie in *September*. His clergy are ignorant, corrupt, and contentious, and he himself has been badly gored by a relentless Bull of Basan, Edward Carey, groom of the Queen's Chamber, who has stripped him of half of his ecclesiastical income.

[2] In this regard, the passage from *Mother Hubberds Tale* might be recalled (a passage which probably also prophetically deals with the Alençon affair) in which the Ape, with the Fox's assistance, seizes the royal throne.

> Then for the safegard of his personage,
> He did appoint a warlike equipage
> Of forreigne beasts, not in the forest bred,
> But part by land, and part by water fed.
>   (1117-20)

These beasts "bred of two kinds" who protect the usurping Ape include such animals as "Griffons, Minotaures,/ Crocodiles, Dragons, Beavers, and Centaures," all of whom are legendary monsters or monstrous because of their amphibious nature. Water, then, to Spenser, in the above-mentioned contexts is a symbol of dangerous falsity and cruelty, of something unnatural.

Elizabeth had a number of animal nicknames for her favorites. Alençon was her "Frog."

Even the fables, which are related by the characters in the eclogues, take a dramatic form, for the action is often realized
through the dialogue of the fabular characters. For instance, in
February's fable, the Briar's abusive words to the Oak and his
subsequent lying complaints to the Husbandman are given in
dialogue. As we have seen, this fable is a dramatization of the
fall of Leicester, a fall tied up with Leicester's leadership of the
group who opposed the Alençon marriage. In the fable, the Oak
is the natural protection of the Briar, as age is the natural protection and wisdom of youth. On an allegorical level, Leicester
is the natural protection and wisdom of England and of younger
courtiers and aspiring statesmen, particularly the Earl of Oxford
who is represented in the Briar. The violence, injustice, and
danger to England of Leicester's fall, and the necessity for his
restoration are implicit in the fable.

Recognition of the dramatic nature of the *Calender* should
correct a common tendency to regard most of the characters in
the poem as spokesmen for Spenser—mirroring diverse aspects
of his mind and character. Spenser, as author, reveals himself
through the plot of his dramatic poem, and the allegory is his
plot. If we discover the allegory, we should, in E. K.'s words, by
marking the compass of Spenser's bent, be able to "judge of the
length of his cast."

XX

Unity of the Shepheardes Calender

FROM THE point of view of this book, the unity of the *Shepheardes Calender* must be considered in relation to its allegory. As Renwick wrote in his study of the *Calender*, the conventional country of the Renaissance pastoral

> was not Sicily, nor an imagined Arcadia, but the poet's own surroundings. The mind was not removed from everyday life and the poet's own interests, but occupied with them. . . . Pastoral was an allegorical disguising that, in a tradition of objective poetry, provided an accepted and acceptable way of treating of personal and contemporary affairs.[1]

We must, then, comprehend the personal and contemporary affairs that the pastoral contains, as well as its historical development, before we can grasp its essential unity.

Spenser's choice of the pastoral form was itself significant, for the pastoral traditionally could accommodate a variety of the poet's interests and offer great scope for allegory and satire, for compliments to the poet's patrons and friends and attacks on his

[1] P. 164.

314

enemies. And for all its rules, the pastoral form was sufficiently loose to allow originality and a personal atmosphere. In the imitations of his pastoral predecessors the poet could pour the new wine of his own age—its specific problems and difficulties—into the old bottles; or, to change the figure, he could set his new matter in the old frames. The conventions were the same, but the content was ever new in its reference to a specific place and time.

Absolute unity, then, a single theme or motif, a single story, is not required of the pastoral and we should not require it of the *Shepheardes Calender*. There is, however, as we have seen, a unity greater than that of the single eclogue. Some themes are more important and extensive than others; the poet has great matters of argument which run through many of the individual eclogues, as well as lesser, more personal matters which are briefly alluded to in the single eclogue.

E. K. recognized the variety of Spenser's interests in the *Calender* and accordingly divided the eclogues into three groups. The first group dealing with Elizabeth as Rosalind and Dido—*January*, *June*, *November*, and *December*—is termed "plaintive." These eclogues are complaints in a double sense. On the surface level they complain of Colin's unrequited love for Rosalind and his sorrow over the death of Dido, the "mayden of greate bloud." On an allegorical level they are political complaints: they mirror England's sorrow over the contemplated Alençon marriage, the metaphorical rejection of the English people by the Queen in favor of a foreign prince, and the prophetic consequences of this marriage —the death of the Queen and her people in the death of Dido and the approaching death of Colin.

The position of the Rosalind eclogues at the beginning, middle, and end of the *Calender*, and the fact that Colin, the main character of the poem, in his double allegorical character as lover and poet represents the people of England and Spenser himself might suggest that Spenser considered the Alençon affair his most important great matter of argument. Rosalind is also referred to in the April and August eclogues. As we have seen, the Fox in May's fable secretly portrays Alençon. The fall of Leicester, the Oak of February's fable, is also tied in with the Alençon controversy. Hence the Alençon affair spills over into E .K.'s other divisions of eclogues. We can if we wish, like Greg, make the Rosalind-Colin drama the controlling center of the poem, but we should not deny the poem unity (like Botting)² just because it contains other material. The pastoral allowed a variety of themes and Spenser did not relinquish his traditional rights.

A second major theme—a full presentation of ecclesiastical abuses—occupies Spenser in three of the moral eclogues (to use E. K.'s classification), May, July, and September. In these eclogues Spenser makes certain of the important bishops of the time, Piers, Aylmer, Cooper, and Richard Davies, dramatic characters who attack ecclesiastical evils. Occasionally other bishops, Grindal and Young, are alluded to as authorities on, and models of, the religious life. Greenlaw would make these eclogues the controlling center of the poem;³ he tries to justify his position by citing E. K.'s final gloss to December on "the keeping of sheepe, which is the argument of all Æglogues," and two verses from Spenser's Epilogue: "To teach the ruder shepheard how to feede his sheepe,/ And from the falsers fraud his folded flocke to keepe." But it should be noted that E. K. is not always exact, for in the same gloss he mentions other themes dealing with Rosalind and Spenser's friendship for Harvey. We could also confront E. K. with his earlier statement in the Epistle where he tells us that

² Roland B. Botting, "The Composition of the Shepheardes Calender," PMLA, L (1935), 423–34.
³ Edwin Greenlaw, "The Shepheards Calender," PMLA, XXVI (1911), 419–51.

Spenser compiled his twelve eclogues "to mitigate and allay the heate of his passion for Rosalind, or els to warne (as he sayth) the young shepheards .s. his equalls and companions of his unfortunate folly." If E. K. himself cannot make up his mind, we should see the wisdom of not stressing one theme at the expense of another or trying to find in a single motif the "heart," or key to the meaning of the *Calender*.

E. K. also lists *February* and *October* among the moral eclogues, "which for the most part be mixed with some Satyrical bitternesse." As we have seen, the bitterness of *February* is largely confined to the political implications of the fable of the Oak and the Briar. And *October*, concerned generally with the "contempt of Poetrie and pleasaunt wits," specifically refers to Edward Dyer, disillusioned Court poet who was friendly with Spenser in late 1579.

E. K.'s third division of eclogues, the recreative (which "conceive matter of love, or commendation of special personages"), includes *March*, *April*, and *August*. In *March* two shepherd boys, Willye and Thomalin, conceive matter of love (which "to springtime is most agreeable") both in their preliminary discussion and in Thomalin's account of his meeting with Cupid. We do not know what special person is represented by Thomalin, but E. K. assures us that he is Spenser's secret friend, one who had long scorned love until he was "unawares wounded with the dart of some beautifull regard, which is Cupides arrowe." In *April* Thenot and Hobbinol "recreate" poetically through the latter's recital of Colin's lay to Elisa, a commendation of the Queen which might counterbalance subtler and more critical representations of her as Rosalind and Dido. In *August* Willye and Perigot recreate in a singing-match, "a delectable controversie" according to E. K., and Cuddie, the umpire, somewhat moderates the recreative aspects of the eclogue by reciting a "doolefull verse of Rosalind that Colin made." E. K. hints that Perigot is a real person and declares that his love deserves no less praise than he gives her in his song.

E. K.'s designation of the three eclogues as "recreative" is surely a hint that they are less serious in their subject matter than the moral and plaintive eclogues. Their allegory is either so clear that one would hesitate to call it allegory—as in Elisa as Elizabeth—or extremely personal and thin. Spenser is also more interested in literary imitations in the recreative eclogues and less interested in the political, social, and religious problems of his age. For instance, *August* gives us the traditional singing-match of Theocritus and Virgil. *March* presents an idyll of Cupid that ultimately goes back to Bion, a story which Spenser (according to most scholars) has not too successfully naturalized or bent to his general allegorical purposes. The panegyric to the monarch in *April* is likewise conventional, going back to Theocritus and Virgil. However, I do not deny that there are allegorical touches or allusions in the recreative eclogues which relate to the life of the time. The allegory is merely less important, less developed, and perhaps more personal.

Even though Spenser had the sanction of the pastoral tradition, he was undoubtedly concerned over the large number of themes and personal interests he incorporated in the *Calender*, for he sought a certain kind of unity through the structural device of the calendar. With this unifying principle in mind, Spenser selected his title, a rather obvious point which many scholars have been inclined to minimize or misinterpret. E. K. tells us that Spenser's twelve eclogues are proportioned to the state of the twelve months and that Spenser hence called his poem the *Shepheardes Calender*, "applying an olde name to a new worke." The correctness of E. K.'s emphasis was not realized until Mary Parmenter published her study of the relationship of the old *Kalendar and*

Compost of Shepherds to Spenser's poem. She pointed out how
the material of Spenser's poem was related to the twelve months
and how the life of Colin Clout was proportioned to the four
seasons. Of the old *Kalendar*, Miss Parmenter writes:

> ... the significance of the months is expressed in two places:
> first in the Prologue of the "Master Shepherd" upon the
> progress of man's life, where each of four ages is likened to a
> season, and then each of twelve ages represented by one of
> the months; and second in the calendar proper, where verses
> in Latin and English, as well as woodcuts of the appropriate
> occupations and of the signs of the zodiac serve to mingle
> the astronomical, the bucolic, and the moral aspects—the
> moral coinciding with the teaching for the special season of
> the Christian year. . . .[4]

With all the points of the above quotation clearly in mind, we
can see that Spenser set himself an extremely difficult task in trying to make his subject matter conform to the calendar pattern.
First of all, the seasons motif does not coincide with that of the
months. According to Spenser's models, the old *Kalendar* and
other allied sources,[5] the first season, spring, generally begins with
the month of March, while the calendar year begins with January.
Let us, to take a single instance, apply January to Colin's life.
According to the division of the seasons, January belongs to man's
last age—winter. But according to traditional calendar material
(division of months),

> The first .vi. yeres of mannes byrth and aege
> May well be compared to Janyvere.
> For in this month is no strength or courage,
> More than in a chylde of .vi. yere.[6]

---

[4] *ELH*, III (1936), 190.
[5] Besides the old *Kalendar*, Miss Parmenter mentions Caxton's *Golden
Legend* and an old primer printed in 1538, a forerunner of the English
Book of Common Prayer. The latter is exceptionally rich in calendar
material and Miss Parmenter analyzes it in considerable detail.
[6] Quoted by Parmenter, p. 193.

Spenser ingeniously solves this difficulty by using the season of winter to symbolize Colin's state of mind, the wintry desolation of unfortunate love. And in his early youth, troubled by misplaced love, Colin, like a child of six years, has "no strength or courage," and casts himself on the ground.

I do not have the space here to discuss further how Spenser fits his material to the familiar framework of the year and its parts. Since Miss Parmenter discusses this subject so well, such a task is unnecessary. I will, however, stress a few general reasons why some scholars find certain eclogues unsuited to their position according to the division of months. First of all these critics completely ignore the old *Kalendar* which Spenser was following. Second, they ignore the woodcuts with the signs of the zodiac and pictures of appropriate occupations for the various months of the year. These woodcuts are necessary to the full understanding of the apportioning of material to various months both in the old *Kalendar* and Spenser's poem. (Herford and Renwick, in their editions of the *Shepheardes Calender*, omit the woodcuts entirely.) Third, seasonal detail in the eclogues must fit the themes or action that Spenser presents. And since most of the eclogues deal with the evils of Church and State in England of 1579, the happy aspects of nature or of the season of the year for these particular months are either suppressed or played down. But since the gloom, storm, and cold of winter are symbolic as well as appropriate to the themes and action of the *Calender* in general, winter is accentuated in *January*, *February*, *November*, and *December*. Finally, the cycle of the seasons applies to Colin alone and not to the other characters of the *Calender*; hence we should not expect them to grow old as Colin does—particularly as summed up in the December eclogue by both E. K. and Colin.

In terms of the calendar pattern and the cycle of the seasons, Colin, on a third level of allegory, is the Christian man, or Everyman (here Colin is similar to the Red Cross Knight), passing through life and experiencing the disillusionment that dependence on things of this world inevitably brings. Even the service of Rosalind is unimportant in relation to man's eternal destiny and his service to God. On this level of allegory, Colin as Everyman declares in *December*:

> The loser Lasse I cast to please nomore,
> One if I please, enough is me therefore. (119–20)

To my mind, it is not particularly important to the unity of the *Shepheardes Calender* whether Spenser invented his underlying calendar plan first and then wrote the eclogues, or wrote certain eclogues before he conceived his plan. (This is a dilemma on which certain critics, who wish to argue that the *Calender* is a relatively inorganic or chaotic poem, try to impale Spenser.) Spenser was artist enough to make the necessary revisions or additions that would fit his earlier eclogues, if such there were, to the later plan. In truth, the *Calender* has as much unity as a series of connected eclogues need have. Besides the unity imparted by the calendar device, it has a unity of tone or mood—of sadness, melancholy, and regret— that his subject matter dictated.

The *Calender* has also a certain unity or coherence of character, as we have seen in the chapters on Piers, Hobbinol, and Cuddie. But the pastoral form does not require that all the characters be fully or consistently developed, or that the same name must necessarily identify the same allegorical character. For instance, Thomalin in *July* is a shepherd, and Thomalin in *March* (a different kind of eclogue, recreative not moral) is a shepherd's boy. The subject matter of these eclogues, E. K.'s explanations, as well as the woodcuts, suggest that the two Thomalins are not the same character. Furthermore, characters like Thenot and Palinode are somewhat shadowy. Spenser needed some opposition figures or contrasts in the debate form of the pastoral. If none from his circle of friends conformed to the type needed, he was free to invent or to borrow from his pastoral models. Besides he had the help of E. K., who could suggest a personal allegory where it was not too obvious and might have been missed. Thus we know that Thomalin of *March* and Perigot of *August* represent actual characters, but not much specific detail is given about them. They would, however, probably be readily identified by the group at Leicester House.

Colin Clout, because he represents at times the English people, Spenser, and Everyman, is much harder to pin down, but he is not any more difficult to understand allegorically than the main characters of the *Faerie Queene*, most of whom lead a double or triple life on the various levels of the poem. If we remember that Colin as lover of Rosalind is the English people; Colin as poet is Spenser; and Colin in the equation of his life to the four seasons of the year is Everyman, we may perhaps have oversimplified Spenser's allegory, but we are getting close to the heart of the poem.

A final unity in the *Shepheardes Calender* is that imposed by the mind of the author on its dramatic form, of the separate eclogues and their relationship to each other and to the poem as a whole. A single personality was at work, a highly articulate poet who possessed a clearly defined Christian philosophy of life, wide humanistic interests, and a mastery of past literatures as well as of the literature of his own day. As an artist Spenser was conscious at all times of what he was doing and how he was doing it. He had definite intentions which he wished to realize through his art form; hence a study of his art form, as well as of his age and personal environment, is necessary in order to realize fully his intentions.

A cautious conclusion on the unity of the *Shepheardes Calender* would be that this poem, for all its complexity and diversity of themes, is as well integrated as need be or as the pastoral genre required, and that there is no series of eclogues in the history of literature, not even those of Virgil, which has a greater unity than the *Calender*.

XXI

Composition of the Shepheardes Calender

THE ORDER and dates of composition of the twelve eclogues of the *Shepheardes Calender* have provoked a great deal of conjecture, most of it based on either a misunderstanding of the allegory or of the kind of unity a pastoral traditionally allows. There is no need to review the scholarship on this subject, for it is conveniently gathered in an appendix of the *Variorum*. The purpose of this chapter is rather to elucidate the problem of the composition of the *Calender* in the light of its allegory.

As we have already seen, the April 10, 1579 date following E. K.'s Epistle to Harvey has been generally accepted without question, whereas it was probably a fiction designed to protect Spenser for his allegorical portrayal of later events. But it is indeed strange that no serious attempt has ever been made to determine whether additions or substitutions were made after this date to mirror "great matters of argument" which occurred in the eight-month interim before licensing on December 5, 1579. This licensing date is, of course, most important. By then we know the *Calender* was probably completed in its present form. Other dates that pertain to the composition and publication of the *Calender* include Spenser's vague reference about the dedication in the letter to Harvey of October 16, 1579, and Harvey's reference to a "certaine famous booke called the newe *Shepheardes Calendar*" in the letter to Spenser of April 23, 1580. By then, apparently, the *Calender* had been printed long enough to have become famous.

The dating of the *Shepheardes Calender* is often studied in relation to Spenser's service with Bishop Young and the Earl of Leicester. Unfortunately, we have no exact information on when Spenser became associated with these men. We know that Young was elected bishop on February 18, 1578, consecrated on March 16, and installed on April 1, and presume that Spenser became his secretary about the time of consecration. By October 5, 1579, Spenser was in Leicester's service and had probably been employed by him for some months, for Leicester was considering sending Spenser abroad on an important errand. Padelford's suggestion that Spenser left Young for employment by Leicester in the spring of 1579 is probably acceptable to most scholars, and I will use this date as the beginning point of Spenser's service with Leicester.

The references to Kent in the eclogues are somewhat ambiguous and, unless qualified in some way, could point to Spenser's service with both Young and Leicester. While secretary to Young, Spenser, of course, resided at Bromley in Kent. While Spenser was in the employ of Leicester, Rosalind (Queen Elizabeth) held court at Greenwich, Kent, and Leicester spent a good deal of time at Greenwich in the crucial period of late 1579. Hence we cannot conclude that a reference to Kent always pertains to the period of Spenser's secretaryship to Young. For instance, in pastoral terms, the reference to Spenser as the Southern Shepherd's boy (in *April*) could apply to Leicester as well as to Young.

Some of the eclogues carry little evidence as to date; others, because of the allegory, can be dated with some assurance. But whether the latter eclogues replaced others of an earlier date, or underwent such thorough revision that they can be considered new, is difficult to determine. And whether Spenser conceived the underlying plan of the *Calender* before he wrote any eclogues is also difficult to determine. The arguments used to sustain the view that the calendar scheme was a last-minute addition to secure unity, to my mind do not hold up, because they are based on a misinterpretation of allegorical hints (such as the sun's being in the Fish's hask in *November*), of the main allegory itself, of the ways the eclogues are proportionable to the twelve months (with the help of the woodcuts), or of the reasons for the omission of pleasant seasonal details in certain eclogues. Spenser may well have written pastorals before he later fitted them to the unifying device of the calendar, but the arguments advanced for this view are either flimsy or totally unacceptable.

My study of the allegory suggests that at least two thirds of the *Shepheardes Calender* was written in the five-month period before the licensing date—December 5, 1579. E. K. probably wrote the glosses, arguments before the eclogues, and the Epistle to Harvey in the ten-week period before December 5. The woodcuts (or at least certain ones) were probably made in the three-week period before this date, for some of them reveal an accurate knowledge of the allegory dealing with late events. Up to the very last minute before the *Calender* was handed to the licensor, Spenser was probably constantly at work revising, adding, or substituting new material. I would suggest that a friendly licensor completed his work within half a day, the manuscript was then rushed to Singleton the printer, and within a two-week period (from December 6 to December 20) the *Calender* was printed and distributed. Its timeliness in regard to the Alençon marriage negotiations made haste imperative for all concerned. Let us now examine the eclogues (according to E. K.'s classification) and attempt to date them by the allegory.

The four plaintive eclogues, *January, June, November, December,* must have been written from July to November, 1579. If there were earlier eclogues for these months, they were totally abandoned and new ones substituted. The names of Colin Clout and Rosalind (the latter based on an anagram of Elisa R. Eng.) must have been invented after the Alençon marriage negotiations took a serious turn in mid-July and August, 1579. Their unity of tone in their focus on the rejection of the English people (Colin Clout as lover) by the Queen in favor of Alençon (Menalcas) emphasizes this view. Elizabeth as Dido in *November,* and her prophetic death in terms of the Alençon marriage, also clearly refer to the thought of the last five months of 1579 as we find it in Stubbs' *Gaping Gulf* and in the letters of the Spanish ambassador. Whether Colin Clout as poet (i.e., Spenser) had an earlier incarnation under another name in eclogues dealing with these months we have no means of knowing. To me the plaintive eclogues seem completely fitted both to the calendar scheme and to the events they allegorically portray. They were probably written *in toto* from mid-July to mid-November 1579, for I find nothing in them dealing with Colin as lover of Rosalind but what refers to events then taking place. Spenser, of course, in terms of the allegory of Colin as Spenser and Colin as Everyman might have merged earlier material with his later allegorical conception of Colin as lover of Rosalind, and I would favor this supposition.

The recreative eclogues are more difficult to date. *March* could well be early work—written while Spenser was secretary to Bishop Young, or even earlier—for I have discovered nothing in the al-

legory to date it. Willye and Thomalin are "shepheards boyes"—
which might suggest someone connected with Bishop Young or
the other neighboring bishops who were friends of his. Thomalin,
a "secrete freende" of Spenser, has been wounded by Love's arrow, a situation not uncommon to youth. Renwick points out
that this eclogue, in its seasonal details, is very well adapted to its
month, and he would date it as one of the last eclogues in order
of composition. I, however, would place it early, precisely because
of its lack of specific identifiable allegorical details.

The lay to Elisa in *April* could be earlier work, but it is more
logical to connect it with Spenser's employment by Leicester.
Likewise it is a necessary balance to Spenser's allegorical treatment of Elizabeth as Rosalind and Dido—which would again suggest late work. The preliminary discussion in this eclogue between
Thenot and Hobbinol is certainly late work, since it refers to
Colin's love for Rosalind and his present misery, with Colin
scorned by the widow's daughter of the glen.

August, too, is hard to date in its entirety. The sestina dealing
with Colin's sorrow over Rosalind (which is mentioned in the
argument but not referred to in the glosses) is certainly late work.
If, as seems likely, Cuddie (the umpire of the singing-match) is
Edward Dyer, it is probable that the eclogue proper was composed, or at least reworked, while Spenser was in the service of
Leicester. Willye and Perigot seem to be members of the Leicester circle, for Colin had earlier defeated Perigot in a competition
of verses. A gloss discreetly indicates that Perigot is a real person
whose love is deserving of the praise that he gives her in his song.
We now come to the moral eclogues.

The three eclogues dealing with church affairs, *May, July,* and
September, give the clearest indication of having been written
during Spenser's service with Bishop Young. For me the strongest
evidence for this dating is not so much their subject matter as

the discrepancies between E. K.'s arguments and glosses and the material in the eclogues. For instance, Palinode in *May* is not the Catholic pastor (as E. K. writes), but the pastoral opposition character who provokes Piers with his defense of May games, thereby allowing Piers to go off on a tangent and attack the clergy who live like laymen and heap up wealth for their children. And this attack is leveled not against the celibate Catholic clergy but against the Anglican clergy. The same is true in *September*. No matter what E. K. says, Diggon Davie is not attacking Popish prelates but the ignorant, corrupt, greedy, and contentious clergy of the Established Church. If Palinode in *May* were truly Catholic, Piers would not be on such friendly terms with him as he is, nor would Palinode so readily accept the moral of the fable.

What has happened is fairly clear. With the exception of the appended fables, Spenser probably wrote the three ecclesiastical eclogues in 1578 while he was Young's secretary. The glosses and arguments were written in the last months of 1579 when the frenzy against the Alençon marriage plus the fears over the success of the Douay mission had created an entirely new climate of religious and political opinion. Spenser allowed the three eclogues to stand unchanged, for the evils represented were still the same. But to bring them up to date in their reflection of later events he added the fable of the Fox and the Kid in *May*, the fable of the Wolf in Sheep's Clothing in *September*, and, presumably for balance, the fable of the Eagle and the Shell-fish in *July*.

The fables, on the whole, represent extremely late work. Esmé Stuart, duc d'Aubigny, did not arrive in Scotland until September 8, 1579, and did not tip his hand for six or seven weeks after that. Hence the fable of the Fox and the Kid, dealing with Aubigny and Scottish affairs, was probably written in late October and early November, 1579. Likewise the fable of the Wolf in Sheep's Clothing deals with events which occurred in late Octo-

ber, 1579, and hence was written shortly after this time. The fable
of *July*, dealing with the sequestration of Archbishop Grindal,
could, of course, have been written early—just as early in fact as
the eclogue proper, for Grindal was suspended and confined in
June, 1577. But since Algrind has been "long ypent," and since
all the other fables in the *Calender* portray events taking place in
the last half of 1579, the presumption would be that Spenser
added the short fable of the Eagle and the Shell-fish to make *July*
harmonize in form with the other ecclesiastical eclogues.

Two more moral eclogues remain. The fable of the Oak and the
Briar in *February*, dealing with Leicester and Oxford, was certainly written after August, 1579. The earlier dialogue between
Thenot and Cuddie was probably touched up, and a new name,
Cuddie, might even have been adopted for the young man in his
controversy with "age" so that he might suggest Edward Dyer.
Thenot seems to be a somewhat conventional type of old age,
being ninety years old just because ninety is a good round number
for old age. The last moral eclogue, *October*, dealing with the
contempt of poetry and presenting Dyer as Cuddie, disillusioned
Court poet, was probably written during Spenser's service with
Leicester and can be dated from July to November, 1579. Bishop
Piers, Cuddie's adversary in *October*, would probably have been
known by Spenser during his service with Young, but as the
woodcut shows, he is presented as Court bishop in relation to
Court poet, with the royal palace in the background.

When the *Calender* appeared, most probably in late December,
1579, it had all the timeliness of the morning newspaper of today,
for many of the great matters of argument it dealt with, some of
them prophetically, were still pending and had yet to be resolved.
On November 24, 1579, Elizabeth and her Council had agreed
on the terms of the marriage contract; they were awaiting the
return of Sir Edward Stafford, emissary to France, for news of

official French approval of the Alençon marriage. According to some political prophets, the marriage would be the death of the Queen and the English people. And now the *Calender* had appeared with Elizabeth (Dido) already dead and the English people (Colin as lover of Rosalind) sadly awaiting "dreerie death." Leicester, the Oak who had been felled by the malice of his enemies and the anger of his sovereign, was still out of favor and hesitated to show his face at Court. In Scotland, Aubigny was proceeding as the fable of Fox and Kid had foretold: the young King James seemed to be completely in his power. Archbishop Grindal, in "lingring payne," was still dazed from the blow of royal sequestration. In a startling fashion Spenser had held the mirror up to nature and had caught the very form and pressure of the times. It is little wonder that Harvey, in April, 1580, could smugly allude to "a certain famous booke called the newe *Shepheardes Calendar*."

In conclusion—to add my full quota of conjecture—I feel that Spenser had certainly accepted his vocation as poet before he became secretary to Bishop Young in the spring of 1578. He was undoubtedly interested in the pastoral as a form of poetry and may even have determined that a series of pastorals would be a good way to introduce himself as a poet. He may have worked out an underlying plan for such a series—the calendar scheme—or may have adopted it later. Some of the more imitative pastorals, such as *March*, were probably written first. While Spenser was secretary to Bishop Young, his interest in the problems of the Church would have intensified. As a result Spenser would probably have studied anew such pastoral poets as Mantuan, Petrarch, Virgil, and Marot, who allegorically attacked those responsible for evils in Church or State, or complimented their friends or patrons. The ecclesiastical eclogues were probably written at this time. The planned cycle may well have been fairly complete be-

fore Spenser left the service of Bishop Young. Next, as one of
Leicester's following, Spenser was surely caught up in the stir
over the Alençon marriage and inspired by his friendship with
Philip Sidney, Dyer, and the rest of their circle. The time was now
ripe to include more recent great matters of argument into his
pastoral cycle. Hence he completely rewrote, or made substantial
changes in the eclogues which now deal with Rosalind, Colin
Clout, and Dido,[1] and to other eclogues added the fables which
portrayed other recent events. Slight changes could also have
been made in other eclogues which, with the help of E. K.'s
glosses, would allude to Spenser's friendships with people of lesser
importance.

Spenser's use of multiple levels of allegory in the Calender may
have been in part a happy accident brought about by the sudden
need of injecting new meanings to old material with a minimum
sacrifice of former meanings. To me this view seems more probable than that Spenser, from the very beginning, should plan that
Colin Clout should represent at different times and in different
ways the English people, Spenser the poet, and the life of man as
proportioned to the four seasons of the year. The new level of
meaning could, as the need arose, be grafted on the old material
to produce a richer, more exciting and complex work of art. And
because of the danger involved in the new level of allegory, it was
much safer to merge the new level with former levels and ride out
the storm. But unlike Cuddie's sad experience in October, Colin's
skill as a poet was happily rewarded. The "Envie" (malice, hostility), which Spenser fully expected to bark at him, and the
"jeopardee"—both mentioned in his dedicatory ("To His Booke")

---

[1] These plaintive eclogues, unlike most of the others, have little or no
connection with the moral teachings for the same months in the old
Kalendar. See Parmenter, "Twelve Æglogues," p. 199. This fact might
suggest that they replaced earlier material.

verses to Sidney—did not, to any great extent, develop. Flaunted authority was forced to smile. Great Rosalind herself was reported to have said that Colin had "all the Intelligences at commaundement, and an other time Christened [him] her Segnior Pegaso." Faithful Hobbinol, ever practical, jocularly prophesied that Colin, through the special favor of "Mistresse Poetrie, . . . and some personall priviledge, may happely live by *Dying Pellicanes*, and purchase great lands, and Lordshippes, with the money, which his *Calender* and *Dreames* have, and will affourde him."[2]

---

[2] The last two quotations are from Harvey's letter to Spenser of April 23, 1580. Spenser's *Dreames* and *Dying Pellicanes*, apparently completed at this time, were never published.

Appendix -- Other Characters

APPENDIX

Other Characters

Here I shall set down a few conjectures on characters in the *Shepheardes Calender* for whom I have offered no identification. As I have mentioned before, E. K.'s allusions to some of Spenser's friends in the arguments and glosses, as well as certain allusions in the eclogues themselves, are so general that it is almost impossible to explain them today. Furthermore, there is no absolute need that every character in the *Calender* should stand for an actual person, for some are probably —at least in part—pastoral opposition characters or types that conform to what Spenser was trying to do in imitation of particular sources.

THENOT OF *FEBRUARY*, *APRIL*, and *NOVEMBER*

The first of the unidentified characters is Thenot, who appears in *February*, *April*, and *November*. In a gloss to *February*, E. K. tells us that Spenser took the name *Thenot* from Marot. (In Marot's famous elegy which is Spenser's model in *November*, Colin and another shepherd, Thenot, mourn in alternate stanzas.) In the argument before *February* E. K. stresses that the eclogue is "rather morall and generall, then bent to any secrete or particular purpose." The introductory flyting between old age and youth does seem rather conventional, and Miss Parmenter has pointed out the influence of the old *Kalendar*,

337

February being the "proper month for the contest between Age and Youth, Winter and Spring, Old and New—as well as for the cutting of trees."[1]

If I singled out a counterpart in real life for Thenot I would choose Richard Cox, the elderly bishop of Ely.[2] All the other moral eclogues have at least one bishop among the speaking characters. E. K. also offers a few hints when he calls Thenot "an olde Shepheard," and Cuddie the unhappy "Heardmans boye." The woodcut also pictures Thenot's sheep and Cuddie's cattle. As I pointed out in my chapter on Cuddie, a careful distinction is normally kept in the use of the terms shepherd and herdman, which might suggest that Cuddie was one of Leicester's following, and Thenot an elderly bishop. And although Cox was entering his eightieth year in 1579, I do not take his "thrise threttie" years in a literal fashion. Ninety is merely a good round number for old age.

Many of Thenot's verses, stressing the world's going from bad to worse, and his philosophic acceptance of life's buffets, his flock being his chief care, would fit Cox, who suffered much from the assaults of the Queen's favorites on his episcopal properties from 1575 to 1579. Lord North was particularly troublesome in trying to wrest certain manors from Cox, a proceeding so flagrant that the Privy Council was forced to intervene in favor of Cox. In 1575 and 1576 Christopher Hatton used the Queen's influence to make Cox surrender to him the episcopal palace at Holborn, the last of the bishops' London residences. (The rest had been appropriated earlier by greedy courtiers.) Thoroughly disgusted with the Court, Cox tried to resign his bishopric in 1578 (a request finally granted in February, 1580). Cox died in 1581. Archbishop Grindal and Bishop Cooper were executors of his will (dated April 20, 1581).

Cox would be a good narrator for the fall of Leicester, the Oak of February's fable, for he had long been a friend of the Dudleys and Sidneys. As tutor to Edward VI, Cox would have known Henry Sidney, Edward's closest companion, and he was apparently involved with Leicester's father in the Jane Grey conspiracy, for he was apprehended on suspicion of treason after the failure of Northumberland's plot to

[1] Parmenter, "Twelve Æglogues," p. 200.
[2] The following details on Bishop Cox can be found in DNB.

unseat Mary Tudor. Cox also opposed the Alençon marriage, writing Elizabeth a letter about it in March, 1579. As a Marian exile, Cox was also an old friend of Archbishop Grindal, John Mullins, and Alexander Nowell, who were close friends of Bishop Young, Spenser's employer in 1578. For these many reasons, I feel that Thenot might suggest Bishop Cox.

In *April* no specific details are given about Thenot, who elicits from Hobbinol the story of Colin's sorrow over Rosalind and the lay of fair Elisa. But again Cox might be thought of, since his episcopal jurisdiction took in Cambridge, and hence he would be an appropriate person to question Harvey, the Cambridge scholar, about the allegorical matter hidden in Colin as lover of Rosalind.

In *November* Thenot encourages Colin to sing of Dido. Since Cox had early protested the Alençon marriage, here too he would be an appropriate person to elicit the elegy that allegorically deals with one of the expected consequences of the Alençon affair, the death of the Queen herself. But the influence of Spenser's model, Marot, is probably present in *November*, for Thenot and Colin are the main characters in Marot's eclogue also.

THOMALIN AND WILLYE OF *MARCH*

As I have before suggested, *March*, of all the eclogues, is least concerned with public affairs and seems to be more of a literary imitation. The personal allegory is thin. All we know is what E. K. tells us—that Thomalin is a "secrete freende" of the author, a friend who long scorned love until he was finally hit by Cupid's arrow. And both he and his companion, Willye, are "shepheardes boyes."

Unfortunately, we do not know who composed Young's episcopal household at Bromley. But even if we did, it would be hard to pin down a Thomas who finally fell in love, because the situation is so commonplace. I studied a number of Thomases and Williams who were undoubtedly known by Bishop Young and Spenser (particularly the London-area clergymen between 1576 and 1580 who were at Cambridge with Spenser), but not one seemed any more probable than another as the Thomalin or Willye of the March eclogue.

PALINODE IN *MAY* AND *JULY*

Palinode appears in the dialogue with Piers in *May* and is mentioned in *July*. As I have pointed out already, Palinode in *May* obviously does not represent the Catholic pastor, as E. K. tells us in his introductory argument (a misleading bit of information probably inserted to tie in with the anti-Catholic campaign stirred up the Alençon marriage negotiations of late 1579). The context makes it clear that Palinode is the usual pastoral opponent who provokes Piers and gives him a chance to speak his mind on ecclesiastical problems. If Palinode were Catholic, he and Piers (the Protestant pastor, according to E. K.) would not be on such friendly terms, nor would Palinode be so enthusiastic about Piers's fable of the Fox and the Kid, which is an attack on Catholics—particularly the French-Catholic schemers, Aubigny in Scotland and Alençon in England.

Since *Palinode* means a recantation, as a type character Palinode probably stands for one whose life of ease, luxury, and frivolity is a recantation of his pastoral vows of complete dedication to his flock. His role seems to be similar to that of Morrell in *July* and Hobbinol in *September*: all make remarks that provoke censure of ecclesiastical evils. And Palinode seems just as friendly with Piers as Morrell and Hobbinol are with their respective antagonists, Thomalin and Diggon Davie. But whereas by name or E. K.'s gloss we can identify all these other characters, neither the name *Palinode* nor a helpful explanation gives us any clue as to his identity. My conclusion, then, on Palinode of *May* would be that Spenser, in the rush to get the *Calender* (with its full freight of recently added allegory) published in late 1579, did not get around to revamping Palinode: he remained the type character, the pastoral interlocutor who prompts Piers to speak out against ecclesiastical evils.

Palinode in *July* does not appear as a speaking character, but his experience is recalled by Thomalin.

> For Palinode (if thou him ken)
>   yode late on Pilgrimage
> To Rome, (if such be Rome) and then
>   he sawe thilke misusage.
> For shepeheards (sayd he) there doen leade,
>   as Lordes doen other where. (181–86)

Thomalin then goes on to particularize the luxury, avarice, indolence, and neglect of flocks of the higher Roman clergy. The parenthetical qualification of Rome, and E.K.'s remark about Palinode ("a shephearde, of whose report he seemeth to speake all thys") make one wonder whether Rome is actually meant or whether there is a reference to ecclesiastical evils much closer to home. At any event, the other ecclesiastical eclogues focus on the ills of the English Church.

But if we accept Palinode's experience as that of an actual person, and perhaps we should, the problem would be to find someone who had recently been to Rome. In his service with Leicester in 1579, Spenser was exceptionally well placed to learn what was going on, especially the news being brought back to England by Walsingham's secret agents. Whether agent or a genuine Catholic convert, Anthony Munday had returned from Rome in July, 1579, and Spenser might well have met him. In the fall of 1578 Munday, on funds supplied by English Catholics and with the encouragement of his patron Lord Oxford, had traveled to Rome, spent some time at the English Seminary there, and on his return was ready to capitalize on his experiences as the "Popes Scholler." He had not long to wait, and in early 1582 contributed two pamphlets to the anti-Catholic campaign. The first was entitled *A Discoverie of Edmund Campion and His Confederates*; the second, *The English Romayn Lyfe*, was an account of his adventures in the English Seminary at Rome.[3]

But there were others, too, who had been to Rome and were waiting to exploit their travels. For instance, John Nichols (or Nicholls), who probably was a spy for Walsingham, had spent some time at Rome

[3] See *DNB* and Celeste Turner [Wright], *Anthony Mundy* (Berkeley, Cal., 1929), pp. 16–23. Eleanor Rosenberg, *Leicester: Patron of Letters*, pp. 233–35, gives a good account of this phase of Munday's life.

In a more recent study, "Young Anthony Mundy Again," *SP*, LVI (1959), 150–68, Celeste Turner Wright more charitably suggests that Munday probably went to Rome not as a spy (her earlier conjecture) but as a convert to Catholicism. She points out that between 1577 and 1580 Munday's printer (John Charlewood) and printing master (John Allde) were Catholic in sympathy, and his patron, the Earl of Oxford, was a crypto-Catholic.

Eustace Conway, *Anthony Munday and Other Essays* (New York, 1927), pp. 23–25, first suggested that Palinode represented Munday.

also, and in 1581 brought out two books relating his experiences. He had been, he testified, "for the space of almost two yeares the Popes Scholer in the English Seminarie . . . at Rome." His first book, his *Recantation*, was devoted to generalizations on Catholic iniquities; the title of the second gives some notion of its tone and contents: *John Nichols Pilgrimage, Wherein Is Displaid the Lives of Proude Popes, Ambitious Cardinals, Lecherous Bishops, Fat Bellied Monkes, and Hypocriticall Jesuites.*[4] Nichols, however, apparently did not return to England until early 1580, so he could not have been the Palinode referred to by Thomalin in *July*, unless we interpret the "report" (of E. K.'s gloss) as an oral or written account sent back by Nichols before his return.

The short section on Palinode in *July*, then, is perhaps an allusion to the experiences of someone like Munday or Nichols: someone who had recently been to Rome and on his return had given a full account to the government of his encounter with Roman religious evils. Spenser, working for Leicester and on friendly terms with such courtiers as Edward Dyer, Daniel Rogers, and Philip Sidney, would be in a position both to pick up such information and to refer to it in the *Shepheardes Calender*—particularly since much was apparently added in the period from July to November, 1579.

PERIGOT AND WILLYE OF *AUGUST*

According to a gloss, Perigot of *August* is a real person whose love deserves no less praise than he gives her in his rollicking complaint— to which Willye supplies the appropriate undersong. The choice of Cuddie (Dyer) as arbiter of the singing-match between Perigot and Willye might suggest that Perigot is of the Court circle. He is possibly Philip Sidney, whom we might expect, even apart from the dedication, to be among the familiar friends and best acquaintance honored in the *Calender*.

According to Perigot's admission, Colin Clout has won a spotted lamb from Perigot in an earlier poetic competition. If we take this competition literally, we might measure Colin's sestina in *August* (in which Colin laments Rosalind's absence from "home") with the sestina in Sidney's *Arcadia* (in which Claius and Strephon lament

[4] See *DNB* and Rosenberg, pp. 241–42.

the departure from the country of the heavenly maid Urania, like Elisa and Rosalind a rural shepherdess, lady, and goddess). Or Spenser's more elaborate lament over Elisa as Rosalind and Dido might be contrasted with Perigot's lament in *August* over the "bonilasse" that he saw tripping over the dale (and consequently, like Colin Clout, he now suffers from "curelesse sorrowe").

There is not much evidence that would connect the subject of Perigot's song with Elisa. However, like Elisa of *April* (with her "Cremosin coronet" of violets) she wears a chaplet of violets. E.K. is perhaps hinting when he defines *chaplet* as "a kind of Garlond lyke a crowne." Also like Elisa, Perigot's bonilass is called a "Bellibone" and in her radiant effects is conventionally equated with Phoebus and Cynthia.

But what more strongly might suggest that Queen Elizabeth is being honored in *August* is the long tradition, from Ovid to the later Latin poets in general, that identifies Astraea, the just Virgin of the golden age, with Virgo, the sign of the month of August[5]—and the subsequent equation of Astraea-Virgo with Elizabeth by the English poets. Also we should remember the interpretation of Virgil's Fourth Eclogue by Christian writers, "wherein the virgin who 'returns' . . . becomes, not merely the virgin Astraea returning to the earth in the new golden age of empire, but the Virgin Mary, Mother of God and Queen of Heaven, whose appearance with her divine Son ushers in the Christian era."[6] This interpretation was later modified by English Protestant writers so that Elizabeth embodied the tradition of sacred empire and became the "returned just virgin Astraea of a new golden age."[7] The common symbols of the Blessed Virgin (Rose, Star, Moon, Phoenix, Ermine, Pearl, etc.) were applied to the English Queen, and in England the veneration of the Queen of Heaven was replaced by the "worship of the 'diva Elizabetta,' the imperial virgin," whose "bejewelled and painted image was set up at Court, and went in progress through the land for her worshippers to adore."[8] Frances A. Yates explains how a concerted attempt was made to draw ancient alle-

---

[5] Frances A. Yates, "Queen Elizabeth as Astraea," *Journal of the Warburg and Courtauld Institutes*, X (1947), 28–31.
[6] *Ibid.*, p. 32.
[7] *Ibid.*, p. 52.
[8] *Ibid.*, pp. 74–75.

giances to Elizabeth by a deliberate substitution of the adulation of the State Virgo Elizabeth for the ancient Catholic veneration of Virgin Mary. In equating the English Queen and the Virgin Mary the point was often made that Elizabeth was born on the eve of the nativity of the Virgin Mary and died on the eve of the Annunciation.[9]

Spenser, of course, was well aware of Virgo-Astraea's connection with August, for he stresses it in the first four lines of *Mother Hubberds Tale* (presumably written about the same time as the *Calender*). He was also aware that the Virgo of August was traditionally equated both with Diana—another poetic name for Elizabeth—whose great feast was August 14, and with the Blessed Virgin whose Assumption was August 15.[10] The first lines of Perigot's song ("It fell upon a holly eve,/ . . . When holly fathers wont to shrieve") connect the lovely subject of Perigot's fascination with both Diana and the Blessed Virgin.

If we study the woodcut before *August*, we see the Virgo of the zodiac with an ear of corn in her hand, and (lower left) Perigot's shapely lass outlined against stacks of wheat. In the song itself, this "bonilasse" is dressed in a frock of gray, which color both Willye and E. K. tell us is a sign of weeping and complaint. However, she also wears a kirtle of green silk, and Willye declares that this "greene is for maydens meete." (Is this a reference to Tudor green—to Tudor sovereignty and independence?) The crown of violets which the bonilass wears is somewhat mystifying (unless we somehow connect it with Elisa's "Cremosin coronet" in *April*), for violets no longer bloom in August.[11]

[9] *Ibid.*, p. 74.

[10] Parmenter, "Twelve Aeglogues," p. 208.

[11] From one point of view, however, Virgo-Astraea brought back the golden age, when spring eternal reigned; hence the flowers of spring can be found at the same time as the signs of autumn. Yates, p. 64.

Another reference to Elizabeth may possibly be found in the passage (after Cuddie calls the singing-match between Perigot and Willye a draw) in which Willye declares:

Never dempt more right of beautye I weene
The shepheard of Ida, that judged beauties Queene. (137–38)
It was a common theme in Elizabethan literature and art that Elizabeth was "beauties Queene," a goddess who excelled all the goddesses of clas-

But perhaps we should not look for more than an occasional hint, for the singing-match of *August* is quite imitative and does not seem to have been written with a clear-cut or detailed allegory in mind. In old calendars we normally find as the picture for August a mysterious maiden who passes through the harvest fields, and it is appropriate that Perigot should sing of this apparition.[12] But it is also true that the Virgo of August was traditionally conflated with Astraea, Diana, and the Blessed Virgin, and all these with the English Queen. Hence, it is quite possible that Spenser wished his readers' minds to make the same leap, and that Perigot's bonilass is another disturbing symbol of the English Queen. In the fall of 1579, Elizabeth in her infatuation with Alençon was a lady who left the land lamenting (as we have already seen in Colin Clout's grief over Rosalind and Dido). The pastoral lady of the August eclogue had a similar effect on Perigot, who, if he represented Philip Sidney, could express Sidney's personal grief over the French marriage negotiations.

Willye, Perigot's antagonist, is a difficult character to identify. Looking over the list of Spenser's and Sidney's friends in 1579, I might suggest William Camden as a possible Willye. Camden and Sidney, fellow students at Christ Church, Oxford (both had Thomas Cooper as their tutor), were good friends, and Camden has testified to the encouragement he received in his antiquarian interests from Sidney. Camden was early recognized as a scholar, for Abraham Ortelius, famous continental geographer and historian, sought him out in his visit to England in 1577 and encouraged him to continue his studies.[13] In the fall of 1579 Spenser was spending some time in Westminster, where Camden was teaching school, in his courtship of Machabyas Chylde (whom Spenser probably married in late October, 1579). Judson thinks that Spenser was probably living in Westminster in late 1579, for the October, 1579, letter to Harvey was partly written

---

sical antiquity. A well-known expression of this theme is the painting (dated 1569) by Hans Eworth at Hampton Court. In this painting (a revised Judgment of Paris), Elizabeth is awarded the golden apple, rather than Venus, Juno, or Minerva. See Yates, p. 60, Plate A.

[12] Parmenter, "Twelve Aeglogues," p. 209.
[13] *DNB*, "William Camden."

there.[14] Camden (whom Spenser highly commends in his *Ruines of Time*) might well have met the poet of the *Calender* as one of Sidney's friends, but Spenser's scholarly and antiquarian interests and his residence in Westminster would have attracted him to Camden even apart from Sidney.

CHLORIS OF *APRIL*

In the April eclogue the ladies of the Court, in pastoral fashion, pay honor to their Queen:

> And whither rennes this bevie of Ladies bright,
> > raunged in a rowe?
> They bene all Ladyes of the lake behight,
> > that unto her goe.
> *Chloris*, that is the chiefest Nymph of al,
> Of Olive braunches beares a Coronall: (118–23)

Chloris most probably represents Lady Margaret, Countess of Derby, granddaughter of Mary Tudor, the younger sister of Henry VIII.

As the only surviving child of Henry de Clifford, second Earl of Cumberland, and his first wife Eleanor, daughter and co-heiress of Charles Brandon, Duke of Suffolk, the Countess of Derby was looked upon by many Englishmen as having a good claim to the English crown.[15] History, however, gives us little information about her. She was born in 1540; in 1555 married Henry Stanley, Lord Strange, who in 1572 became the fourth Earl of Derby; separated from him in 1567; and died in 1596. Stanley kept his wife's claims to the throne well in the background and apparently suffered no molestation on this account.[16]

Chloris, "the chiefest Nymph of al," I take to be the most important lady at Court next to the Queen. As granddaughter to Mary Tudor, a first cousin once removed from the Queen, and a legal heir to the throne, the Countess of Derby was undoubtedly prominent enough to warrant special mention in the *Calender*. In his listing of New Year's gifts to the Queen for January 1579, John Nichols has organized the donors in groups according to their political and social

[14] *Spenser*, p. 60.
[15] See *DNB*, "Henry de Clifford."
[16] *DNB*, "Henry Stanley."

importance. At the top of this list in the first category of three names comes Margaret, Countess of Derby, Elizabeth's chief matron of honor, followed by Sir Nicholas Bacon and Lord Burghley. In the listing of the Queen's New Year's gifts to others in 1579 (the year of the *Calender*), the Countess of Derby is again first and receives a more expensive gift than any other woman.[17]

Apart from the fact that the Countess of Derby was, after the Queen, the first lady of Elizabeth's Court and, as such, would be recognized as the "chiefest Nymph of al," what reason would Spenser have to honor her in such covert and mysterious fashion? The real reason was undoubtedly her opposition to the Alençon marriage—and its unfortunate consequences. In a letter to his King dated August 22, 1579, Mendoza, the Spanish ambassador to England, wrote that the Countess of Derby was placed under arrest for discussing, against the Queen's edict, Alençon's coming to England and his projected marriage to Elizabeth.[18] The Countess was a prisoner for well over a year and apparently never afterwards regained her place at Court or the Queen's favor.[19] This extended punishment was probably due to the fact that the Countess had the misfortune to share the

[17] John Nichols, *Progresses and Public Processions of Queen Elizabeth*, 3 vols. (London, 1788–1805), III, 313, 327. (In the more common 1823 edition: II, 65, 81.) Nichols' listing of the Queen's New Year's gifts for 1579 (as well as for other years) suggests the current favorites. In January, 1579, for instance, the second category of recipients, Earls, reveals that Oxford (enemy to the Leicester-Sidney group) and Ormonde (who was largely responsible for Henry Sidney's ignominious recall from Ireland in 1578) stood highest in the Queen's favor.

E. K.'s mysterious gloss on Chloris emphasizing the color green and sovereignty is possibly a veiled reference to the Tudor colors and Tudor sovereignty, to which the Countess of Derby, as a Tudor, would be a qualified claimant.

[18] *C.S.P.*, Spanish, 1568–79, p. 692.

[19] See my study of the Countess of Derby, in which I gather pertinent information about her, and review her complicated relations to Leicester's group in 1579: "Spenser's Chloris," *HLQ*, XXIV (1961), 145–150.

I here point out that Leicester in late 1579, apparently without the Queen's knowledge or permission, arranged the marriage of the Countess's oldest son, Ferdinando Stanley, to Alice Spencer (daughter of Sir John Spencer of Althorpe), who was related to the poet of the *Calender*.

Blood Royal. The Alençon affair was perhaps a pretext for severity towards one whose greatest sin was her legal claim to the crown as a successor to Elizabeth.

WRENOCK OF *DECEMBER*

The context of the reference to Wrenock in *December*—the "good olde shephearde" who made Colin more skillful in writing verses (1. 41)—would fit Spenser's school days rather than his Cambridge period. Apparently Spenser was proficient in verse-composition while he attended Merchant Taylors' School in London, for his translations for Jan van der Noot's *Theatre* were published in 1569, the year he went up to the university.

The most plausible conjecture on Wrenock is Richard Mulcaster, the famous headmaster of Merchant Taylors' School during the term of Spenser's residence there.[20] The greatest difficulty in this conjecture is Mulcaster's age, Mulcaster (1530?–1611) being only about twenty-two years older than Spenser. Mulcaster would have been about thirty-nine when Spenser left Merchant Taylors' and about forty-nine when the *Calender* appeared, and hence might not qualify as an "olde shephearde."

Mulcaster's theory of poetry, "to cover truth with a fabulous veil," was in accord with Spenser's practice. Furthermore, Mulcaster believed that boys with an aptitude for poetry should study the poets. He also had an exceptionally high regard for English.[21]

G. C. Moore Smith has suggested that Wrenock is an anagram of one of the variant forms of Mulcaster's name "Mowncaster." (Other spellings were "Mouncaster," "Moncaster," and "Muncaster.") As an anagram, "Mowncaster" works out to Mast. Wrenoc.[22] In view of other anagrams in the *Calender*, this suggestion is attractive.

[20] Var., p. 421.
[21] See Judson, *Spenser*, pp. 15–18.
[22] "Spenser and Mulcaster," *MLR*, VIII (1913), 368. Roland M. Smith strengthens this suggestion by pointing out Spenser's habit of writing *ow* before a nasal—hence "Mowncaster." "Spenser's Scholarly Script and 'Right Writing,'" *Studies in Honor of T. W. Baldwin* (Urbana, Ill., 1958), p. 67.

Bibliography

The following abbreviations have been used:

CHEL	Cambridge History of English Literature
C.S.P.	Calendar of State Papers
DNB	Dictionary of National Biography
ELH	A Journal of English Literary History
HLQ	Huntington Library Quarterly
HMC	Historical Manuscripts Commission
JEGP	Journal of English and Germanic Philology
MLN	Modern Language Notes
MLQ	Modern Language Quarterly
MLR	Modern Language Review
MP	Modern Philology
NED	New English Dictionary
NQ	Notes and Queries
P.L.	Patrologia Latina
PMLA	Publications of the Modern Language Association of America
PQ	Philological Quarterly
RES	Review of English Studies
SP	Studies in Philology
Var.	Variorum edition of Spenser, The Minor Poems, I

The following list includes only those works which are referred to in this book.

Albright, Evelyn May. "Spenser's Reason For Rejecting the *Cantos of Mutability*," *SP*, XXV (1928), 93–127.

Atkins, John William Hey. *English Literary Criticism of the Renaissance*. London, 1947.

Austin, Warren B. "Spenser's Sonnet to Harvey," *MLN*, LXII (1947), 20–23.

———. "William Withie's Notebook: Lampoons on John Lyly and Gabriel Harvey," *RES*, XXIII (1947), 297–309.

Bennett, Josephine W. "Oxford and *Endymion*," *PMLA*, LVII (1942), 354–69.

Botting, Roland B. "The Composition of the *Shepheardes Calender*," *PMLA*, L (1935), 423–34.

Bradner, Leicester. *Edmund Spenser and the Faerie Queene*. Chicago, 1948.

Brooke, C. F. Tucker, ed. *The Life of Marlowe and the Tragedy of Dido Queen of Carthage*. London, 1930.

Buchanan, George. *Opera omnia*, 2 vols. Ed. Pieter Burman. Leyden, 1725.

Buxton, John. *Sir Philip Sidney and the English Renaissance*. New York, 1954.

Byrom, H. J. "Edmund Spenser's First Printer, Hugh Singleton," *The Library*, Fourth Series, XIV (1933), 121–56.

Campbell, Lily B. *Shakespeare's "Histories": Mirrors of Elizabethan Policy*. San Marino, California, 1947.

Carpenter, Nan. "Spenser and Timotheus: A Musical Gloss on E. K.'s Gloss," *PMLA*, LXXI (1956), 1141–51.

Carrick, Elizabeth. "The Life and Works of Fulke Greville." Unpublished M.A. thesis. University of London, 1936.

Carroll, W. M. *Animal Conventions in English Renaissance Non-Religious Prose, 1550–1600*. New York, 1954.

Chamberlin, Frederick. *Elizabeth and Leycester*. New York, 1939.

Chambers, E. K. *Sir Henry Lee*. Oxford, 1936.

Collins, Joseph B. *Christian Mysticism in the Elizabethan Age*. Baltimore, Md., 1940.

Conway, Eustace. *Anthony Munday and Other Essays*. New York, 1927.

Courthope, W. J. *CHEL*. 1909. "The Poetry of Spenser." Vol. 3, 239–280.

Craik, G. L. *Spenser and His Poetry*. 3 vols., London, 1845.

Croll, Morris W. *The Works of Fulke Greville*. Philadelphia, 1903.

Darbishire, Helen. Review of W. L. Renwick's edition of the *Shepheard's Calendar*. *RES*, VIII (1932), 326–29.

Dawley, P. M. *John Whitgift and the English Reformation*. New York, 1954.

Draper, John W. "The Glosses to Spenser's *Shepheardes Calender*," *JEGP*, XVIII (1919), 556–74.

Edgerton, W. L. "The Calender Year in Sixteenth-Century Printing," *JEGP*, LIX (1960), 439–49.

Ferne, John. *Blazon of Gentrie*. London, 1586.

Fleay, F. G. *Guide to Chaucer and Spenser*. London, 1877.

Friedland, Louis S. "A Source of Spenser's 'The Oak And The Briar,'" *PQ*, XXXIII (1954), 222–24.

———. "Spenser As a Fabulist," *Shakespeare Association Bulletin*, XII (1937), 85–108, 131–54, 194–207.

———. "Spenser's Fable of 'The Oake and the Brere,'" *Shakespeare Association Bulletin*, XVI (1941), 52–57.

Garrett, C. H. *Marian Exiles*. Cambridge, 1938.

Greenlaw, Edwin. "The Shepheards Calender," *PMLA*, XXVI (1911), 419–51.

Greg, W. W. *Pastoral Poetry and Pastoral Drama*. London, 1906.

Greville, Fulke. *Life of Sidney*. Ed. Nowell Smith. Oxford, 1907.

———. *Poems and Dramas*, 2 vols. Ed. Geoffrey Bullough. London, 1938.

Grindal, Edmund. *The Remains of*. Ed. Rev. W. Nicholson for Parker Society. Cambridge, 1843.

Hall, Herbert. *Society in the Elizabethan Age*. London, 1886.

Haller, William. *The Rise of Puritanism*. New York, 1938.

Hartman, Herbert, ed. *Surrey's Fourth Boke of Virgill*. New York, 1933.

Harvey, Gabriel. *Ciceronianus*. Ed. Harold S. Wilson. Lincoln, Neb., 1945.

———. *Letter-Book of, 1573–1580*. Ed. E. J. L. Scott for Camden Society. Westminster, 1884.

——. *Marginalia.* Ed. G. C. Moore Smith. Stratford-Upon-Avon, 1913.

——. *Works of,* 3 vols. Ed. Alexander B. Grosart. London, 1884–85.

Herford, C. H., ed. *Shepheards Calender.* London, 1895.

Higginson, James J. *Spenser's Shepherd's Calender in Relation to Contemporary Affairs.* New York, 1912.

Hill, Christopher. *Economic Problems of the Church.* Oxford, 1956.

Hind, A. M. *Engraving in England in the Sixteenth and Seventeenth Centuries.* 2 vols. Cambridge, 1952.

Hughes, Philip. *The Reformation in England.* 3 vols. London, 1950–54.

Hughes, William. *A History of the Church of the Cymry.* London, 1916.

Hulbert, Viola Blackburn. "Diggon Davie Again," *JEGP,* XLI (1942), 349–67.

Hume, M. A. S. *The Courtships of Queen Elizabeth.* London, 1898.

Jenkins, Raymond. "Rosalind in Colin Clouts Come Home Againe," *MLN,* LXVII (1952), 1–5.

Jones, H. S. V. *A Spenser Handbook.* New York, 1930.

Judson, A. C. *A Biographical Sketch of John Young, Bishop of Rochester, With Emphasis on His Relations to Edmund Spenser.* Indiana University Studies, XXI (1934). Study No. 103.

——. *The Life of Edmund Spenser.* Baltimore, 1945.

——. *Thomas Watts, Archdeacon of Middlesex (and Edmund Spenser).* Bloomington, Ind., Indiana University Publications. Humanities series, No. 2, 1939.

Kennedy, W. P. M. *Elizabethan Episcopal Administration.* 3 vols. London, 1924.

Kermode, Frank. *English Pastoral Poetry.* New York, 1953.

Kinsman, Robert S. "Skelton's Colyn Cloute: The Mask of Vox Populi." *Essays Critical and Historical Dedicated to Lily B. Campbell.* Berkeley and Los Angeles, 1950. Pp. 17–23.

Knappen, T. W. *Tudor Puritanism.* Chicago, 1939.

Legouis, E. *Edmund Spenser.* Paris, 1923.

Lewis, C. S. *English Literature in the Sixteenth Century.* Oxford, 1954.

Long, Percy W. Review of James J. Higginson's *Spenser's Shepherd's Calender in Relation to Contemporary Affairs*. *JEGP*, XIII (1914), 344–50.

———. 'Spenser and the Bishop of Rochester," *PMLA*, XXXI (1916), 713–35.

McElderry, Bruce Robert, Jr. "Archaism and Innovation in Spenser's Poetic Diction," *PMLA*, XLVII (1932), 144–70.

McGinn, D. J. *The Admonition Controversy*. New Brunswick, N. J., 1949.

McLane, Paul E. "Diggon Davie Again," *JEGP*, XLVI (1947), 144–49.

———. "Spenser's Chloris: The Countess of Derby," *HLQ*, XXIV (1961), 145–50.

Mohl, Ruth. *Studies in Spenser, Milton, and the Theory of Monarchy*. New York, 1949.

Mounts, Charles E. "Two Rosalinds in *Colin Clouts Come Home Againe*," *NQ*, New Series, II (1955), 283–84.

Mullinger, James Bass. *St. John's College*. London, 1901.

———. *The University of Cambridge*. 3 vols. Cambridge, 1884.

Nashe, Thomas. *Works of*, 5 vols. Ed. Ronald B. McKerrow. London, 1910.

Nicholas, Sir Harris. *Memoirs of the Life and Times of Sir Christopher Hatton*. London, 1847.

Nichols, John. *Progresses and Public Processions of Queen Elizabeth*. 3 vols. London, 1788–1805.

Padelford, F. M. "Spenser and the Puritan Propaganda," *MP*, XI (1913), 85–106.

Parmenter, Mary. "Colin Clout and Hobbinoll: A Reconsideration of the Relationship of Edmund Spenser and Gabriel Harvey." Unpublished dissertation. Johns Hopkins University, 1933.

———. "Spenser's 'Twelve Æglogues Proportionable to the Twelve Monethes,'" *ELH*, III (1936), 190–217.

Pearson, A. F. Scott. *Thomas Cartwright and Elizabethan Puritanism*. London, 1925.

Peel, Albert, ed. *Notebook of John Penry 1593*. London, 1944.

Phillips, James E. "George Buchanan and the Sidney Circle," *HLQ*, XII (1948), 23–55.

Pierce, William. *John Penry.* London, 1923.

Pollen, J. H. *English Catholics in the Reign of Queen Elizabeth.* London, 1920.

Puttenham, George. *Arte of English Poesie.* Ed. G. D. Willcock and A. Walker. Cambridge, 1936.

Read, Conyers. *Mr. Secretary Walsingham.* 3 vols. Cambridge, Mass., 1925.

Renwick, W. L., ed. *The Shepheard's Calendar.* London, 1930.

Rosenberg, Eleanor. *Leicester: Patron of Letters.* New York, 1955.

Rowse, A. L. *England of Elizabeth.* New York, 1951.

Ruutz-Rees, Caroline. "Some Notes of Gabriel Harvey's in Hoby's Translation of Castiglione's *Courtier* (1561)," *PMLA*, XXV (1910), 608–39.

Sargent, R. M. *At the Court of Queen Elizabeth: The Life and Lyrics of Sir Edward Dyer.* London, 1935.

Sidney, Philip. *Complete Works,* 4 vols. Ed. A. Feuillerat. Cambridge, 1923.

Smith, G. C. Moore. Review of W. L. Renwick's edition of the *Shepheard's Calendar. MLR,* XXVI (1931), 456–59.

———. "Spenser and Mulcaster," *MLR,* VIII (1913), 368.

Smith, Hallett. *Elizabethan Poetry.* Cambridge, Mass., 1952.

Smith, Roland M. "Spenser's Scholarly Script and 'Right Writing,'" *Studies in Honor of T. W. Baldwin.* Urbana, Ill., 1958. Pp. 66–111.

Spenser, Edmund. *Complete Works.* Ed. Alexander B. Grosart. 9 vols. London, 1882–84.

———. *The Poetical Works of.* Ed. J. C. Smith and E. De Selincourt. Oxford, 1912.

———. *The Works of. A Variorum Edition. Faerie Queene, Books Six and Seven.* Ed. Edwin Greenlaw et al. Baltimore, 1938.

The Minor Poems, I. Ed. C. G. Osgood and H. G. Lotspeich (assisted by Dorothy E. Mason). Baltimore, 1943.

Prose Works. Ed. Rudolf Gottfried. Baltimore, 1949.

Starnes, DeWitt T., and Ernest W. Talbert. *Classical Myth and Legend in Renaissance Dictionaries.* Chapel Hill, N. C., 1955.

Starnes, DeWitt T. *Renaissance Dictionaries.* Austin, Texas, 1954.

Steeholm, Clara and Hardy. *James I of England.* New York, 1938.

Stein, Harold. "Spenser and William Turner," MLN, LI (1936), 345–51.

Stowe, John. Annals of England. London, 1615.

Strype, John. Annals of the Reformation. 4 vols. Oxford, 1824.

———. History of the Life and Acts . . . of Edmund Grindal. Oxford, 1821.

———. The Life and Acts of John Aylmer. Oxford, 1821.

———. The Life and Acts of Mathew Parker. 3 vols. Oxford, 1821.

———. Life and Acts of John Whitgift. 3 vols. Oxford, 1822.

Stubbs, John. The Discoverie of a Gaping Gulf . . . . London, 1579.

Thomas, Sidney. "Hobgoblin Runne Away With the Garland From Apollo," MLN, LV (1940), 419–20.

Thoms, W. J., ed. Early English Prose Romances. 3 vols. London, 1858.

Tillyard, E.M.W. Elizabethan World Picture. London, 1948.

Usher, Roland G. The Reconstruction of the English Church. 2 vols. New York and London, 1910.

Victoria History of County of Kent. 3 vols. Ed. William Page. London, 1908–32.

Waldman, Milton. Elizabeth and Leicester. London, 1946.

Wallace, M. W. The Life of Sir Philip Sidney. Cambridge, 1915.

Ward, B. M. The Seventeenth Earl of Oxford. London, 1928.

Webbe, William. A Discourse of English Poetrie. 1586. In Smith, Elizabethan Critical Essays. London, 1904. I, 226–302.

Whitaker, Virgil K. The Religious Basis of Spenser's Poetry. Stanford, California, 1950.

White, F. O. Lives of Elizabethan Bishops. London, 1898.

Wilkerson, William. A Confutation . . . . London, 1579.

Wilson, Elkin Calhoun. England's Eliza. Cambridge, Mass., 1939.

Wilson, Harold S. "Harvey's Orations on Rhetoric," ELH, XII (1945), 167–82.

———. "The Humanism of Gabriel Harvey," Joseph Quincy Adams Memorial Studies. Washington, D. C., 1948. Pp. 707–721.

Wilson, Mona. Sir Philip Sidney. New York, 1932.

Wood, Anthony à. Athenae Oxonienses, 5 vols. Ed. Philip Bliss. London, 1813–20.

Wrenn, C. L. "On Re-Reading Spenser's *Shepheardes Calender*," *Essays and Studies* by Members of the English Association, vol. 29 (1943), 30–49.

Wright, Celeste Turner. *Anthony Mundy*. Berkeley, Cal., 1929.

———. "Young Anthony Mundy Again," *SP*, LVI (1959), 150-68.

Yates, Frances A. "Queen Elizabeth as Astraea," *Journal of the Warburg and Courtauld Institutes*, X (1947), 27–82.

Zurich Letters. Ed. Rev. Hastings Robinson for Parker Society. Cambridge, 1846.

Index

Index

THE
SEES OF ENGLAND
AND WALES
AS RE-ARRANGED
IN 1541
AND
1555

THE HEAVY LINE SHOWS THE BOUNDARIES OF THE NEW SEES FOUNDED
BY HENRY VIII IN 1541 AND RECOGNISED BY POPE PAUL IV IN 1555

THE STIPPLE MARKS THE AREA OF THE SEE OF WESTMINSTER, i.e., MIDDLESEX, FOUNDED
BY HENRY VIII IN 1541 AND SUPPRESSED BY EDWARD VI IN 1550